THEATERS OF JUSTICE

Cultural Memory
in
the
Present

Mieke Bal and Hent de Vries, Editors

THEATERS OF JUSTICE

Judging, Staging, and Working Through

in Arendt, Brecht, and Delbo

Yasco Horsman

STANFORD UNIVERSITY PRESS

STANFORD, CALIFORNIA

Stanford University Press
Stanford, California

Printed in the United States of America on acid-free, archival-quality paper

Library of Congress Cataloging-in-Publication Data

Horsman, Yasco.
    Theaters of justice : judging, staging, and working through in Arendt, Brecht,
and Delbo / Yasco Horsman.
        p. cm.
    Includes bibliographical references and index.
    ISBN 978-0-8047-7031-6 (cloth : alk. paper) — ISBN 978-0-8047-7032-3
(pbk. : alk. paper)
    1. Holocaust, Jewish (1939-1945), in literature. 2. Trials in literature. 3. Justice
in literature. 4. Arendt, Hannah, 1906–1975. Eichmann in Jerusalem. 5. Brecht,
Bertolt, 1898-1956. Massnahme. 6. Delbo, Charlotte—Criticism and interpretation. 7. Psychoanalysis and literature. I. Title.
    PN56.H55 H687
    809'.93358405318—dc22
                                    2010020247
Typeset by Thompson Type in 11/13.5 Garamond

For Hanneke

Contents

Acknowledgments

This book could not have been completed without the support, encouragement, and feedback of a group of people to whom I would like to express my gratitude. First and foremost, I thank Shoshana Felman for her support during the initial stages of this project and for being a continuing source of inspiration. Ernst van Alphen, Mieke Bal, Katerina Clark, Geoffrey Hartman, Michael Holquist, Frans Willem Korsten, Sara Suleri Goodyear, and Hent de Vries read parts of the manuscript and gave valuable comments. I am grateful to Dori Laub for our inspiring conversations on trauma and memory. Luc Kinsch, Lance Duerfahrd, and Dan Friedman read and reread large chunks of the earliest version of this book. Their feedback proved invaluable. Thanks to James Gibbons for his meticulous editing. Special thanks to Herschel Farbman, Carolina Sanin, Eugene Chang, Tessa Lee, George Katsaros, Laure Goldstein, and Bram Ieven. I would like to thank my colleagues at the Department of Literary Studies at Leiden University: Maria Boletsi, Isabel Hoving, Madeleine Kasten, Stefan van der Lecq, Liesbeth Minnaard, and Peter Verstraten. Finally, I thank my friends Lucas and Thomas Taris, Arjan Gunst, Nicolien Herblot, Ralf Mohren, and Henri Drost; my parents Dick and Willy Horsman; Minke Horsman, Sebas Huisman, Ruud and Mariëtte Grootenboer, Roel and Kim Grootenboer, Juul Grootenboer, Arnold van Rooij, and my son Kees Horsman. I am grateful to Hanneke Grootenboer for her criticism, suggestions, feedback, and encouragement—more than I can express on this page. This book is dedicated to her.

THEATERS OF JUSTICE

Coming to Terms with the Past

TRIAL, THERAPY, AND THE THEATER

In 1959, Theodor Adorno published the now-famous essay entitled "Was bedeutet: Aufarbeitung der Vergangenheit?" ("What Does Coming to Terms with the Past Mean?").[1] The essay opens with Adorno's explanation of what "coming to terms with the past" had come to mean in postwar West Germany:

"Coming to terms with the past" does not imply a serious working through of the past, the breaking of its spell through an act of clear consciousness. It suggests, rather, wishing to turn the page and, if possible, wiping it from memory. (115)

In his essay Adorno draws the by-now familiar picture of postwar West Germany as a country firmly in denial of its Nazi past. Although the Adenauer government had officially recognized the nation's responsibility for the Holocaust and had agreed to pay reparations to survivors, Germans privately sought to sidestep the question of the Holocaust as much as possible. Adorno observes that in the early years of postwar West Germany many of its key political figures were former Nazis, and certain Nazi ideas were still accepted as common truths, albeit ones that were not spoken publicly. Moreover, many people maintained a strong psychological investment in the ideas and leaders of the past, which leads Adorno to state that the West Germany of the late 1950s had not gone through a process of "serious working through," a process that would help it liberate itself from what he calls the "spell" of the past. Rather than confronting its past,

West Germany had evaded the question and treated the past as a closed chapter no longer affecting the present.

Adorno's essay discusses a wide range of defensive strategies of "unconscious and not-so-unconscious" (115) denial and repression found in West Germany, ranging from the use of euphemisms to refer to the past to outright denial of what had happened.[2] Whereas some of these denials were neurotic defenses against feelings of guilt, others were semiconscious attempts at exculpation. For Adorno, the patent idiocy with which these strategies were applied testifies to "a lack of psychic mastery and an unhealed wound." He continues: "One wants to get free of the past: rightly so, since one cannot live in its shadow, and since there is no end to terror if guilt and violence are only repaid, again and again, with guilt and violence" (115). But such yearnings to break free of the past should not cause one to close one's eyes to a history that was still so intensely alive. "National Socialism lives on, and to this day we don't know whether it is only the ghost of what was so monstrous that it didn't even die off with its own death, or whether it never died in the first place" (115).

What Germany needed, Adorno famously suggested, was a process of public *enlightenment*, which would confront the persistence of certain fascist patterns, prepare the nation for democracy, and, most crucially, "work against a forgetfulness that too easily goes along with and justifies what is forgotten"(125).[3] By using the word *enlightenment* and by giving his essay the title "Was bedeutet: Aufarbeitung der Vergangenheit?" Adorno obviously alludes to Kant's 1784 essay "Beantwortung der Frage: Was ist Aufklärung?" in which Kant defines enlightenment as "humanity's exodus from its self-imposed immaturity." Adorno's essay thus raises the question of how to conceive the project of "coming to terms with the past" along the lines of a Kantian-Schillerean project of "public education." The German situation calls for more general reflections on how exactly such public education should be organized. Indeed, how do we enlighten a nation that has shown itself to actively *resist* the process of learning? Conventional teaching as it is customarily understood, as a rational process in which information is conveyed, does not suffice; as Adorno puts it succinctly, it is exactly the confrontation with historical facts that gave rise to the most stubborn denials:

Here I choose to sidestep a question that is very difficult and burdens us with the greatest kind of responsibility: namely, the extent to which we've succeeded, in attempts at public enlightenment, to explore the past and whether it is not the case that precisely such insistence on the past does not awaken a stubborn resistance and bring about the exact opposite of what is intended. (126)

The paradox is that as information about the past accumulates, there emerges ever stronger forms of resistance against accepting this information and its implications. Therefore, Adorno concludes, "one should not expect too much from recourse to facts, for they'll often either not be admitted or be neutralized as exceptions" (128). What Germany needed was an altogether different project of public education, one that would use different strategies and require a different type of intellectual work.[4]

*

Although he remains vague about how to envision such a project of public enlightenment, Adorno suggests that a good starting point for conceptualizing this program would be psychoanalysis, a field that has traditionally struggled with the question of how one overcomes resistance to a certain insight (126).[5] Indeed, the word Adorno uses for the psychological work that is needed to come to terms with the past, *Aufarbeitung*, alludes to the Freudian concept of *Durcharbeitung* (working through).[6] Freud introduced this term in an essay written in 1914, entitled "Remembering, Repeating, and Working Through," asking for the individual what Adorno would later ask for the nation: How does one get free from a past not fully remembered, yet under whose spell one still lives? In his essay, Freud opposes two ways of relating to the past, the conscious process of recalling the past and the unconscious process of acting out. In the process of acting out, past events that one cannot consciously remember return and find expression in the idiotic repetition of gestures, phrases, acts, and behavioral patterns. In short, the past is manifested via a set of symptoms. That which is not remembered returns on the level of action. The third term of the triad of the essay's title, the enigmatic "working through," is introduced to conceptualize the transition from the (unconscious) repetition of the past to its (conscious) remembrance. This transition is at the heart of the psychoanalytic cure.[7]

Freud originally wrote his essay to analyze a deadlock that he repeatedly observed during the psychoanalytic process. He had discovered that the articulation of an accurate interpretation of a patient's past did not always lead to the dissolution of the patient's symptoms. Much as Adorno does, Freud lists a plethora of strategies of forgetting employed by his patients to avoid facing the reality of the past, from "dissolving through-connections, failing to draw the right conclusion" to "isolating memories"

(149). Because simply telling a patient the "truth" about his or her past has proved insufficient, something else is needed, Freud suggests, a particular type of psychic "work" that he labels *durcharbeitung*, an "experience which convinces the patient of the existence and power of such impulses" (155). This experience takes the shape of acting out in a particular *scene*, namely the psychoanalytic setting, which Freud compares to a *playground* where the patient can enact his or her repressed memories (154). The result is a moment of learning that is, according to Freud, "a piece of real experience, but one which has been made possible by especially favorable conditions" (154). The moment of learning, then, is not a moment of cognition; it takes the shape of a certain *event*, a sudden insight whose impact transforms the patient's relation to his or her past. This event, furthermore, takes place not in the patient's "real life" but rather in the controlled setting of the therapy room. Beneath the gaze of the therapist, acting out is transformed into a theatrical scene, a *Spiel* (play), which has a didactic-therapeutic effect.[8] It is precisely the artificiality of the psychoanalytic setting, and the distance it implies, that enables the patient to work through his or her impulses—and learn about them—without regressing into a compulsive, blind acting out.[9]

In this study I would like to return to Adorno's essay and to the question at its heart: Would it be possible to organize a process of public education so that it resembles the psychoanalytic process of working through? How can we organize a public "scene" that is both part of "real life" and distinct from it and that allows for a transformative, didactic event to take place that would enable a community to liberate itself from the spell of the past? I am particularly interested in the question, How should such a didactic scene be structured if it is to be a *public* event? As Freud emphasizes, psychoanalysis takes place in a highly formalized setting in which a set of rules and conventions assigns specific speaking and listening positions to the analysand and the analyst. What set of "fundamental rules" is required for a scene of public enlightenment? In what type of mise-en-scène can a moment of public enlightenment take place? Indeed, the question I want to raise is, What type of theater do we need to liberate ourselves from the past?

Trials as Didactic Events

In May 1960, a year after Adorno's essay was published, the Israeli secret service captured the former chief of the Gestapo's Division of Jewish

Affairs, Adolf Eichmann, in Buenos Aires and transported him to Jerusalem to stand trial for his role in the mass deportation of European Jews to concentration and extermination camps during World War II.[10] The trial, which began on April 11, 1961, was an event that attracted worldwide publicity. The proceedings were broadcast live on Israeli radio and filmed for later screenings on television. Although the trial sought primarily, of course, to judge Eichmann and to mete out punishment for his crimes, the ways it was brought to the public's attention clearly showed that the trial was also an effort in mass education. David Ben-Gurion, Israel's prime minister at the time, stated in an interview shortly after Eichmann's capture that he hoped that the trial would have a didactic effect: "There is no punishment great enough for Eichmann's deeds, but we want the trial to educate our youth. In addition, this trial is needed because the world has started to forget the Nazi horrors."[11] From the very outset, the trial was meant to be more than a series of legal proceedings; it was organized as a didactic event, which eventually changed the way Israel remembered the Holocaust and understood itself as a nation. As Israeli historian Idith Zertal writes, the trial "changed the face of Israel, psychologically binding the pastless young Israelis with their recent history and revolutionizing their self-perception."[12]

The Eichmann trial was the first in a series of widely publicized trials against former Nazis or their collaborators that took place from the 1960s through the 1990s: the Auschwitz trials in Frankfurt; the Touvier, Papon, and Barbie trials in France; the prosecutions against Priebke in Italy and Menten in the Netherlands.[13] These trials differed from the international tribunals in Tokyo and Nuremberg in that they were explicitly organized as *national* events, meant to assist in a process of national education— and sometimes even a process of national healing.[14] The Barbie trial was regarded by the French government as a "pedagogical trial," containing a "history lesson."[15] Nancy Wood writes that Papon's trial generated so much publicity that the event's didactic nature threatened to overshadow its legal goals:

The trial was a mass-mediated event of an unprecedented scale in France, enjoying daily newspaper coverage and regular television, radio and magazine commentary. For the more voracious consumer, a glut of information related to the trial could be accessed through hundreds of sites on the World Wide Web. At one point a tally noted that 146 accredited journalists had attended the trial; 1,413 scholars had abandoned lessons or libraries to witness History-in-the-making, and 8,827 members of the general public had been admitted. With this kind of saturated media and public attention, there was the attendant expectation that Maurice Papon's trial would yield lessons of a pedagogic, historical and symbolic nature for French society as a whole.[16]

The assumption that trials can assist in the (re)construction of the nation and its relation to the past has become so widespread that they have become the "focal point for the collective memory of whole nations," as Mark Osiel has argued.[17] For Osiel, trials have become "secular rites of commemoration," during which the nation redefines itself. Employing anthropologist Victor Turner's term, he understands trials as "social dramas": "cultural performances involving the wholesale disruption, self-examination and reconciliation of a society by means of legal or other ritual procedures."[18] Whereas the didactic-therapeutic function was considered a desirable side effect of the legal proceedings in the 1960s and 1970s, for the truth commissions, a new type of semilegal institution first established in Argentina in 1983 and subsequently emulated in several countries, it has become the explicit goal. As they have evolved over the last quarter-century, truth commissions seek not to punish criminals but to support a process of working through the past, which is often understood as a moment of "healing" for the nation.[19] The South African Truth and Reconciliation Commission (TRC), one of the best-known truth commissions, explicitly used therapeutic vocabulary to refer to this process.[20] The chairman of the commission, Bishop Desmond Tutu, described the goal of the TRC as the laying to rest "the ghosts of that past so that they may not return to haunt us . . . [thereby] healing a traumatized and wounded nation."[21]

*

In the discourse produced by several decades of war crimes trials that led up to the South African TRC, three distinct subdiscourses can be distinguished, namely a legal, a didactic, and a therapeutic one. A trial—or hearings administered by new, innovative legal institutions such as truth commissions—is believed both to serve justice and to teach the public as part of a national process of psychic healing. These varying ambitions are knotted together by a belief that trials can help bring about a moment of *closure*. As a verdict is pronounced or amnesty is granted, one closes the books on the past, as it were, thereby satisfying a desire for an ending that has psychological, legal-political, and aesthetic components. Judging the past, or reconciling oneself to it, makes it possible to both face the past— often in its full horror—and to close it off as distanced history by way of a similar gesture. One can be liberated from what Adorno called the spell of the past, which is transformed into something that is consciously remembered.

As the few examples mentioned above show, these subdiscourses are closely intertwined, and over the years the relations among the processes of learning, judging, and coming to terms with the past have become ever more intricate. The interrelated subdiscourses raise a wide range of issues regarding the didactic and therapeutic functions of the trial-as-spectacle. Three sets of questions are crucial for this study.

*

First, what kinds of assumptions about the nature of teaching are (implicitly) made when we expect a trial to be didactic? How do we understand the nature of the "lessons" to be learned from these spectacles if we wish to maintain, with Freud and Adorno, that the teachings of a didactic trial should go beyond the simple transmission of information and assist, instead, in a radical transformation of our relation to the past? Does learning about the past necessarily entail translating it into a story that one fully comprehends? Furthermore, through what *scenes* does one learn about the past? What trajectory is followed by the process of public education that addresses a repressed or traumatic past? As Shoshana Felman points out, psychoanalysis teaches us that learning amounts to an overcoming of (unconscious) resistances and therefore does not necessarily proceed as a linear progression—an accumulation of data. Rather, as a largely unconscious process, it relies on "breakthroughs, leaps, discontinuities, regressions and deferred action."[22] In short, one learns during unexpected moments that are beyond conscious control; learning, therefore, may be hard to script. Organizing a scene that would allow for these moments may be a daunting task, in particular when these lessons concern a history of massive trauma.[23]

Second: How are we to understand the therapeutic impact of a trial? What does it mean to expect it to "heal" the wounds of a nation, a people, a community—or even humanity? Does "healing" necessarily imply closure? Or is it possible to conceive of something approximating a "coming to terms with the past" that does not amount to "closing the book on the past"?[24] I should note here that it is exactly the call for closure that has been deemed suspicious by various scholars and thinkers, who have put forth objections to it on the basis of legal arguments (Minow), on ethical grounds (Hartman, Friedländer, LaCapra), for psychological reasons (Caruth, Laub, Felman, Langer), and on the basis of philosophical arguments (Derrida).[25] Finding closure in relation to massive trauma is at best unlikely, and at worst it constitutes a betrayal of the past. As Geoffrey Hartman states, in the wake of the disasters of the twentieth century, the challenge, precisely, is to envision a mode of "coming to terms with the past" that does *not* amount to finding closure yet that also prevents desensitization and the emergence of a new set of resistances resulting from what he calls the "secondary traumatization," which can be the effect of a confrontation with images of suffering.[26]

Third: How do the preceding questions relate to the specific nature of a trial's theatricality? A trial has a very specific theatrical structure, as Alain Finkielkraut rightly observes in an essay on the Barbie trial.[27] The ceremonial opening of a trial, the calling of "La Cour" by the bailiff— Arendt calls him the courtroom usher—serves not only to announce the judges' entrance and the beginning of the legal proceedings; it also symbolically separates the courtroom from everyday life, transforming it into a highly structured space that ascribes different speaking and listening positions to its participants. The scene of justice depends on this "original cut," Finkielkraut maintains. It "can take place anywhere—a table suffices—as long as a symbolic gesture sets it apart from the profane realm of the everyday."[28] Finkielkraut argues that a similar cut, though ostensibly not articulated by a ceremonial utterance, can be found at the core of three other symbolic spaces: the theater, the classroom, and the church. Teaching, acting, performing a religious ritual, and handing down justice— these can happen everywhere, as long as the space in which they take place is symbolically rendered distinct from the realm of mundane life.[29] What, then, are the relations among these different symbolic spaces? To use Finkielkraut's metaphor, a table suffices to stage a scene of justice, but this table entails a particular arrangement, a highly conventional set of "table manners," and a precisely defined group of companions. What is the relation between this scene and the didactic scene? And how do they differ from the psychoanalytic scene, which similarly relies on a separation from the everyday? Furthermore, how are we to understand the endpoints of didactic-therapeutic legal theaters? Pronouncing a verdict or giving amnesty are totalizing gestures, both of which seek to establish the truth about the past and to radically alter our relation to it. How do we combine these totalizing gestures with the aforementioned demand to resist understanding the past in terms of what Dominick LaCapra calls "redemptive narratives," teleological stories that emphasize the "positive" or "just" outcome of history while overlooking or marginalizing the history of suffering and trauma?[30]

Outline

In this study, I reflect on this set of interrelated questions through extensive close readings of texts that are particularly invested with the pedagogical and therapeutic implications of a legal trial: *Eichmann in Jerusalem* (1963) by the political philosopher Hannah Arendt; *La mémoire et les jours* (1985) and *Auschwitz et après* (published in three volumes, 1965–1972) by Auschwitz survivor and poet Charlotte Delbo; and one of the so-called *Lehrstücke* of Bertolt Brecht, entitled *Die Maßnahme* (1930/1998). These three texts offer, I argue, profound reflections on the theatrical aspects of the legal trial as well as its didactic and therapeutic functions, and in doing so they challenge some of the assumptions that are currently made about the cultural role of legal trials. Read together, these works enable me to rephrase some of the questions that play key roles in contemporary discussions about coming to terms with the past. Let me briefly introduce my "cases" as an outline of the project that I will shortly embark on.

Arendt's *Eichmann in Jerusalem* is, of course, perhaps the best-known post-Holocaust trial report and has remained a recurring topic of debate in the humanities. This study opens with an analysis of *Eichmann in Jerusalem* to acknowledge the centrality of both the Eichmann trial and Arendt's report on it in current debates about law and cultural memory. As is well known, Arendt was highly critical of some of the didactic ambitions that accompanied Eichmann's trial. Her book may therefore seem less useful for this study than those of recent legal scholars who study the "extralegal" functions of a trial and in particular its national-didactic and therapeutic functions.[31] What is useful, however, for my purposes is, precisely, Arendt's overly dogmatic or even conservative stance on the nature of the trial. Her emphasis on (legal) judgment—rather than rushing to understand the trial as something else altogether—helps us understand the precise nature of the legal theater. As I will demonstrate, it is not with theatricality per se that Arendt takes issue, but with the particular *type* of theater that the Eichmann trial was presumed to be. Arendt's understanding of the Eichmann trial differs from those of her contemporaries, most of whom considered it to be the staging of the "tragedy of the Jewish people" and thus designed so that a moment of catharsis—or even redemption—could take place. In contrast to her fellow reporters at the trial, Arendt emphasizes the staging of a scene of judgment, which, as a consequence, needed to be viewed from the particular perspective of a judge-spectator who regards the proceedings with a detached and rational gaze. Adopting such a position herself, she sees a different type of spectacle unfold in Jerusalem, one that resembles not a tragedy but a *comedy*. The "comic scenes" she observes nevertheless allow her to spell out a specific lesson that can be learned from the trial, albeit one that differs in both content and structure from the lessons scripted by the prosecution. In my first chapter, I propose to read *Eichmann in Jerusalem* as a report on the surprising and unexpected lesson that the trial taught Arendt. As I will demonstrate, the scenes that taught her this lesson broke through the legal-didactic framework of the trial, and—surprisingly—challenged Arendt's own assumptions about the nature of Nazi evil.

Shifting emphasis, Chapter 2 focuses on the way in which Arendt's book itself performatively stages a scene of justice. By opening her trial-report with a citation of the words of the courtroom usher that transform the courtroom into a "legal theater" and ending with the pronouncement of her own verdict in which she directly addresses the accused, Arendt mimics the structure of the scene that she is reporting on. I therefore claim that in addition to offering an analysis of the trial's theatrical nature, *Eichmann in Jerusalem* reads as a reenactment of the trial. Yet, as I will demonstrate, in her restaging of the scene of justice, Arendt slightly displaces some of the questions at the heart of the historic trial, rearticulating in particular the trial's demand for justice as voiced by the prosecution. Her book thereby sheds new light on the political and legal function of the Eichmann trial as well as on the nature of the community that it hopes to heal.

Chapter 3 offers a reading of various poems of Auschwitz and Ravensbrück survivor Charlotte Delbo, which I propose to understand as her attempt to create a literary "supplement" to the trials of her time. Delbo worked as assistant to the playwright Louis Jouvet before being arrested in 1942 because of her involvement with the French Resistance. After her return from the camps in 1945, Delbo published plays, poetry, and three books of memoirs, collectively entitled *Auschwitz et après*. One of the characteristics of Delbo's writing style in the memoirs, as critics such as Lawrence Langer and Ernst van Alphen have pointed out, is her refusal to narrate her experience from a retrospective point of view. As van Alphen puts it, "In her stories, she does not narrate 'about' Auschwitz, but 'from' it,"[32] frequently presenting her readers with present-tense reenactments of the past, which interrupt past-tense narratives. Van Alphen proposes to call this technique "theatrical" because a "conventional dramatic text is by definition located in a fictional present. Even if an actor talks in the past tense, each sentence is implicitly embedded in the sentence: 'I say.' This 'I say' situates each dramatic sentence in the present."[33] Following van Alphen in this regard, my chapter analyzes the "theatrical scene" constructed by Delbo's poetry by focusing on two poems included in *La mémoire et les jours*, "Kalavrita des mille Antigone," and "Les folles de mai." Both poems evoke Sophokles' *Antigone*, a tragedy that dramatizes a conflict between the law of the polis and the demands on the living made by the dead. I propose that both poems could serve as a model for understanding the particular structure of address in Delbo's writing. In her poetry, as well as in her autobiographical trilogy *Auschwitz et après*, Delbo attempts to give a voice to the dead so that they might address the living with a demand for justice. Such an exhortation expresses itself in a cry for justice that ultimately remains silent. Delbo, I argue, thereby poetically creates what I would like to call her own literary "theater of justice," which allows the voicing of a particular demand for justice that has traditionally remained unspoken within the idiom of the courtroom.

To further understand the strategies of staging and dramaturgy in theaters of justice, I examine Bertolt Brecht's work of the late 1920s and early 1930s, in particular *Die Maßnahme* (1930/1998). In this period, Brecht created didactic theater that sought to transform its audience. Understanding the moment of learning as a moment of judgment, Brecht modeled his theater on a courtroom hearing. An excellent example of this new model, *Die Maßnahme* consists of a set of trials and verdicts embedded within each other. The play concerns the verdict and execution of a young communist during a revolutionary mission, reenacted in front of Party members by the comrades who judged and killed him. The comrades ask the Party to judge their actions, and the audience in turn is invited to make a third verdict, judging the other two verdicts. In his play, Brecht thoroughly investigates the didactic possibilities of theater as trial, and trial as theater, by a tripling of a moment of judgment in a theatrical setting, or rather, of a theater modeled after a trial. Whereas the play itself consists of a complex set of verdicts, its historical reception even complicates it furthermore, embedding it in yet another set of trials.

When Brecht was summoned to appear before the House Un-American Activities Committee (HUAC) in 1947, he was cross-examined specifically about *Die Maßnahme*, which, I argue, was taken as an anticipation and justification of the Stalinist show trials that took place several years after Brecht wrote his play. My chapter analyzes this complex web of trials and verdicts—historical as well as fictional—in relation to the central dramatic event of *Die Maßnahme*: the execution of the play's central character and the subsequent disposal of his body. Framed by the two historical trials, I argue, the episode of the disposal of a body obtains an unexpected resonance, thereby raising questions that could not have been scripted by the play's overt didactic structure, such as—once again—the nature of our responsibilities to the dead. Placed last, this chapter reprises a theme that is central to this study, namely literature's ability to ask for justice in ways that are not available to judges and lawyers and to go beyond the socially important task of providing closure.

The nonchronological organization of the book—it opens with a discussion of the Eichmann trial in 1961 and ends with an analysis of a play from 1930—testifies to the centrality of the Holocaust as a defining event in the legal and political culture of the twentieth century. The Holocaust (and in particular the Eichmann trial in its aftermath), I contend, has become the prism through which we now regard past trials addressing massive violence and victimization. It has therefore become a central reference point for all discussions about the possibilities of working through trauma by legal means.

*

These three widely divergent texts—a trial report, a play, and a series of poems—contain, I argue, profound reflections on the relations among pedagogy, the trial, and the theater, as well as the attempts to "dramatize" that which escapes the dimension of the law. As may be clear from the preceding outline, in my readings I will pay attention to the ways in which these questions are not only reflected on discursively or thematically, but also, perhaps more implicit, how they are *staged* performatively by the dramatic and theatrical structure of these texts. Even though *Die Maßnahme* is the only text in this study that "officially" belongs to the theater, the memoirs, poems, and journalistic and philosophical texts central to this book will thus be probed for their theatrical dimensions.

By giving voice to a different set of demands for justice, verdicts, and accusations, the works of Arendt, Delbo, and Brecht respond to key trials of the twentieth century: to the Eichmann trial in Arendt's case, the Nuremberg trials in Delbo's case, and the Moscow trials, in the case of Brecht. Yet, more than responses, I argue, they are to be understood as quasi-Freudian reenactments, reopening the cases that the historic trials sought to close, bringing to center stage aspects that had escaped the confines of the legal framework. Instead of reading these works in the context of their times, framing them by what historically has happened, I aim to look for the precise moments when these trials broke through the governing legal, ethical, and theatrical frameworks of their times— sometimes even breaking through the dramatic frameworks of the text themselves—so as to open up to what I would like to call "law's other scene." I aim to develop a practice of reading that is attentive to these ruptures because it is precisely in these moments that the works of Arendt, Delbo, and Brecht work find their surprising didactic—and perhaps even therapeutic—potential.

The source of inspiration for this method of reading is the critical practice developed in the last decennia under the name of "trauma studies."[34] Inspired by Freudian psychoanalysis as well as by deconstruction's suspicion of totalizing schemes, trauma studies has developed a hermeneutics that is attentive to the mode in which a text's performance exceeds its own intentions and enacts a truth that it cannot relate via narrative. As Cathy Caruth explains, the term *trauma*, originally a Greek word that refers to a wound inflicted on the body, underwent a radical shift when Freud started using it to describe a psychic state of woundedness. For Freud, *trauma* points to a paradoxical structure of experience. Caruth writes,

What seems to be suggested by Freud in *Beyond the Pleasure Principle* is that the wound of the mind—the breach in the mind's experience of time, self and the world—is not like the wound of the body, a simple and healable event, but rather an event that . . . is experienced too soon, too unexpectedly, to be fully known and is therefore not available to consciousness until it imposes itself again, re-peatedly, in the nightmares and repetitive actions of the survivor.[35]

Freud's notion of trauma points to an experience that was missed when it "originally" happened and therefore resists integration into conscious narrative memory; it can become present only through its repetitions, re-stagings, and reenactments. By focusing on that which a text unwittingly stages, trauma studies reveals how cultural phenomena can testify to an experience that cannot be conveyed as a story. This implies a shift of inter-est from a text's narrative structure to its dramatic nature and performative dimension. It pays attention to what is enacted by a text in excess of what it narrates in its own voice.

Although my project shares trauma studies' interest in performance and performativity, its emphasis is slightly different. Whereas trauma studies have predominantly concentrated on individual cases, stressing the irreducible singularity of each trauma, I choose to focus on the public nature of the texts I analyze. Staged in the public sphere, the cases I discuss can be understood as theaters of justice that raise political as well as ethical questions. As Hannah Arendt reminds us, theater is the most worldly of literary genres.[36] Whereas poetry speaks to us as individuals, and the novel concentrates on humanity's social dimension, theatrical plays tend to address us as citizens—as members of a community. My question is, What happens when stories of trauma are enacted in the public sphere? How do they speak to us? What call do they make to us? Following Mieke Bal's suggestion in *Traveling Concepts* to take the theatrical term of mise-en-scène as a theoretical concept that enables one to analyze the way in which cultural texts are put to "work" in a particular scene, I propose to study the scenes constructed by Arendt, Delbo, and Brecht as particular, *dated* performances.[37] Through the particular, historic mise-en-scène of each, they implicate various audiences. *Eichmann in Jerusalem*, *Die Maßnahme*, and Delbo's poetry and memoirs are not taken as third-person artifacts but as first-person speech acts that, when staged in the public arena, give voice to particular demands for justice.

Read together, the works of Arendt, Brecht, and Delbo reopen cases that the historic trials to which their works respond sought to close. It is precisely in this gesture of reopening that these texts find their literary dimension. "Law is a discipline of limits and of consciousness," Shoshana Felman writes in *The Juridical Unconscious*, and the function of a trial is to "close a case and to enclose it in the past."[38] We need art and literature, she suggests, to face up to a past that cannot be closed, to those aspects of the past that legal closure effaces. In their writings Arendt, Brecht, and Delbo have opened a different scene, a literary theater of justice in which the past can be staged, mourned, and, eventually, worked through.

1

Arendt's Laughter

THEATRICALITY, PEDAGOGY, AND COMEDY
IN *EICHMANN IN JERUSALEM*

> The great political criminals must be exposed and exposed especially to
> laughter. . . . One may say that tragedy deals with the sufferings of mankind
> in a less serious way than comedy.
> —Bertolt Brecht

> Laughter always bursts, and loses itself in its peals. As soon as it bursts out,
> it is lost to all appropriation, to all presentation.
> —Jean-Luc Nancy

In a letter to Mary McCarthy, written shortly after the publication of
Eichmann in Jerusalem, Hannah Arendt confesses to her lifelong friend:

You were the only reader to understand what I have otherwise never admitted—
namely that I wrote this book in a curious state of euphoria. And that ever since
I did it, I feel—after twenty years—light hearted about the whole matter. Don't
tell anybody; is it not proof positive that I have no "soul"?[1]

Years later, during an interview in Germany, Arendt repeated this admission and so acknowledged publicly the lightness of her tone. She describes
how she often laughed uncontrollably while studying the case, as when
she read in her Jerusalem hotel room "the transcript of the police investigation, thirty-six hundred pages, read it, and read it very carefully, and
I do not know how many times I laughed—laughed out loud!"[2] This eruption into laughter is of course described as a private response, taking place
in the solitude of a hotel room; and the earlier revelation of her lightheartedness is confessed from within the intimacy of a correspondence with

a dear friend. Nevertheless, the laughter Arendt describes did not remain external to her report on the Eichmann trial. In a sense, its echoes reverberate throughout the pages of *Eichmann in Jerusalem*.[3] One can hear its resonances when she calls Eichmann a "clown" (54), characterizes certain aspects of the trial as "outright funny" (48, see also 50, 288), and refers to the proceedings as "sheer comedy" (3), a "horrible comedy" (198), and a "comedy" whose "macabre humor easily surpasses that of any Surrealist invention" (50). More generally, a tone of laughter permeates her book and can clearly be discerned in the irony with which she depicts not just the figure of Eichmann but also his Israeli prosecutors and even the dramatic gestures of some of the holocaust survivors who took the witness stand during the trial.

This slightly mocking tone scandalized her critics when her report was first published.[4] Now that the dust over the debate over the content of *Eichmann in Jerusalem* seems to have settled, this tone appears to be the most enduring curiosity about the book. Arendt writes that the Eichmann trial presented itself to her as a comedy, rather than as, for example, a tragedy. To indicate how crucial the comic dimension is for her understanding of the trial as a whole, she selected as the book's epigraph Brecht's "O Germany— / Hearing the speeches that ring from your house, one laughs. / But whoever sees you, reaches for his knife."

Reading Arendt's report in the context of her contemporaries' responses to the trial, Arendt's emphasis on the trial's comic aspect is conspicuous indeed. The journalists covering the case tended to write about it with a pious solemnity. More significantly, *Eichmann in Jerusalem*'s ironic tone distinguishes it from that of Arendt's earlier exploration into the evils of fascism in *The Origins of Totalitarianism* (1951). Whereas that book had been written in a tone of high moral seriousness and expressed a patent sense of indignation, and therefore seemed to bear itself heavily under the "burden of our times," (its original title), *Eichmann in Jerusalem* displays by contrast that aura of lightheartedness that typically follows a moment of laughter.

Although *Eichmann in Jerusalem* wears this laughter on its sleeve— and received disapproving comments from her contemporaries because of it—her tone is rarely acknowledged and almost never analyzed by current Arendt scholarship.[5] Most critics who nowadays champion Arendt's report go through rather painstaking efforts to defend the book's moral seriousness—the publisher's copy on a recent paperback edition praises Arendt for her "compassion," her "outrage," and her "true sense of tragedy"— thereby going against everything the text so clearly flaunts about itself.[6]

Yet I would contend that if Arendt's book still speaks to us now, more than forty years after its publication, it is exactly because of the roaring laughter that sounds in it, which we have not yet assimilated.

The aim of this chapter, then, is to analyze Arendt's laughter, or rather, what I would like to call, in her terms, "the precision of her laughter."[7] What exactly does her laughter entail, and to what does it respond? I would be reluctant to reduce it to a "distancing" device as is suggested by, among others, Shoshana Felman, Deborah Nelson, and Alan Rosen.[8] As Arendt herself indicates in the interview with Gauss quoted above, her laughter was not a means to control her emotions; her bursting into laughter caught her by surprise and overcame her. Coming to grips with such roaring laughter may be a daunting task because, as Nancy has reminded us, laughter poses a challenge to conceptual thinking. It is rarely fully present, he writes: It slips away and disappears almost as soon as it sounds, falling out of our hands at the very moment we seem to grasp it.[9] The question that I would like to raise in this chapter is: What is the relation between Arendt's laughter and the particular mode of understanding implied by the tone of her book? Or rather, to employ Arendt's own terminology, what is the relation between her laughter and the particular *lesson* that she said the trial taught her?

Despite the criticism of the trial's overtly didactic ambitions (which I will discuss in the next paragraph), Arendt claims at two separate moments in her report that the proceedings taught her a lesson (she explicitly uses this term), namely that Eichmann's crimes were driven not by fanaticism, anti-Semitic hatred, or some "profound diabolical" nature but rather stemmed from his incapability to judge, speak, and think for himself. The particular nature of the Nazis' crimes should therefore not be understood of manifestations of a Kantian Radical Evil, as she had suggested in *The Origins of Totalitarianism*, but rather as fairly banal cases of "thoughtlessness."[10] She summarizes this newly gained insight in the renowned and often misunderstood phrase "the banality of evil." *Eichmann in Jerusalem* became, of course, famous—or notorious—for coining the term "the banality of evil," and most Arendt scholars tend to treat this phrase as a summary of the book's "claim," interpreting it as a philosophical, psychological, or legal concept employed to analyze Eichmann's behavior.

Overlooked in almost all of these discussions, however, is the phrase's peculiar status in Arendt's book. Grasping its nature may perhaps be as difficult as getting a grip on Arendt's laughter itself. As she explains in the introduction to the first part of *Life of the Mind* (1971, 1978), the phrase, when used in her report on the Eichmann trial, implied neither a "thesis" nor a "doctrine" about the nature of evil, nor was it a psychological concept explaining Eichmann's behavior. It was simply a shorthand expression referring to a particular type of *scene* that "struck her" as a spectator of the trial.[11] As she writes in the postscript to *Eichmann in Jerusalem*: "When I speak of the banality of evil, I do so on a strictly factual level, pointing to a phenomenon *which stared one in the face* at the trial" (287, my emphasis). She goes on to elaborate what she means not by defining this banality conceptually but by contrasting it to other theatrical scenes of evil:

Eichmann was not Iago and not Macbeth, and nothing would have been farther from his mind than to determine with Richard III "to prove a villain." Except for an extraordinary diligence in looking out for his personal advancement, he had no motives at all . . . He *merely*, to put the matter colloquially, *never realized what he was doing.* (287, emphasis in original)

The above formulations suggest to me that the phrase "the banality of evil," when used in *Eichmann in Jerusalem*, does not in the first place refer to the (philosophical, political, or legal) content of the lesson that she learned in Jerusalem but rather to the theatrical structure of a surprising scene that *struck* her, as a spectator, with an impact that she describes as didactic. She continues:

That such [that is, Eichmann's] remoteness from reality and such thoughtlessness can wreak more havoc than all instincts taken together which, perhaps, are inherent in man—that was, in fact, the lesson one could learn in Jerusalem. *But it was a lesson, neither an explanation of the phenomenon, nor a theory about it.* (288, my emphasis)

Hence, in *Eichmann in Jerusalem* the phrase "the banality of evil" points to a lesson that is not (yet) articulated in conceptual terms and transposed into a set of assertions that would add up to an explanation or a theory. As a lesson it is (still) marked by the first-person *experience of learning*, of being struck by something unexpected and new whose impact has not (yet) been solidified into a thesis or a doctrine articulated in the third person. The phrase seems to point to what she had called earlier, in "Understanding and Politics" (1954), a "preliminary understanding": a grasping of the newness of a phenomenon, which precedes its analytical understanding. This preliminary moment of understanding typically results in a new coinage: "Whenever we are confronted with something frighteningly new, our first impulse is to recognize it in a blind and uncontrolled reaction, strong enough to coin a new word."[12] New phrases, such as "the banality of evil," do not, then, express a full conceptual understanding but merely acknowledge the recognition of something "frighteningly new." They are spontaneous responses to an experience that attempt to express something on the threshold between understanding and not (yet) understanding.[13]

*

In this chapter I propose to understand *Eichmann in Jerusalem* as a report on an *unexpected didactic event* and as an attempt to render the *experience* of learning its lesson without translating it into an explanation or theory that would explain away its shocking impact. I seek to demonstrate that the experience of learning is intricately bound up with Arendt's bursting into laughter and her understanding of the trial as comedy. Hence *Eichmann in Jerusalem* is (implicitly) an investigation into the relations among a unique trial, its peculiar theatrical nature, and the unexpected way in which the event became pedagogical. To indicate how Arendt's understanding of both the didactic impact of the Eichmann trial and its theatrical nature differs from way the Israeli government understood it, I will first describe some of that government's stated goals for the Eichmann trial, as well as Arendt's criticism of these aims. Second, I will analyze Arendt's own understanding of the theatrical nature of the trial. *Eichmann in Jerusalem* implicitly contains, I argue, a theory about the didactic nature of the legal theater. I will explicate this theory by comparing her book to Rolf Hochhuth's play *Der Stellvertreter* (1963), a comparison Arendt herself invites in the postscript to her book. Third, I will discuss what was, according to Arendt, the trial's "lesson"—or rather the lesson that *she* learned as a spectator of the trial, linking it precisely to her eruption into laughter. My chapter concludes with a reflection on the question: How, according to Arendt, did the Eichmann trial become a didactic event? There I will return to the very precise meaning possessed by the notion of "understanding" in Arendt's work.

Beth Hamishpath! The Courtroom as a Theater

Eichmann in Jerusalem (1963) opens by citing the call of the bailiff who announces the judges' arrival into the courtroom:

"*Beth Hamishpath*"—the House of Justice. (3)

These words, uttered on April 11, 1961, opened the proceedings of the Jerusalem District Court against Adolf Eichmann, the former chief of the Gestapo's Division of Jewish Affairs, under indictment for crimes against the Jewish people, for crimes against humanity, and for having been a member of criminal organizations. As Arendt indicates in the book's introduction, from the very beginning there was confusion about the precise goals that the trial was supposed to achieve, some of which exceeded strictly legal goals. The Knesset had announced that the widespread dissemination of the proceedings through all available media was a highly desirable social objective.[14] In addition, shortly before the opening of the legal proceedings, Prime Minister Ben-Gurion declared that for Israel the verdict of the trial mattered less than the spectacle staged for a global audience, a spectacle intended to teach Israel and the world a few lessons about the Holocaust. In pretrial statements Ben-Gurion spelled out how these various lessons would be directed toward different audiences. For the non-Jewish world, the trial was supposed to provide a lesson about the Holocaust and their implication in it; Jews in the Diaspora would be instructed that Israel was the only certain protection for Jews in an anti-Semitic and hostile world; and finally, for the younger generation of Jews inside Israel who had not lived through the war, the trial was going to be a history lesson about what had happened in the 1930s and 1940s (10).

If the exclamation *"Beth Hamishpath"* had, in Arendt's words, the effect of a "rising curtain" (4), what followed was a highly complex, multilayered theatrical scene, meant to stage various lessons addressed to different audiences inside and outside the courtroom, in Israel as well as the rest of the world. This theater was to extend outside the spatial confines of the courtroom and was to be preserved for the future: The entirety of the proceedings was transcribed, archived, audiotaped, and filmed. Arendt describes the mise-en-scène of the trial in cinematic detail, as if to trace the building's transformation under the impact of those inaugural words. She introduces the central figures of the legal drama that would unfold in the following months: the black-robed judges, flanked by court stenographers, who have taken their seats at the long table that soon will be covered with books and documents; directly below them, the translators and radio equipment; the accused, surrounded by a protective glass booth; and finally, occupying the lowest tier, the prosecutor and the counsel for the defense (3).

As is well known, Arendt was critical of the Israeli attempt to turn the Eichmann trial into "didactic theater." A large part of the polemical thrust of her book is aimed at the efforts of Ben-Gurion—the "invisible stage manager" (5) directing the proceedings—and prosecutor Gideon Hausner to make this legal event a "show trial" (4). Patiently she spells out the differences between a "house of justice," opened by the *Beth Hamishpath* of the bailiff, and the legal theater envisioned by the Israeli government. Although a courtroom resembles a theater in many ways because legal proceedings take place before an audience separated from the legal scene (coincidentally, the design of the auditorium of the *Beth Ha'am* was modeled on a theater "complete with orchestra and gallery, with proscenium and stage, and with side doors for the actors' entrance" [4]), a trial, if it is a theatrical event, is one oriented toward a very particular goal: "The purpose of a trial is to render justice; even the noblest of ulterior purposes . . . can only detract from this" (253). Even if, she writes, the rendering of justice requires a theatrical scene, as "justice must not only be done, but must be seen to be done" (277), its theatricality differs from that of the dramatic show trial envisioned by the prosecution. Justice needs seclusion; it prescribes "the most careful abstention from all the nice pleasures of putting oneself in the limelight" (6). The trial's success, Arendt maintains, would be largely due to the presiding judges' refusal to fall into the trap of playacting.[15]

Hence, from the very first pages of her book onward, Arendt is critical of both the trial's didactic ambitions and its particular theatrical nature. This criticism was not limited to what she calls the prosecutor's "love of showmanship" (4). It also extended to the large number of witnesses whom the prosecution called to testify. Unlike the Nuremberg Tribunal, which relied largely on written documents that were believed to be more reliable than eyewitness testimony, the Eichmann trial contained sworn accounts by a large group of eyewitnesses called to take the stand. Over the course of sixty-two sessions, the presiding judges, along with the audience gathered in Jerusalem's House of the People, heard the testimonies of more than a hundred survivors from all over Europe, ranging from those confined to ghettoes to those incarcerated in the death camps. No small part of the trial's historical impact was in its providing a forum for these stories to be told, for the first time, in a public sphere whose reach was global in scope.[16]

Some testimonies were given not for strictly legal reasons. Twenty-three sessions were devoted to those Arendt calls "background witnesses" (207, 225), referred to by the Israeli authorities as "sufferings-of-the-Jewish-people-witnesses" (207), witnesses whose testimony served to "paint a picture" of the Holocaust in general without necessarily providing evidence of Eichmann's particular responsibility for specific atrocities. Largely impatient with what she calls the "huge panorama of Jewish sufferings" put up by the prosecution (8), Arendt offers descriptions of what she considers the overly melodramatic gestures of some of the witnesses that can at times come off as somewhat cruel. She suspects that these are yet further elements of the scripted didacticism of the trial, or the "spectacle" that Ben-Gurion had hoped for. The world, represented by the journalists and magazine writers who had "flocked to Jerusalem from the four corners of the earth" were promised a "spectacle as sensational as the Nuremberg trials" (6). This time, however, she adds, citing a pretrial statement by Ben-Gurion, "the tragedy of Jewry as a whole was to be the central concern" (6). For Arendt, the problem with this "spectacle of suffering" is that it diverts attention from the accused, whose acts, after all, should be at the center of a trial ostensibly meant to pass judgment on him. In fact, the very question of Eichmann's responsibility was obscured under the weight of the victims' individual stories:

As witness followed witness and horror was piled upon horror . . . the more "the calamity of the Jewish people in this generation" unfolded and the more grandiose Mr. Hausner's rhetoric became, the paler and more ghostlike became the figure in the glass booth, and no finger-wagging: "And there sits the monster responsible for all this," could shout him back to life. (8)

Arendt insists that it is Eichmann's deeds, and not personal accounts of suffering, that should be held up for judgment. Comparing the spectacular trial to a play, she maintains that its central character should be the perpetrator who stands accused because of his acts and asserts that it should end in the pronouncement of a verdict.[17] But here the central role assigned to the victims, Arendt argues, threatens to close the particular theatrical space opened up by the *Beth Hamispath* of the bailiff and to turn its protagonist into a specter. Hence her report skips most of the scenes of witness testimony, preferring to focus on a detailed analysis of the intricate bureaucracy of the Nazi machine of killing to assess Eichmann's role within it.

*

As obvious as Arendt's insistence on the centrality of the perpetrator and the delivery of a verdict may be from a legal point of view—recent commentators on the trial even called her stance conservative and overdogmatic—as a report on the Eichmann trial as a *theatrical* spectacle,

Arendt stands virtually alone.[18] A quick glance at the responses to her book, as well as other journalistic or literary essays on the trial, reveals that Arendt's vision of the Eichmann-trial-as-play is distinctly different from her peers in selecting Eichmann as its protagonist, as well in her understanding of the type of closure that it should provide. Responding as willing spectators, most journalists did indeed focus their attention on the spectacle of Jewish suffering that was staged in Jerusalem. Some even compared the trial's impact with that of a classic Greek tragedy, precisely following the prosecution's rhetoric by pointing to moments of catharsis and redemption as the trial's possible outcomes.[19] A notable example of a tragic reading of the trial would be Susan Sontag's, which argues that the Eichmann trial, in fact, is an attempt to deal in a theatrical way with the "supreme tragic event of modern times," that is, the Holocaust, which she calls a "wound that will not heal."[20] Provocatively calling the Eichmann trial "the most interesting and moving work of art of the past ten years," she explains that in the wake of World War II, the trial has assumed the historical function of tragic poetry that traditionally served to make the pathetic and terrifying past live again in the mind.[21] The large number of witnesses heard in Jerusalem indicates to her that the cultural role of the trial exceeded that of the mere rendering of a judgment. The function of the trial, to her, was its offering of a moment of catharsis:

The truth is, that the Eichmann trial did not, and could not, have conformed to legal standards only. . . . Masses of facts about the extermination of the Jews were piled into the record; a great outcry of historical agony was set down. There was, needless to say, no strictly legal way of justifying this. The function of the trial was rather that of the tragic drama: above and beyond judgment and punishment, catharsis.[22]

For Sontag, what is crucial about the trial's cultural impact is its staging of a different scene, *above* and *beyond* the legal drama that was to culminate in a verdict. She locates the trial's literary and perhaps even therapeutic dimension on a different plane, one that ends in a moment of catharsis. In a similar gesture, Lionel Abel—one of Arendt's fiercest critics—also saw the Eichmann trial as tragedy; but, in contrast to Sontag, he perceived its closure not as a moment of catharsis but rather as a marker pointing to a scene of redemption that has been achieved outside of the courtroom, through the founding of the State of Israel:

When we think of tragedy we must remember that the best critics of tragedy considered as an art have told us that at the end of tragedy there must be a moment of reconciliation. . . . Some good must come of so much evil; and for the Jews, this good was found only in the setting-up of the state of Israel. What came out of the Holocaust was the success of Zionism.[23]

Eichmann in Jerusalem can be understood as a polemic against such a "tragic" understanding of the trial. Throughout her book Arendt insists that the political and cultural role of a trial is to provide a different moment of closure than that which occurs in a tragedy; it ends in a verdict, a scene of *justice*, rather than a moment of catharsis or redemption. Furthermore, as she implicitly states, such a scene requires a specific type of spectator. The critics who castigated Arendt's book for its cold and unsympathetic tone generally assumed that the trial self-evidently scripted a compassion-ate observer; the trial's cultural function was to foster feelings of compas-sion for the Holocaust's victims.[24] *Eichmann in Jerusalem*'s epitaph from Brecht—an author who in Arendt's eyes always fought the temptations of compassion[25]—as well as its judgmental, ironic, and somewhat impa-tient tone testify to the author's resisting of the appeal to compassion and sympathy that the trial's "spectacle of suffering" made on its spectators. Instead of the sympathetic audience of a tragedy, who feel for the victims, the theater of judgment put up by a trial, Arendt seems to be suggesting, needs a cold and rational spectator who observes the scene with detach-ment and is ready to pronounce her own independent verdict. To indicate that her report is indeed written from this perspective, Arendt opens her book by citing the *Beth Hamispath*—the very words pronounced by the bailiff, which transformed the "house of the people" into a courtroom—and ends the reportage section with a three-page address to Eichmann in which she pronounces her own verdict, concluding with "and therefore you must hang," thereby mimicking the very structure of the trial.

As Deborah Nelson has convincingly demonstrated, Arendt's insis-tence on judgment and the ostentatious display of lack of sympathy in her report stem not so much from "coldness" or "heartlessness" on her part, as some critics have suggested, but should rather be understood in rela-tion to her overall suspicion toward the role assumed by the sentiment of pity in the public sphere.[26] *Eichmann in Jerusalem* was written as she prepared *On Revolution* for publication. This latter book contains a sus-tained reflection on what Arendt considers to be the "disastrous" effects of the politicization of feelings of pity in revolutionary discourse from the end of the eighteenth century onward.[27] Because it is boundless, pity for the poor and the destitute, Arendt argues in a chapter entitled "The Social

Question," forms a threat to the political sphere. Feelings of pity tend to engulf the subject and thus close the distance between self and others, thereby threatening the worldly space in between people on which politics relies.[28] A revolutionary "politics of pity" that seeks to act on behalf of the needy therefore threatens the political realm as a separate sphere.[29] It understands political action as a response to "natural" feelings of pity that one cannot argue with and furthermore implies a transition from a republican notion of the body politic as a sphere of differences into an understanding of "the people" as a monolithic unity.[30] We may extrapolate that the trial, an event whose political function in Arendt's eyes is to protect the public realm, thus relies on coldness and must, precisely, resist engendering feelings of sympathy and compassion.[31] Moreover, because the Eichmann trial was organized in the wake of the massive onslaught on the public realm by the Nazis its contribution to a process of overcoming this past may need to rely on a judgmental coldness rather than on empathy. Indeed, responding to a letter by Gershom Scholem, who had criticized her judgmental tone and lack of sympathy, Arendt states that the cultural function of the trial lies precisely in the judgmental attitude that it encourages: "I believe we shall only come to terms with *this* past," she writes, "if we begin to judge and to be frank about it."[32]

*

Hence, much of the debate over *Eichmann in Jerusalem* can be understood as a disagreement over the exact theatrical "genre" after which the trial was modeled, and consequently what type of spectator it would therefore require, and finally how to understand the didactic, therapeutic, or political impact on this spectator. On one side of this debate, we find critics like Abel, Sontag, and Scholem, who considered the trial to be staging a tragedy of suffering that hence called for a spectator's empathy and, as a consequence, allowed for mourning or some sort of catharsis to take place. On the other side stands Arendt, virtually alone in the view that the spectacle mounted in Jerusalem required a spectator who observed its scenes with detachment and who, precisely because of her coldness and lack of sympathy, is ready to pronounce her own verdict on the case, thereby effectively redoubling the very scene that she observes. These different interpretations of the trial's theatrical nature also imply divergent ideas about its possible didactic-therapeutic function. The tragic conception of the trial, here represented by the remarks made by Sontag and

Abel, holds that it helps us come to terms with the past in a cathartic moment of emotional cleansing by giving voice to what Sontag calls a "cry of agony." Going a step further, Lionel Abel even indicates that the trial's implicit reference to the founding of Israel allows for a redeeming moment of reconciliation with the Holocaust. Arendt, in contrast, sticks to the idea that only by adopting the cold attitude of a judgmental spectator could the legal spectacle in Jerusalem acquire its didactic function.

Implicit in the debate over *Eichmann in Jerusalem* is thus a confrontation between two different understandings of the pedagogical scene put up by the trial: a learning-through-catharsis versus a learning-through-judgment. Because Arendt did claim that she learned a lesson in Jerusalem, as I indicated above, this raises the question: What exactly is the relation between learning and judging? How are the specific lessons she learned made possible by the position she assumed as a spectator? To put it in more general terms, the questions at the heart of the debate over *Eichmann in Jerusalem* are as follows: What are the relations between the legal scene and the scene of teaching? Under what circumstances can the quasi-theatrical space, opened up by the *Beth Hamispath* of the bailiff, become a didactic space?

Dramas of Judgment: Reading *Eichmann in Jerusalem* with *Der Stellvertreter*

In the postscript to the book, Arendt reflects on the controversy when her report was first published in *The New Yorker*. By suggesting that the reactions to her work show strong similarities to those provoked by Rolf Hochhuth's play *Der Stellvertreter* (1963), she implies that what is at stake in the "affair" may indeed be her understanding of the particularly theatrical nature of the trial.[33] In evoking Hochhuth's play, Arendt effectively inserts the debate over *Eichmann* into a heated discussion about the political-didactic potential of the theater. *Der Stellvertreter* was to become the first in a series of documentary plays written by young German playwrights, such as Peter Weiss and Heinar Kipphardt, who sought precisely to transform the theater into a site of learning.[34] Finding their inspiration partly in Bertolt Brecht's and Erwin Piscator's political theater of the 1930s, these authors nevertheless differed from their predecessors in that they focused their attention for a large part on the recent (German)

past. The plot of *Der Stellvertreter*, first staged in West Berlin's Freie Volks-
bühne in 1963 by Piscator, the éminence grise of German political theater,
revolves around the refusal of Pope Pius XII to publicly denounce Nazi
policy toward the Jews, even though he was fully informed about the de-
portations. The irresponsible attitude of the pope is contrasted to that of
a fictional character, the Jesuit priest Riccardo Fontana, who assumes the
responsibility the pope refuses. In a dramatic moment in act five, Fontana
pins the Star of David to his cassock and announces that he will accompany a group of Jews who are to be deported to Auschwitz. In the play, the
motivation behind the young priest's decision remains partly a mystery.
His act is depicted not as a planned and calculated choice but rather as an
impulsive decision that overcomes him after he has witnessed too much
suffering.

Although the published text of the play included a sixty-five-page
supplement with "historical sidelights" that sought to establish the historical accuracy of the play, Piscator argues in his preface that its didactic
nature is not to be found in the information it conveys but rather in the
theatrical structure in which it presents this information to its audience
and the verdict it seems to demand from them.[35] Hochhuth's *The Deputy*
is one of the few substantive contributions toward "mastering the past,"
Piscator holds, because it "confronts society as a theater audience" and
asks it to judge specific individuals "with names." Hochhuth's insistence
on the question of individual responsibility is set in opposition to the theater of the absurd, whose "tragedies of *Ohnmacht*" (powerlessness, impo-
tence) sought to stage the impossibility of individual's acting responsibly.
Piscator states that the understanding of history in absurdists plays effectively erases the question of guilt:

> *The Deputy* makes liars of all those who assert that a drama as a drama of decision
> [*ein Drama der Entscheidungen*], given the featureless anonymity of social-political
> arrangements and pressures in an absurd construction of human existence that
> sees everything as predetermined [*in welchem alles im vorhinein entschieden sei*]
> Thus to blot out historic action [*eine solche Theorie der Auslöschung geschichtlichen
> Handelns*] is a theory that recommends itself to those who today would like to
> escape the truth of history, the truth of their own historic acts.[36]

Against sweeping statements such as "we are all guilty" or "humanity is
on trial," Hochhuth insists on the importance of staging a drama of
Entscheidungen—a drama of decisions or distinctions.[37] Because the German

word *Entscheidungen* carries legal connotations, one could also call *Der Stellvertreter* a legal drama, a play that revolves around verdicts and judgments made by the characters on stage, as well as by the spectators in the auditorium.[38]

Perhaps because of its judgmental character, the performance of the play caused a huge row. The extensive discussion that ensued spilled over into the West German Bundestag, and even the Vatican issued a strong statement about the play.[39] In an essay in the *Herald Tribune*, Arendt seems to agree with Piscator that the controversy over the play was provoked not so much by the facts presented in the play, which she claims were never in dispute, as by the play's embedding of these indisputable facts in a theatrical structure that challenges the audience to judge the behavior of the characters on stage.[40] Returning to the case of *Der Stellvertreter* in *Eichmann in Jerusalem*, Arendt points out that while *Der Stellvertreter* asked its audience to pronounce a verdict on the pope's actions, most of the play's commentators went to great lengths to argue that we, as viewers, are in no position to judge the pontiff. Motivations for this sort of comment ranged from the clichés such as "we cannot judge if we were not present and involved ourselves" (295) to claims asserting that it is "superficial" to insist on the guilt of individuals (297) and proposing that all sorts of larger entities should "really" have been on trial in the wake of the Holocaust—humanity, Christianity, even God. These responses shared a desire to erase the aim at the very heart of Hochhuth's play: the task of judging an identifiable individual with a name, a grand position, and a title. Arendt remarks:

About nothing does public opinion everywhere seem to be in happier agreement than that no one has the right to judge somebody else. What public opinion permits us to judge and even to condemn are trends, or whole groups of people—the larger the better—in short, something so general that distinctions can no longer be made, names can no longer be named. (296)

Arendt concludes that a similar set of responses were elicited by the Eichmann trial. As a trial, it staged a scene of judgment, yet journalists, novelists, and philosophers who wrote about it were quick to sidestep the specific question of Eichmann's guilt by arguing that, actually, various larger groups were "really" on trial: Germany, the West, or, indeed, humankind as a whole. This mode of reasoning was adopted as well by the prosecution—the very figure responsible for articulating an accusation—in its remark that "it is not an individual that is in the dock at this historic trial, and not the Nazi regime alone, but anti-Semitism throughout history" (19), an observation that was followed by a broad historical outline of this "abstract category," starting with the Egyptian pharaohs. For Arendt this strategy absolved Eichmann of guilt by insinuating that he was a mere "innocent executor of some mysteriously foreordained destiny" (19). Such strategies allowing for an "escape from the area of judgment" can also be found in the many sweeping, nonspecific "explanations" of Eichmann's behavior and of the Holocaust in general offered in the press. These commentaries invoked all sorts of generalities to account for the Holocaust: the notion of *Zeitgeist*, the typicality of German national character, the submissive ghetto mentality of the Jews. Obsessively invoked by the popular press, these ready-made explanations showed a widespread desire to sidestep the question of judgment. As Arendt phrases it: "All these clichés have in common that *they make judgment superfluous* and that to utter them is devoid of all risk" (297, emphasis mine).

The general discomfort with the prospect or obligation of having to make a judgment, apparent in commentaries about the Eichmann trial as well as Hochhuth's play, is, I feel, significant. Both the fictional and the legal trial revolve around accused individuals whose "crime" precisely consists of their attempt to disavow their responsibility to judge. The pope, in Hochhuth's view, was neither a fanatic nor "a criminal for *raisons d'état*, but rather a political neuter, an over-industrious careerist," whose "clever," calculating attitude led him to an attitude of neutrality. *Der Stellvertreter*, careful to avoid the larger question of the Vatican's anti-Semitism, refuses to place this story in the broader context of Catholic anti-Semitism and concentrates on Riccardo as a Catholic hero.[41] Likewise, in Arendt's portrayal, Eichmann is neither a fanatical anti-Semite nor a perverse sadist. Rather, his evil resulted from his "thoughtlessness," his refusal to think and judge for himself. The drama of "thoughtlessness," displayed by Eichmann's life story, reaches its climax during the Wannsee conference, which authorized the Final Solution. This was surely the most important decision ever witnessed by Eichmann, but when he saw that all the people whom he held in high regard did not object to the Final Solution, he felt absolved of all responsibility. "At that moment, I sensed a kind of Pontius Pilate feeling, for I felt free of all guilt," he thought. "*Who was he to judge?*" (114). In *Der Stellvertreter* this "Pontius Pilate feeling" manifests itself in the pope's neurotic obsession with washing his hands, a trope with its basis in the scriptural record that becomes, in Hochhuth's treatment, a sign of the Holy Father's attempt to absolve himself (380).

As Arendt acknowledges, Eichmann's "thoughtlessness" should be understood in context. Eichmann commits his crimes "under circumstances that make it well-nigh impossible for him to know or to feel that he is doing wrong" (276). Although Eichmann was not a criminal in the limited sense of the term, his crimes were nevertheless "committed under a criminal *law*" (262) and under the complete breakdown of morality in Nazi Germany. Eichmann could feel like a "law-abiding citizen" who simply "did his *duty*" (135) as he understood it. He no longer regarded himself as master of his own deeds. Or, as Eichmann himself puts it in his final statement, his "guilt came from his obedience, and obedience is praised as a virtue" (247). Whereas Eichmann's defense sought to exculpate him from guilt on this basis, it is precisely under such circumstances that one should apply one's faculty of judgment, Arendt explains. The capacity to judge only becomes a *responsibility* in situations in which general rules simply do not apply. When the whole world seems to offer its complicity with grave injustice, we can rely only on our own judgments. People who acted responsibly during the war did so out of a certain "arrogance"— they "dared" to take the risk to judge:[42]

Those few who were still able to tell right from wrong went really only by their own judgments, and they did so freely; there were no rules to be abided by, under which the particular cases with which they were confronted could be subsumed. They had to decide each instance as it arose, because no rules existed for the unprecedented. (295)

Judging becomes a genuinely ethical-political decision only when we do it *freely*—when a judgment cannot be determined by calculation or by the application of a rule. In other words, our capacity to act responsibly is possible only if we dare to sidestep what was for Eichmann the essential question: "Who are we to judge?" In a series of philosophical texts written after the trial, which were intended to culminate in the final part of *Life of the Mind*, Arendt turns to Kant to conceptualize the faculty of judgment.[43] Kant's *Critique of Judgment* (1790), originally a study on aesthetics, offers Arendt a starting point for rethinking political and moral judgment as something other than the mere application of general rules to specific situations.[44] Judging always implies dealing with the singularity of a situation in a scenario in which general rules seem not to apply. Therefore, it implies a leap.

An instance of such a leap is exemplified by the story of Anton Schmid (misspelled "Schmidt" in *Eichmann*), narrated by a witness during the trial. Schmid was a *Feldwebel* (sergeant) in the German Army on the Eastern Front who, witnessing the ongoing massacre of the Jews, felt obliged to help the Jewish Resistance in Poland by providing them with forged papers, weapons, and trucks. He did so without asking them for money.[45] Arendt emphasizes that nothing, indeed, had prepared Schmid for this surprising heroic action; his decision to act on the Jews' behalf was precisely *not* based on a following of moral guidelines or an observance of honor codes. Schmid acted freely. When his actions were discovered by the Nazis, he was executed. The narrating of this heroic story was one of the "dramatic highpoints" of the trial, Arendt holds, and when it was revealed that he had been executed, a hush settled over the courtroom, as if "the crowd had spontaneously decided to observe the usual two minutes of silence in honor of the man named Anton Schmidt [sic]" (231):

And in those two minutes, which were like a sudden burst of light in the midst of impenetrable, unfathomable darkness, a single thought stood out clearly, irrefutable, beyond question—how utterly different everything would be today in this courtroom, in Israel, in Germany, in all of Europe, and perhaps in all countries of the world, if only more such stories could have been told. (231)

During these unexpected dramatic moments, which could not have been scripted by the prosecution, the trial became truly a didactic event. Arendt even uses the word *lesson* to describe the impact of this story:

For the lesson of such stories is simple and within everybody's grasp. Politically speaking, it is that under conditions of terror most people will comply but *some people will not*, just as the lesson of the countries to which the Final Solution was proposed is that it "could happen" in most places, but *it did not happen everywhere*. Humanly speaking, no more is required, and no more can reasonably be asked, for this planet to remain a place fit for human habitation. (233, emphasis in original)

I would argue that for Arendt, the story of Anton Schmid constitutes more than a history lesson. The heroic actions of Schmid are singular historical events, but when brought into the public limelight of the trial they assume a different status and become didactic examples. In "Truth and Politics," written as a further reflection on the Eichmann trial, Arendt explains that precisely because the act of judging cannot be reduced to the mere application a set of preexisting rules to a specific situation, the capacity to judge cannot be taught by merely explicating moral principles. We can only *train* our ability to judge by turning to the examples of previous judgments made by others.[46] These examples acquire an "exemplary validity"; that is, they can demonstrate and teach us something in a setting that I would call theatrical. When singled out as examples in front of the gaze of an audience of judge-spectators, the particularity of these historic examples is retained, yet their universal dimension is revealed and preserved for posterity.[47] This preservation is important because for Arendt the memory of others' judgments guides us through our lives and forms the background against which we employ our own faculty of judgment. This background, then, constitutes our "common sense"—the Kantian *sensus communis*—which is precisely *not* a set of rules or principles but an imaginary company of exemplary judgments made in the past. As Arendt remarked during a course on "Basic Moral Propositions" in 1971: "Our decisions about right and wrong will depend upon our choice of company, with whom we wish to spend our lives. And this company is chosen through thinking in examples, in examples of persons dead or alive, and in examples of incidents, past or present."[48]

By bringing Schmid's story to the legal stage, another such example was added to our collective memory, and as such it fulfilled a specific didactic function.

*

Hence the controversies over Arendt's book and Hochhuth's play revolve around the problem of judgment in several ways. First, the Eichmann trial and *Der Stellvertreter* present stories that dramatize the importance of judging and the disastrous consequences of a disavowal of the responsibility to judge. Second, these stories are embedded in dramatic structures that elicit a judgment, either from the court (as in Eichmann's case) or from the audience (as in *Der Stellvertreter*). As Piscator and Arendt suggest, it is precisely because of this shared structure that the play and the trial have didactic impact. By inviting the audience to judge the behavior of two pairs of named individuals, Pope Pius XII and Adolf Eichmann on the one hand and Riccardo Fontana and Anton Schmid on the other, these historical figures become examples that teach us lessons. These lessons are neither philosophical nor theoretical (or cognitive), but they are practical in that they teach us how to make our own judgments. Yet, in an uncanny repetition of precisely the dramas staged by the Eichmann trial and Hochhuth's play, the responses at the time and for some time thereafter culminated in a emphatic refusal to render a verdict, articulated in the ubiquitous exclamation: "Who am I to judge?" Arendt's report on the Eichmann trial, as well as her short essay on Hochhuth's play, differ from these responses in that she explicitly assumes the role of judge, which is evident in her judgmental style as well as the very structure of her report, an account that, as I've said, ended in a verdict. Like Piscator, Arendt holds that precisely because the Eichmann trial solicits a verdict, it is transformed into a site in which the past can be worked through.

*

In Chapter 2 I will discuss the precise content of Arendt's own verdict, to analyze the relations between judging and working through. Referring to Karl Jaspers's *The Question of German Guilt*, an essay that exerted a crucial influence on both Hochhuth and Arendt, I will spell out differences among legal, political, and moral judgments.[49] In the remainder of this chapter I will analyze the theater that Arendt's judgmental attitude allowed her to see. As I indicated in the beginning of this chapter, because she watched the proceedings from a certain distanced vantage and did not fully give in to empathy Arendt saw in Jerusalem not a spectacle that resembled a tragedy but rather one that was at times close to a comedy. "Despite all efforts of the prosecution," Arendt writes, "everybody could see that this man [i.e., Eichmann] was not a 'monster,' but it was difficult not to suspect that he was a clown" (54).

At the heart of the drama put up by the trial, according to Arendt, is the conflict between the laughable nature of Eichmann's personality and the terrible consequences of his acts. She explains that this "dilemma between the unspeakable horror of the deeds and the undeniable ludicrousness of the man who perpetrated them" (54) posed such problems for the prosecution, the judges, and those who came to Jerusalem to report on the trial that most of them chose to remain blind to it. The prosecution, which followed its own agenda, simply declared Eichmann a monster and a "clever, calculating liar—which he obviously was not" (54). The judges found it difficult to take Eichmann's banality into account because they sensed, as Arendt suggests, that recognizing it would have been fatal to their whole enterprise (54). For criminal proceedings are based on the assumption that human beings are capable of judging right from wrong, "even when all they have to guide them is their own judgment" (295), which Eichmann clearly could not do. The spectators and reporters in the auditorium, empathizing with the suffering of the victims, could not see anything "funny" about Eichmann either. As Arendt acknowledges, it was an observation "rather hard to sustain in view of the sufferings he and his like had caused to millions of people" (54). As a result, Eichmann's "worst clowneries were hardly noticed and almost never reported" (54).

Among the reporters at the trial, Arendt is unique in her decision to take seriously Eichmann's ludicrousness. She takes the bursting into laughter he provokes as an occasion for learning something new because, as she states in the postscript, the spectacle of Eichmann's banality, as staged in Jerusalem, did teach a *lesson*. This lesson, however, differs in content from the lesson that was exemplified by Anton Schmid and is taught in a different theatrical scene. The lesson of Anton Schmid only receives its full didactic force, she suggests, once it is transformed into a story and committed to (collective) memory. The silence that followed the telling of Schmid's story in Jerusalem, then, is precisely the time that is necessary for his story's implications to sink into the audience's consciousness. The staging of Eichmann's banal refusal to judge, on the other hand, seems to elicit—at least in Arendt—an altogether different response: that of an uproarious laughter. As a didactic event, the Eichmann trial consists of a juxtaposition of two examples that teach two different lessons, whose pedagogical structure, however, seems for each to be profoundly different from the other's. Whereas the "positive" lesson taught by the case of Schmid is something that can be collectively received, the "negative" lesson offered by Eichmann's case seems to culminate in a scene of comedy. Obviously, the lesson exemplified by Anton Schmid serves in *Eichmann in Jerusalem* as a counterpoint to the lesson that emerges from Eichmann's banal refusal to judge for himself: The darkness of this latter lesson becomes visible only when seen in the light of the counterexample of Anton Schmid, just as the pope's irresponsibility assumes its full clarity when set against the heroic decision of the fictional priest in Hochhuth's play.[50] At first sight, the examples of Schmid and Riccardo and those of Eichmann and the pope seem to relate as figure to ground, as the banal refusal of judgment serves only to make more visible the contours of the heroic priest and *feldwebel*. Yet, the precise nature of this "negative" lesson remains a bit of an enigma in the book. Indeed, what type of "understanding" is embodied by laughter?

In the discussion that follows I will analyze the paradoxical pedagogical nature of the "lesson" of Eichmann's banality. I am interested in the question as to how the experience of learning this lesson relates to a moment of *bursting into laughter*. My question is: What type of understanding (or nonunderstanding) does Arendt's laughter represent? And second, how does her laughter erupt out of the particular position she assumes as a spectator of this trial? The starting point for my discussion will be a specific moment during the proceedings—a singular moment, perhaps marginal to the legal proceedings itself, that nonetheless staged, according to Arendt, everything that could be learned in Jerusalem, namely the scene in which Eichmann, standing at the gallows, pronounces his last words. It is in relation to this moment, and, perhaps surprisingly, *only* in relation to this scene, that she uses the phrase "the banality of evil."

"Long Live Germany, Long Live Argentina": Eichmann's Funniest Moments

But what if irony is always of understanding, if what is at stake in irony is always the question of whether it is possible to understand or not to understand?
—Paul de Man

Kant . . . seems to have been unique among the philosophers in being sovereign enough to join in the laughter of the common man.
—Hannah Arendt

In a chapter entitled "Judgment, Appeal, and Execution" (234–252), Arendt relates, with some irony, how Eichmann went to the gallows with great poise. He drank some wine and refused to talk with a Protestant minister because, as he claimed rather pompously, he had two more hours to live, and thus "no time to waste" (252). He walked to the execution chamber calm and erect and refused the black hood that was offered to him. "He was in complete command of himself," Arendt writes, adding with a hint of sarcasm, "nay, he was more: he was completely himself" (252):

Nothing could have demonstrated this more convincingly than the grotesque silliness of his last words. He began by stating emphatically that he was a *Gottsgläubiger*, to express in common Nazi fashion that he was no Christian and did not believe in life after death. He then proceeded: "After a short while, gentlemen, *we shall all meet again*. Such is the fate of all men. Long live Germany, long live Argentina, long live Austria. *I shall not forget them*." (252, emphasis in original)

If Eichmann is completely himself and shows no anxiety when faced with his own death, his behavior is an emblem of his profound inauthenticity and his inability to fully become himself. In the hour of his death, confronted with his own mortality, he is capable only of uttering empty phrases. These clichés, moreover, contradict each other. How can he first declare that he is a *Gottsgläubiger*, suggesting that he does not believe in life after death, only then to state "we shall all meet again"? And what does it mean to announce that he will *never* forget Germany, Austria, and Argentina at the very moment when his death is imminent? Arendt comments on this almost black-comic moment by noting that while Eichmann was now more "himself" than the audience of the trial had previously seen, he had forgotten the situation he was in. Even now, his thoughtlessness was apparent: "In the face of death, he had found the cliché used in funeral oratory. Under the gallows, his memory played him the last trick; he was 'elated' and forgot that this was his own funeral" (252). She concludes:

It was as though in those last minutes he was summing up the lesson that this long course in human wickedness had taught us—the lesson of the fearsome, word-and-thought-defying *banality of evil*. (252, emphasis in original)

When Arendt uses the phrase "the banality of evil" in the postscript to the book, which is the only other place where it is mentioned in *Eichmann in Jerusalem*, she again singles out this scene of black comedy to illustrate her point. Eichmann's banality should not be equated with stupidity, nor can we simply call it something common:

It surely cannot be so common that a man facing death, and moreover, standing beneath the gallows, should be able to think of nothing but what he has heard at funerals all his life, and that these "lofty words" should completely becloud the reality of his own death. (288)[51]

Again, she concludes that this scene of comedy dramatizes the lessons that could be learned in Jerusalem:

That such remoteness from reality and such thoughtlessness can wreak more havoc than all evil instincts taken together, which, perhaps, are inherent in man—that was, in fact, the lesson one could learn in Jerusalem. But it was a lesson, neither an explanation nor a theory about it. (288)

Obviously, Eichmann's final words summarize the overall lesson of the trial, that is, that a banal "thoughtlessness," rather than "evil instincts," is responsible for the gravest atrocities of our era. Yet what strikes me, beyond the content of this lesson—which Arendt would reflect on philosophically in her later publications—is the remarkable fact that this lesson—that would otherwise remain word-and-thought defying—is taught through a precise theatrical figure: dramatic irony. When Eichmann exclaims "Long live Germany . . . I shall not forget them" at his own execution scene, he does not seem to grasp the implication of his words; or rather, he does not understand his implication *in* his own words. He finds the right words to utter, but he misunderstands the position of enunciation he is involved in. He seems not to realize that the position from which he speaks undermines the content of his words. What makes the scene silly and grotesque is that he finds the words that would be appropriate to recite at a funeral, but he forgets that he is speaking at his own execution. The comedy of this scene results from the spectators—or at least Arendt as a spectator—understanding far better than Eichmann himself the full implication of his words. As a scene of dramatic irony, its effect relies on a discontinuity between Eichmann—the character on stage—and the audience in the auditorium. Our laughter responds, perhaps, to the realization that we can no longer understand Eichmann's words by concentrating on his intentions because the true meaning of his words lies beyond the grasp of the speaker himself.

Furthermore, the baffling foolishness of Eichmann's final words is characteristic of what Arendt singles out as the main source of humor during the trial: Eichmann's peculiar use of language, more precisely his incapacity to speak in terms other than banalities or clichés. Throughout the cross-examination and during the police investigation, Eichmann consistently used worn-out phrases and colloquialisms, often in idiosyncratic ways or in a manner that seemed at odds with the gravity of what he was talking about. Much to the frustration of his judges, he stuck to the euphemistic Nazi terminology and referred to expulsion as "migration," identified other Nazis by their full official titles, and delighted in using jargon to explain the "complex of matters of migration." Even though Eichmann's memory proved to be rather limited because he did not seem to remember key events of his life story during the trial, he showed a remarkable ability to recite the different stock phrases—or the "winged words," as he called them—used on these occasions, most of which he could reproduce verbatim. These stock phrases appealed to him, Arendt suggests, because of the enormous sense of "elation" he felt when he heard them uttered. They had the additional function of shielding him from the consequences of his acts. In fact, the precise function of the Nazi "language rules"—the set of euphemisms for murderous activities used both in official documents and everyday life in Nazi Germany (such as "Final Solution," "special treatment," and "resettlement" for extermination, liquidation, and forced deportation, respectively)—was to prevent perpetrators understanding their acts in terms of their old "normal knowledge of murder and lies" (86). "Clichés, stock phrases, adherence to conventional, standardized codes of expression and conduct," she writes in *Life of the Mind*, "have the socially recognized function of protecting us against reality, that is, against the claim on our thinking attention that all events and facts make by virtue of their existence."[52]

Eichmann may have shared these habits of language with other Germans of his generation; yet typical of him, Arendt suggests, is his response to Nazi language that triggered in him "a mechanism that had become completely unalterable" (50). At one point during the cross-examination, when it dawned on him that his bureaucratic language irritated his judges, he apologizes: "Officialese [*Amtssprache*] is my only language." "The point here is," Arendt adds, "that officialese became his language because he was genuinely incapable of uttering a single sentence that was not a cliché" (48). Even when he was not quoting phrases he had overheard and finally managed to construct a sentence of his own, he repeats himself until his own words become clichés. Comparing Eichmann's use of language during the cross-examination, the police investigation, and in an autobiographical text written before his capture, Arendt notices a striking repetition of exactly the same sentences, phrased using exactly the same words.[53]

Arendt does not hesitate to compare Eichmann's mechanical, cliché-ridden speech to a mild case of aphasia (48). Eichmann, according to Arendt, was not only incapable of judging for himself, he had also lost the human capacity to speak because he proved genuinely incapable of producing sentences that were not merely *citations*. His words, even though they come out of his own mouth, *are not really his*; they are what Arendt calls, in *The Human Condition*, mere speech—empty phrases that do not disclose anything about the speaker.[54] To use the terminology employed by French linguist Emile Benveniste, Eichmann is not capable of subjectivizing himself in his discourse.[55] When Eichmann uses the first-person pronoun, he seems to be speaking as if in *the third person*; he seems to be merely the mouthpiece of a speech that finds its origin elsewhere. This is indeed most poignantly illustrated by the ludicrousness of his final words. When Eichmann shouts "Long live Germany, long live Austria, long live Argentina. I shall not forget them," the "I" who proclaims that he will not forget cannot be the same person who uttered this sentence because he is about to die. His speech suggests a splitting because the grammatical "I," the subject of the statement, cannot be the same as the subject of the utterance. In rhetorical terms, Eichmann's final words have the effect of an anacoluthon—a figure in which a syntactical pattern is unexpectedly interrupted by another before the first is allowed to complete itself.[56] The most common example of this kind of linguistic event occurs when a first-person construction shifts midsentence into a third-person construction. Precisely this mode of speech, this quasi-ungrammatical shift in person, enables Eichmann to stage his absence from the scene of his own execution. Citing "winged words," he felt so elated that he could erase himself from the mise-en-scène of his own death.

The Scandal of Eichmann: Thinking in the Third Person

I would argue that the scene of Eichmann's execution serves as a summary of the "lesson" taught by the trial because the figure of the anacoluthon is in a precise way symptomatic of Eichmann's "thoughtlessness." Unlike the prosecution and the judges, Arendt argues that Eichmann's vacuous talk does not hide other, more hideous thoughts; it rather points to his inability to produce thoughts of his own: "The longer one listened to him, the more obvious it became that his inability to speak was closely connected with an inability to *think*, namely, to think from the standpoint of somebody else" (49). Going against a long philosophical tradition that understands thinking as a solitary activity, Arendt holds that genuine thinking is always inherently dialogic. One's thoughts, she claims elsewhere, are always articulated in dialogue with others. As I pointed out in the previous paragraph, Arendt, in a series of philosophical afterthoughts to the Eichmann case, turns to Kant's notion of judgment to conceptualize this mode of thinking. What attracts her in the Kantian conception of judgment is his suggestion that our judgments are not purely subjective but rather based on a "*sensus communis*," a common sense shared by all of us. Our judgments are articulated in dialogue with others, and by judging we place ourselves in a human community. In "Truth and Politics" she cites Kant: "We think, as it were, in community with others to whom we communicate our thoughts as they communicate theirs to us" (234–235).[57] Thinking, I extrapolate, has a theatrical dimension, it relies on a mise-en-scène in which others are imaginatively evoked.

Eichmann's incapacity to talk in the first person can therefore be seen as symptomatic of his incapacity to think *in the first person*. Or rather, as I would like to put it, what typifies Eichmann's thoughtlessness is a *thinking in the third person*. This oxymoron captures, I think, precisely the type of reasoning that Arendt had earlier called "ideological thinking." Typical of totalitarian ideologies, she argued in *The Origins of Totalitarianism*, is a promise of a "total explanation" of all past, present, and future phenomena under the rubric of one idea, whether this be survival of the fittest in a Darwinian sense or the survival of the most progressive class in history:[58]

Ideologies always assume that one idea is sufficient to explain everything in the development from the premise, and that *no experience can teach anything* because everything is comprehended in this consistent process of logical deduction.[59]

These ideologies produce an explanation of the world split off from the subject and his or her experiences; a genuine moment of learning—something that is dependent on an *experience*—is made impossible. Such ideologies invite a mode of thinking "emancipated from the reality that we perceive with our five senses" and suggest we need a "sixth sense," namely ideology itself, to understand reality.[60] Returning to this argument in "Understanding and Politics," Arendt writes that ideology replaces common sense with "stringent logicality." Ideologies may be internally coherent but make the question of *truth* superfluous.[61] She suggests, perhaps ironically, that this disregard for the truth of utterances has affinities with the work of certain (unnamed) logicians, who define the truth of a statement in terms of its logical *consistency*:

This equation [of truth as consistency] actually implies the negation of the existence of truth insofar as truth is always supposed to reveal something, whereas consistency is only a mode of fitting statements together, and as such lacks the power of revelation.[62]

Ideological reasoning has the logic of a *grammar* that enables one to fit statements together. These statements are disconnected from common sense because "common sense presupposes a common world in which we all fit . . . whereas logic . . . can claim a reliability altogether independent of the world and the existence of other people."[63] Typical of totalitarian ideologies, then, is their production of "knowledge" that is radically cut off from common sense and from the illocutionary situation in which thinking usually takes place. Ideological thinking takes place *in the third person* and demands from its subjects a constant anacoluthon-like shift into the third person.[64]

Eichmann's cliché-ridden speech, with its verbatim repetition of "winged words" and his faithful adherence to "language rules," is symptomatic of his thoughtlessness precisely because it has the effect of an anacoluthon. His words are continuously interrupted by the machinelike logic of Nazi ideology, which has the effect of erasing the speaker out of his own words, thereby, perhaps, absolving him from the responsibility to judge and think for himself. If this taints his speech with a certain comedy, it also makes his words, in a sense, incomprehensible. As Paul de Man points out, the anacoluthon is not a trope of meaning, like metaphor or metonymy, but it is rather a disruption in a meaningful pattern. It confronts us with a linguistic element—in this case a shift in person—that remains unreadable because it cannot be integrated in a coherent hermeneutic understanding of an utterance.[65] When we listen to Eichmann's words in a commonsensical way, ascribing meanings, intentions, and motivations to them, we are faced with a stupefying absence that makes it impossible to relate to him in the first person. Hence, if it is indeed the case that the baffling silliness of Eichmann's exclamation "Long Live Germany . . . I will never forget you" at the scene of his execution serves as a summary of everything that could be learned during the trial, as Arendt holds, the pedagogical impact of this scene lies precisely not in its enabling us to understand Eichmann. The effectiveness of its "lesson" relies rather on its confronting us with a breakdown in understanding.

*

In an earlier essay entitled "Social Science Techniques and the Concentration Camps" (1950), Arendt testifies to a comparable breakdown in understanding when she states that the rigid logical nature of Nazi ideology is an affront to those who seek to understand the Holocaust in a humanistic way. The camps present, as she put it, a "serious perplexity" when we apply our commonsensical judgments to them because our common sense operates on the assumption that human behavior is driven by utility, and it is hard to find a utilitarian rationale behind the camps—if anything, they undermined the war effort. Yet from the "third-person" vantage point of Nazi ideology, the camps are only too understandable:

If on the other hand, we make an abstraction of every standard we usually live by and consider only the fantastic ideological claims of racism in its logical purity, then the extermination policy of the Nazis makes almost too much sense.[66]

The "perplexity" of the camps lies in their being incomprehensible when we employ our commonsense judgments—and yet they seem completely understandable in terms of the machinelike logic of Nazi ideology. Studying the camps confronts us with a tension between what we can follow logically and what we are capable of understanding humanly. Arendt calls the tension between these two incommensurable modes of comprehension a "stumbling block" that disrupts our attempts to formulate a coherent theory of the camps because every attempt to resolve the tension at a higher meta-theoretical level would amount to an explaining away of its unique historical affront to understanding.

*

I would claim, then, that Arendt's laughter during the trial points to a similar moment of stumbling she describes when writing about concentration camps. Her laughter testifies to the breakdown of her capacity to understand, which occurs when Eichmann's banality stares her, as she puts it, in the face (287). When we watch Eichmann as "judge-spectators," applying our commonsense judgments, attempting to understand his motives, we stumble over his banal refusal to think for himself:

> Out of the unwillingness or inability to choose one's examples and one's company, and out of the unwillingness or inability to relate to others through judgment, arise the real *skandala*, the real stumbling-blocks which human powers cannot remove because they were not caused by human and humanly understandable motives. Therein lies the horror and, at the same time, the banality of evil.[67]

The phrase "the banality of evil," then, is not a concept that serves to explain Eichmann's behavior. It describes a "stumbling block" that makes it impossible to understand him in a human way; it points to a moment of *nonunderstanding*, which occurs precisely when we seek to apply our faculty of judgment and are confronted with its failure. This experience of a breakdown in understanding—as Arendt insists—*nevertheless* teaches a *lesson*, but it is a radically negative lesson that remains heterogeneous to knowledge. It cannot be assimilated into a *theory* or an *explanation* because it cannot be translated into a set of assertions, nor be phrased in the third person, without explaining away the stupefying and thought-defying aspect of it. As she writes in her letter to Scholem:

> It is indeed my opinion now that evil is never "radical," that it is only extreme, and that it possesses neither depth nor any demonic dimension. It can overgrow

and lay waste the whole world precisely because it spreads like a fungus on the surface. It is "thought-defying," as I said, because thought tries to reach some depth, to go to the roots, and the moment it concerns itself with evil, it is frustrated because there is nothing. That is its "banality." Only the good has depth and can be radical.[68]

Arendt's report, *Eichmann in Jerusalem*, is an attempt to preserve the impact of this thought-defying lesson, precisely by *not* translating it into conceptual language. Because the stumbling can be experienced only in the first person, every attempt at explaining it would necessarily entail an explaining away of its shocking impact. The lesson of the trial, I would therefore argue, comes across though her ironical tone.[69] It is performed through the "laughter" that permeates her book. This laughter, which scandalized her critics, is an attempt to render the *skandala* at the heart of the trial without resolving its scandalizing nature.

Conclusion: The Lessons of *Eichmann in Jerusalem*

> It remains perhaps to think of laughter, as, precisely, a remains.
> —Jacques Derrida

How, then, are we to understand the Eichmann trial's didactic impact, according to Arendt's book? I would argue that *Eichmann in Jerusalem* points to a lesson that goes beyond the political and historical lessons that were scripted by the Israeli court, one that is in excess of the philosophical lessons that could be learned from the positive examples of the importance of judgment that were brought to the legal stage in the figure of Anton Schmid. This lesson, however, is not a full cognition, nor is it articulated as a piece of (scientific) knowledge that one can own, remember, and communicate. It is not of the order of an *understanding* but is tied to the singular experience of a stumbling that leads one to erupt into laughter. Yet this overwhelming laughter, precisely because it does *not* constitute an understanding, has an ethical dimension. Understanding, Arendt argues in "Understanding and Politics," is a highly subjective process, an "unending activity by which . . . we come to terms with and reconcile ourselves to reality, that is, try to be at home in the world" (307–308).[70] It should not be confused with being informed or acquiring knowledge.[71] "Understanding," she writes, "makes knowledge meaningful,"[72] and meaning is only revealed in retrospect, "when the action has come to an end and become a story susceptible to narration."[73] Understanding is thus only possible after our relation to the past has changed:

Such memory can speak only when indignation and just anger, which impel us to action, have been silenced—and that needs time. We can no more master the past than we can undo it. But we can reconcile ourselves to it.[74]

I claim that Arendt's laughter, then—or rather, the *precision* of her laughter and the nonunderstanding it represents—allows her to face the scandal of Eichmann's banality without *completely* reconciling herself with it. In an essay on Lessing, entitled "On Humanity in Dark Times," Arendt suggests that laughter, like anger, has a unique capacity to expose the world. Hope and fear, she argues, are attempts to turn away from reality:[75]

But anger, and above all Lessing's kind of anger, reveals and exposes the world just as Lessing's kind of laughter . . . seeks to bring about reconciliation with the world. Such laughter helps one to find a place in the world, but ironically, which is to say, without selling one's soul to it.[76]

The Eichmann trial, then, was for Arendt a paradoxical didactic event in which she "came to terms" with the reality of Eichmann's crimes, *but not quite*—that is, she relates to it ironically—without "selling her soul to it." The incomprehensible scandal of it remains fully there, as something to be stumbled over, as something that cannot be integrated into a moment of cognition or be translated into a story that, with its retrospective point of view, would ascribe meaning to it.

The scandalous nature of these lessons is, perhaps, not so much preserved by the narrative of her report but rather by its style. Style, Arendt argues in a letter to Eric Voegelin, who had criticized the indignant tone of *The Origins of Totalitarianism*, is not something that is external to one's writing. Style dramatizes how the author is implicated in that which she seeks to describe. She illustrates this by citing an example: When one describes the phenomenon of excessive poverty in a society of great wealth, such as, for example, the poverty of the British working class during the early stages of the Industrial Revolution,

the natural human reaction to such conditions is one of anger and indignation because these conditions are against the dignity of man. If I describe these conditions without permitting my indignation to interfere, I have lifted this particular phenomenon out of its context in human society and have thereby robbed it of part of its nature, deprived it of one of its important inherent qualities. For to arouse indignation is one of the qualities of excessive poverty insofar poverty occurs among human beings.[77]

"Totalitarianism did not occur on the moon," she continues, "but in the midst of human society."[78] The response it provokes in a human being is therefore not external to a true understanding of it but an essential part of it. One's writing style, then, is precisely the mise-en-scène of one's particular mode of understanding. If *Eichmann in Jerusalem* marked a change in Arendt's understanding of the characteristics of Nazi evils, this shift is indicated by a *change of tone*: from indignant outrage to laughter. It is precisely this laughter that embodies the particular mode of (non)understanding that Eichmann's banality provokes.

It is perhaps this tone of laughter that makes *Eichmann in Jerusalem* such a singular literary text. Despite the various interpretations of the book that have sought to distill theories or ideas from it, it speaks to us because it exposes Eichmann's banality to laughter. This gesture of exposure makes the book into more than a constative report on the trial. Exposing, as Mieke Bal defines it, is implicitly theatrical and thus differs from the act of narrating. Whereas a narration is a third-person construct, an act of exposure involves a mise-en-scène in which a first person invites a second person to look at something that is put on display.[79] The lasting force of *Eichmann in Jerusalem* inheres in its preservation of the scandal at the heart of the Eichmann case. It exposes to us, the readers of the report—to the extent that it *stares us in the face*—something we can neither master nor purge ourselves from in a moment of catharsis.

Founding a Nation, Healing a Wound

ON CRIMES AGAINST HUMANITY

In Chapter 1, we noted that Arendt, in the postscript to *Eichmann in Jerusalem*, suggests that the dynamics of the controversy over her book could be clarified by comparing it to the storm that raged over the publication of Rolf Hochhuth's play *Der Stellvertreter*. The intensity of the public fury that greeted both texts, in which both authors were said to have put forth all sorts of claims that they had clearly never made, suggested to her that the Nazi years constituted, indeed, a past that had not been "mastered." This past continued to evoke a range of uncontrolled defense mechanisms whose main function was to provide excuses to disavow the responsibility to judge. As we saw, Arendt maintained that learning from the past—and working through the grip it has over us—starts by adopting a judgmental stance.

Instructive as the comparison between the receptions of *Der Stellvertreter* and *Eichmann in Jerusalem* may be, they differ sharply as cases of collective refusals to face the past. As theatrical events, the Eichmann trial and *Der Stellvertreter* were staged in front of audiences whose subjective positions vis-à-vis the Nazi years were profoundly different. *Der Stellvertreter* was first performed in West Germany, the country of the perpetrators, whereas the Eichmann trial took place in Israel, the country of the victims. Both countries had different sets of issues to work through and hence variant types of resistance to overcome in their relation to the past.[1] Most obviously, Germany needed to come to terms with its guilt, whereas the Jews, having established a sovereign nation-state as their homeland, had to cope with the trauma of massive loss and displacement.[2]

Another crucial difference is that Hochhuth's play deals with the question of its characters' *moral* responsibility, whereas the Eichmann trial sought to establish the *criminal* guilt of its defendant. On the final pages of *Eichmann in Jerusalem*, Arendt argues that these moral and legal realms should not be confused. In fact, many of the misunderstandings about the trial have resulted from a conflation of these two types of culpability and the misguided attempts to invoke a rather vague notion of "collective guilt" to assert that not merely Eichmann but "humanity" should be tried in the wake of the Holocaust. Arendt acknowledges the existence of political accountability that exceeds personal liability as each government assumes responsibility for the deeds of its predecessor. But she insists that this is not to be confused with guilt that can be adjudicated in a courtroom:

Many people today would agree that there is no such thing as collective guilt or, for that matter, collective innocence, and that if there were, no one person could ever be guilty or innocent. This, of course, is not to deny that there is such a thing as *political* responsibility which, however, exists quite apart from what the individual member of the group has done and can therefore neither be judged in moral terms not be brought before a criminal court.[3]

Arendt's classification of different types of accountability alludes to her friend Karl Jaspers's philosophical exploration of the notion of guilt in his famous essay *The Question of German Guilt*, published in 1947.[4] As historian Anson Rabinbach points out, Jaspers wrote this essay in the context of the democratic "reeducation" of Germany being undertaken by the Allied forces, for which he worked as one of the selected "reliable dignitaries" advising the Allies.[5] Jaspers argues in his book that the democratization of postwar Germany would depend on the degree to which it can work through its guilt. For this process to be successful, it is crucial that one distinguishes four modes of being guilty, as each requires a different scene in which guilt can be acknowledged and (if possible) overcome. The first category, criminal guilt, pertains to the actions of individuals. Second is political guilt, determined by the implication of Germany's public institutions in the Nazi atrocities. Insofar as these institutions still existed, they could be held accountable for past actions, even if the individuals who governed them in the postwar years were not directly responsible for actions committed in the past.[6] Third, most Germans were morally guilty, according to Jaspers, insofar as they could be said to be responsible for not intervening in what they had seen happening. Jasper's fourth category, metaphysical guilt, refers to the breach of the basic solidarity among human beings that had taken place during the Nazi years, which implicated every human being in the Holocaust, whether personally responsible for crimes or not. This is not to be confused with "collective guilt" because establishing guilt always implies dealing with a specific individual (40). Jaspers continues:

There can be no collective guilt of a people or a group within a people—except for political liability. To pronounce a group criminally, morally or metaphysically guilty is an error akin to the laziness and arrogance of average, uncritical thinking. (42)

Jaspers contends that a true transformation of Germany into a decent democratic nation would require that its citizens work through all four types of guilt. Yet only the first two types—criminal and political—could be established or acknowledged publicly: through trials (in cases of criminal guilt) and via the postwar German government's decision to assume political responsibility for Nazi atrocities by paying reparations to its victims. One's moral guilt can only be examined in the tribunal of one's consciousness, as it pertains to the relation of the individual to him- or herself, or in front of the loving gaze of one's friends and family. Coping with metaphysical guilt demands the "transformation of human self-consciousness before God" (36). Because moral and metaphysical guilt are private matters, according to Jaspers, they are not "theatricalizable": "No one needs to acknowledge a worldly tribunal in points of moral and metaphysical guilt," he writes. "What is true before God is not, therefore, true before men. For God is represented by no authority on earth—neither in ecclesiastic nor in foreign offices, nor in world opinion announced by the press" (42).

Hochhuth's *Der Stellvertreter* seems to subscribe to Jaspers's program because it raises both the question of the moral responsibility of the pope as an individual and, more generally, the question of the accountability of his office. As such, it contributes to a moral education as well as a renewed reflection on the role of our quasi-political institutions. As Jaspers remarked during a radio discussion broadcast in 1963, the play's true contribution to a "working through of the past" consists, however, in its evocation of the question of metaphysical guilt toward the end of the play.[7] When, at the beginning of act five, an old man addresses God with the question, "How was this possible?" Hochhuth's "drama of decisions" (to use Piscator's characterization of the play) opens up to a different scene, in which a set of responsibilities, wounds, and breaches are addressed, none of which can be fully captured in legal or moral terms. As Jaspers indicates, this direct address to God is not to be understood as a prayer or as a dispute with God, such as the one that takes place in the book of Job; it is, rather, an *entreaty* that lacks confidence that God will respond.[8]

*

In Chapter 3, I will return to this notion of guilt that exceeds moral, political, and criminal categories and that of a collective wound (or a "breach in human solidarity," to use Jaspers's phrase) that lies beyond the boundaries of legal repair, through a brief discussion of prosecutor Gideon Hausner's opening address during the Eichmann trial. Although I won't employ Jaspers's Christian terminology, I will reflect on the way the Eichmann trial implicitly attempts to cope with a traumatic wound the impact of which cannot be exhaustively articulated sheerly in worldly terms. This chapter focuses on the issue that is at the heart of Arendt's book on the Eichmann case: the particular nature of the defendant's criminal guilt. As Arendt reiterates, time and again, it is around the question of criminal guilt that a trial revolves. The trial's success should therefore be measured according to the degree to which it presented Eichmann's actions as crimes. The first thing to note, then, is that a crime has a very specific definition in the legal sphere. Neither an act simply considered morally objectionable by the majority nor something that hurts an identifiable victim, it is legally defined as an offense against the *community* whose laws are broken. Arendt quotes from an essay by Telford Taylor, the prosecutor at the Nuremberg trials, to highlight the legal definition of a crime:

Criminal proceedings, since they are mandatory and thus initiated even if the victim would prefer to forgive and forget, rests on laws whose "essence"—to quote Telford Taylor, writing in *The New York Times Magazine*—is that "a crime is not committed only against the victim, but primarily against the community whose law is violated." The wrongdoer is brought to justice because his act has disturbed and gravely endangered the community as a whole, and not because, as in civil suits, damage has been done to individuals who are entitled reparation. The reparation effected in criminal cases is of an altogether different nature; it is the body politic itself that stands in need of being "repaired," and it is the general public order that has been thrown out of gear and must be restored, as it were. It is, in other words, the law, not the plaintiff that must prevail. (261)

Thus, a criminal trial is a ritual through which the legal order is reconstituted. It seeks to repair the "body politic," the juridico-political community protected by a set of laws, which was "wounded" by the crime.

According to this definition, a crime is not in the first place committed against a victim but against the body politic, as *performed on the body of the victim*. Arendt is critical of the prosecution's emphasis on the victims—on the "spectacle of Jewish suffering," as she calls it—because it gives the impression that the trial was conducted in the name of the victims, rather than in the name of the community whose laws were broken.

Hence, the verdict at the end of a trial does more than simply declare someone guilty and announce a punishment. The "scene of judgment" serves to reinstate the public order that has been "thrown out of gear." Its aim is to reinstate the law and to recreate the community through a moment of judgment. As Pierre Bourdieu and Pierre Legendre, among others, have pointed out, the "body politic" is always constructed through these very scenes of reconstitution. The trial is a ritual in which the institution creates itself.[9] To put it in speech-act terms: In a trial, the verdictive speech act has a double function.[10] As a constative, it seeks to speak the "truth" about the past; it uses its institutional power to create an "official" version of the past. As a performative, however, it is aimed at the future: By pronouncing a judgment, the legal community is reconstituted. Its illocutionary force depends exactly on this doubleness: A verdict speaks the truth about the past for the sake of the future.

*

The Eichmann trial, however, was a unique legal event that complicates this model in two ways. Firstly, Israel, as a nation-state, was founded after the Holocaust: The trial sought to repair a body-politic that did not exist as such when the crimes were committed. Second, the crimes for which Eichmann was tried included crimes against *humanity*, a community altogether different from the juridico-political community of Israel. These two complications can be understood in relation to the two main indictments against Eichmann: He stood trial for crimes against the Jews—a community that is *not quite* a juridico-political community—and for crimes against humanity that exceed the limited legal definition of a crime. The verdict, then, aimed to reinstitute a legal community that did not exist when the crime took place in the wake of a crime that exceeds the very definition of crime.

Eichmann in Jerusalem ends with a postscript in which Arendt reflects on these legal-political complications of the trial. In this chapter I will discuss Arendt's attempt to answer the questions posed by these complications in order to analyze the uniqueness of the legal theater that was mounted in Jerusalem. In the first part, I will examine the notion of "crimes against the Jews" in the context of the then-recent founding of the state of Israel. The second part concentrates on the notion of "crimes against humanity." I propose that it is exactly in the tension between these two indictments, and in the attempt to pronounce a judgment in the name of the two different communities involved in these indictments, that we can understand the unique theatrical space opened up in Jerusalem, as well as Arendt's equally unique response to it.

Crimes against the Jewish People

A large part of the postscript to *Eichmann in Jerusalem* consists of a discussion of the various objections raised against trying Eichmann in Israel. Some of these objections, Arendt points out, can easily be dismissed, such as the claim that Israeli judges can't be objective because they are Jews. The most substantive objection, according to Arendt, is that Eichmann should have been tried before an international tribunal rather than a national one because his crimes were international in scope. This suggestion was made by Karl Jaspers as well as by Telford Taylor in his *New York Times Magazine* essay, which Arendt quotes extensively in her report (see above). Without explicitly responding to Taylor, Arendt seems to be in dialogue with his argument and even takes up his specific examples.

In his essay, Taylor cites the limited legal definition of the crime to argue that the prosecution's emphasis on the victims is problematic—something with which Arendt wholeheartedly agrees. Unlike Arendt, however, Taylor claims that the very terms of the indictment for "crimes against the Jewish people" is problematic from a legal point of view as well. True justice, according to Taylor, always makes a claim to universality. Ben-Gurion's suggestion that Eichmann's crimes need to be framed as crimes against the Jewish people and must therefore be tried in a Jewish court undermines the claim to universality implicit in legal proceedings. He illustrates his point with a simile that was topical at the time:

If racial hatreds lead to the lawless killing of a Negro in the South, in Ben-Gurion's sense no doubt that is a crime against the Negro people. But no one would suggest that "historic justice" requires the perpetrators to be tried before a court in a "Negro state," such as Ghana or Guinea.[11]

Taylor argues that this position is ridiculous. "On the contrary," he writes, "true justice declares that such an act is as much a crime against whites as against blacks."[12] Similarly, he writes that calling Eichmann's crime a "crime against the Jews" carries the dangerous implication "that it is not a crime against non-Jews." Taylor adds ironically that "such indeed was the philosophy of old Teutonic law under which murder offended only the victim's kinsmen. But that is far from satisfactory as the basis of an enlightened system of law in the modern world."[13] He concludes that Eichmann should therefore have been tried before an international tribunal such as Nuremberg: "Nuremberg was based on the proposition that atrocities against Jews and non-Jews are equally crimes against world law."[14]

Arendt's postscript about the legal-political implications of the Eichmann trial is partly an unacknowledged argument against Taylor. Arendt disagrees with Taylor's point that the notion of "crimes against the Jews" differs from the standard legal definition of a crime. Like Taylor, she cites the U.N. resolution that states that "persons charged with genocide . . . shall be tried by a competent tribunal of the States in the territory of which the act was committed" (262) and that crimes that could not be localized should be tried by an international tribunal such as the one in Nuremberg.[15] Unlike Taylor, however, she argues that Eichmann's crimes do fall within Israel's jurisdiction if we understand "territory" as a "political and a legal concept, and not merely a geographical term" (262). "Territory" refers to a symbolic space:

It relates not so much, and not primarily, to a piece of land as to the space between individuals in a group whose members are bound to, and at the same time separated and protected from, each other by all kinds of relationship, based on a common language, religion, a common history, customs and laws. Such relationships become spatially manifest insofar as they themselves constitute the space wherein the different members of a group relate to and have intercourse with each other. (262–263)

The Jews, according to Arendt, are neither simply a *tribe* (as in Taylor's example of Teutonic law) nor just a *race* (as in his Negro example). The relation among the Jews, she argues, exceeds that of kinship—which has connotations of both *race* and *family*. According to Arendt, Jews, even before the founding of Israel, were already a *political* community. The political sphere is defined by Arendt as a radical departure from kinship; it is the sphere of differences—where people are bound together not because they are kin but because they share the same symbolic space.[16] As a political community, the Jews were not so much "akin" in the familial or racial sense; rather, they maintained historically this symbolic space among them, which made them comparable to a nation even before the founding of Israel. "No State of Israel would ever have come into being if the Jewish people had not created and maintained its own specific in-between space throughout the long centuries of dispersion, that is, prior to its seizure of its old territory" (263). She argues at length that the Jews can be considered a de facto people who had claims to sovereignty as a political community even before the state of Israel was founded.[17]

In this respect, the Eichmann trial, Arendt continues, is not different from the other national trials held in formerly Nazi-occupied countries such as Poland, Hungary, Greece, France, or Yugoslavia. Because of the territorial dispersion of Jews, Eichmann's crimes can be considered an international concern in the limited, legal sense of the Nuremberg Charter (259). However, once the Jews had their own state, Eichmann's crimes could be judged in a national trial:

Once the Jews had a territory of their own, the State in Israel, they obviously had as much right to sit in judgment on the crimes against their people as the Poles had to judge the crimes committed in Poland. (259)

Arendt concludes that the prosecution of Eichmann in a national trial was made possible by the founding of the state of Israel, an unprecedented political event. Legally, she claims, there was nothing unprecedented in bringing Eichmann before a court in Jerusalem. In fact, the only unprecedented legal aspect of the trial was the kidnapping of Eichmann in Argentina, which "was the least entitled ever to become a valid precedent" (264). In an ironic wink to Taylor, she adds, in parenthesis, "What are we going to say if tomorrow it occurs to some African state to send its agents into Mississippi and to kidnap one of the leaders of the segregationist movement there? And what are we going to reply if a court in Ghana or the Congo quotes the Eichmann case as a precedent?" (264)

Human Rights and the Rights of Citizens

Even though, as Arendt suggests, the trying of Eichmann was not unprecedented from a *legal* point of view, it was made possible by a historical event that implied a radical transformation of the legal-political status of the Jews, namely the founding of the state of Israel. Because the Jewish people now had their own state, and thereby their own national court, they could try Eichmann's crimes as *crimes*, without having to fall back into what she calls the "phraseology of human rights":

Jews were able to sit in judgment on crimes committed against their own people, . . . for the first time, they did not need to appeal to others for protection and justice, or fall back upon the compromised phraseology of the rights of man— rights, which, as no one knew better than they, were claimed only by people who were too weak to defend their "rights of Englishmen" and to enforce their own laws. (271)

Arendt locates the unprecedented nature of the legal event in the context of the history of the political position of the Jewish people and the "compromised history of human rights." In her earlier books, Arendt had already discussed how the bankruptcy of the notion of human rights between the world wars was the immediate legal-political context that made the Holocaust possible. In *The Origins of Totalitarianism* (1951), she describes how, in the period after World War I, after the collapse of the larger multiethnic states and the denationalization of large groups of ethnic and national minorities, large groups of stateless persons arrived, as it were, on the political scene. The most important among these stateless groups were the Jews, who formed, in Arendt's description, an "extraordinary spectacle of a people . . . without a government, without a country and without a language."[18] The emergence of these groups of stateless people, she argues, was a political testing ground for the discourse of human rights because the claim that a member of the human race, regardless of his or her political status, has inalienable rights acquires a political urgency only when people appear on the scene who can claim no other rights but their human rights. Furthermore, human rights have always been articulated in relation to refugees and people without political status. Within the law, the "sacred right to asylum" had always figured as the symbol of human rights (280):

If a human being loses his political status, he should, according to the implications of the inborn and inalienable rights of man, come under exactly the situation for which the declarations of such general rights provided. (300)

However, when statelessness became a mass phenomenon, and large groups of people had not only lost their political homes but had found it impossible to find new ones, the discourse of human rights proved to be politically bankrupt. Arendt describes how these groups were handed over to the direct administration of the police and placed in camps for displaced persons, ultimately to lose their "inalienable" human rights. "The world found nothing sacred in the abstract nakedness of being human," she writes (299). All solemn declarations by commissions and tribunals proved "unenforceable . . . whenever people appeared who were no longer citizens of any sovereign state" (293):[19]

No paradox of contemporary politics is filled with a more poignant irony than the discrepancy between the efforts of the well-meaning idealists who stubbornly insist on regarding as "inalienable" those human rights which are enjoyed only by the citizens of the most prosperous and civilized countries and the situation of the rightless themselves. (279)

The principle of human rights, though it should be higher and more "sacred" than that of civil rights, turns out to be utterly dependent on supposedly secondary civil rights. "Prepolitical" or "extralegal" rights—sacred as they may be—are safe only within the framework of a nation-state with the force to protect them. The history of human rights effectively shows that "a man who is nothing but a man has lost the very qualities which make it possible for other people to treat him as a fellow-man" (300). Arendt continues by approvingly quoting Burke, who wrote in response to the French declaration of the *Droits de l'homme et du citoyen* that he preferred his rights of an Englishman to his supposedly "inalienable" human rights. "Rights spring from within the nation," Burke writes, "so that neither natural law, nor divine command, nor any concept of mankind such as Robespierre's 'human race,' 'the sovereign of the earth,' are needed as source of law."[20]

We may conclude with Arendt that a paradox lies at the basis of the notion of human rights. The term points to a right that preexists citizenship and emanates from one's "naked human being."[21] Yet, as it turns out, it can be codified only in positive law and politically enforced only within the framework of citizenship.[22] Arendt concludes her chapter by pointing to the founding of the state of Israel. The case of Israel proves that the "restoration of human rights . . . has been achieved so far only through the restoration of the establishment of national rights" (299).

The Revolutionary Transformation
of the Jewish People

In this context, it is crucial that Eichmann was tried in Israel, the state of the formerly stateless Jews, rather than in an international tribunal, because the very act of trying him was a response to the history that had made Holocaust possible. In Arendt's words:

(The very fact that Israel had her own law under which such a trial could be held had been called, long before the Eichmann trial, an expression of "a revolutionary transformation that has taken place in the political position of the Jewish people"—by Mr. Rosen on the occasion of the First Reading of the Law of 1950 in the Knesset.) It was against the background of these very vivid experiences and aspirations that Ben-Gurion said: "Israel does not need the protection of an International Court." (271–272)

Hence the Eichmann trial, as a political-legal event, points to the history of the Jews as a stateless people as well as to the "revolutionary transformation" in which the Jewish people survived the European wars to become something different: the citizens of a nation-state and a republic. It is no coincidence that Arendt wrote *Eichmann in Jerusalem* while completing *On Revolution*, a book that focuses on the revolutionary moment in which new political bodies are founded. A central chapter in this book, "The Pursuit of Happiness," analyzes the moment of constitution of a new state as a framing of a set of laws that both create and protect the political space.[23] The word *constitution*, Arendt emphasizes, can refer to the discursive act that creates a political community—the act of framing a constitution—and to the document that protects this community. She takes as model the American Declaration of Independence; this is a declaration in the name of "the people," which through its very declaration constitutes the people as a political community.[24] Arendt argues that no "American people" existed prior to this declaration; on the contrary, the American people as a political body finds its origin in this declarative speech-act. In a beautiful passage, she writes:

No doubt there is a grandeur in the Declaration of Independence, but it consists not in its philosophy and not even so much in its being "an argument in support of an action" as in its being the perfect way for an action to appear in words. . . . And since we deal here with the written, and not with the spoken word, we are confronted with one of the rare moments in history when the power of action is great enough to erect its own monument. (130)

The Eichmann trial, then, took place against the background of the revolutionary transformation in which the Jewish people, which had been a de facto political community, became, de jure, a legal-political entity, protected by laws. This "revolutionary transformation" made it possible to "frame" Eichmann's crime in the limited legal sense, and it made the legal event a moment in which the legal-political space was reconstituted.

Crimes against Humanity

Eichmann's crimes, in fact, were made possible because of the state-lessness of the Jewish people. Similarly, Eichmann's prosecution depended on a "revolutionary transformation in the political status of the Jews." Only retroactively were the Jewish people capable of framing Eichmann's crimes in the proper sense of the term, namely as crimes against "a people." Yet how are we to understand the second indictment proposed in Jerusalem, namely that Eichmann had committed "crimes against humanity"? If we follow Arendt's earlier suggestion that human rights always need to be codified as citizens' rights to be enforced, then how can a criminal trial prosecute "crimes against humanity"? If the "revolutionary transformation" of the political position of the Jewish people made it possible to try Eichmann's crimes in a national court, should we define his crimes as having been com-mitted against a people, rather than against "humanity"? Can Eichmann's crimes be prosecuted as crimes against humanity, or must they necessarily be understood as crimes against the Jewish people so as to be subject to legal proceedings? If so, what are the implications of the translation from *humanity* to *the Jewish people*? Can we consider crimes against humanity as crimes in the limited sense *without remainder*?[25]

Eichmann in Jerusalem seems to be haunted by this question, as Ar-endt's report traces the various stages of Nazi policy toward the Jewish people, from the destruction of their judicial person to the Final Solution. Arendt reaches a crucial point in her elaboration when she asks whether Eichmann's participation can still be expressed in legal terms or whether his acts exceed the definition of a crime in the proper legal sense. She sug-gests that there was a radical, unprecedented newness to the Nazi policy toward the Jews that was not fully recognized by the Israeli prosecutor who cast the Final Solution as the outcome of centuries of anti-Semitism, po-groms, and persecutions. Arendt argues that Nazi anti-Semitism was new not in terms of magnitude but in essence. "None of the participants ever arrived at a clear understanding of the actual horror of Auschwitz, which is of a *different nature* from all the atrocities of the past," she writes (267). It was a radically different type of crime:

It was when the Nazi regime declared that the German people not only were unwilling to have any Jews in Germany but wished to make the entire Jewish people disappear from the face of the earth that the new crime, the crime against humanity—in the sense of a crime "against the Human status," or against the very nature of mankind—appeared. Expulsion and genocide, though both are international offenses, must remain distinct; the former is an offense against fellow-nations, whereas the latter is an attack upon human diversity as such, that is upon the characteristic of the "human status" without which the very words "mankind" or "humanity" would be devoid of meaning. (268–269)

This new type of crime, which includes "the blotting out of whole peoples and the 'clearance' of whole regions of their native populations" (257), exceeds the traditional notion of a crime. The Nazi atrocities went further than an offense against the legal order and the political space it protects. In fact, the Nazis were bent on deciding who can inhabit Earth. As such, the Nazi crimes attacked the very conditions that have made the political possible, or, in Arendt's terms, the fact that "men, not Man live on the earth."[26] "Politically and legally," Arendt continues, "these were 'crimes' different not only in degree of seriousness but in *essence*" (267, emphasis mine). Whereas "the essence" of a crime—in the narrow sense—threatens the "worldliness" of the political sphere, these crimes were visited on the people who live on *Earth*. As such, the Final Solution was a crime against a different community, namely *humanity*, and it should be understood, according to Arendt, as being directed not so much against human nature or humanenness but the being together on *Earth* that precedes every political community:

For just as a murderer is prosecuted because he has violated the law of the community, and not because he has deprived the Smith family of its husband, father, and breadwinner, so the modern, state-employed mass murderers must be prosecuted because they *violated the order of mankind*, not because they killed millions of people. (272, emphasis mine)

With these new crimes an "altogether different order is broken and an altogether different community is violated" (272). She concludes with the remarkable suggestion that Eichmann's crimes have to be understood as crimes against humanity *"perpetrated upon the body of the Jewish people"* (269).[27] This puzzling formulation indicates that the newness of Eichmann's crimes is to be found not only in the character of the acts he perpetrated but in their status as *crimes*. According to the legal definition, a crime is a wounding of the body politic, performed on the body of the specific victim. Eichmann's crimes, Arendt seems to suggest, are directed against a different community, namely humanity, and are perpetrated on the body politic itself. The newness of Eichmann's crimes can be understood only in relation to a different body, a different community, which cannot be reduced to the political legal community without remainder. The Eichmann trial has broken with the logic of the trial that I outlined in the introduction to this chapter because it sought to pass judgment on something that exceeds the definition of a crime and hoped to "repair" a community that is "altogether different" from the political community.

Echoing remarks made by Karl Jaspers in the German magazine *Der Monat*, Arendt goes on to suggest that "insofar as the victims were Jews, it was right and proper that the Jewish court should sit in judgment; but insofar as the crime was a crime against humanity, it needed an international tribunal to do it justice" (269).[28] Her analysis, however, leaves us with a number of questions not answered fully in *Eichmann in Jerusalem*. For example, how are we to understand "humanity" as a community "altogether different" from the juridico-political community? How should we understand a crime against this different community as the breaking of a law, if one of its characteristics is that, as a *prepolitical* order, it is not yet politically articulated?[29]

As she makes plain, the notion of a "crime against humanity" should not be confused with the breaking of a "natural law." She disagrees with Yosal Rogat, whose pronouncement "that a great crime offends *nature*, so that the very *earth* cries out for vengeance; that evil violates a *natural harmony* which only retribution can restore" (277, emphasis mine), she calls barbaric. Humanity, to Arendt, is a community that is not political—not codified in positive laws—yet not simply natural either.

An Altogether Different Community

How can this new "crime" be articulated in terms of positive law without effacing that which makes it radically different from a crime in the limited sense of the word? In the postscript to the book, Arendt takes issue with several attempts to frame the notion of "crimes against humanity" within traditional legal categories. She disagrees with the Nuremberg trials, which sought to understand crimes against humanity as a particular set of acts that were considered inhuman, such as murder, extermination, enslavement, deportation. She points out that the standard German translation of humanity during the Nuremberg trials was *Menschlichkeit*, rather than *Menschheit*. *Menschlichkeit* means humaneness, which suggests that the Nazi crimes were crimes against a certain humaneness, whereas she insists that they were crimes against *Menschheit*, or *humanity as such*. She also disagrees with the attempt to articulate the notion of a crime against humanity as a version of the old legal category of universal jurisdiction, a category that had been used to prosecute pirates and was indeed invoked during the Eichmann trial. This notion suggests that a crime against humanity is a crime that would harm everyone in the same way. Yet, Arendt argues, this does not explain how this crime is *essentially* different from other crimes because there is a difference between a crime that offends all humanity and a crime that offends Humanity as such. All these attempts efface that which makes a crime against humanity different from a traditional crime.

*

We are left with an opposition between a community constituted and sustained through reiterated speech-acts and something that exists prior to this community and functions as its *guarantee*. The two indictments of Eichmann, that is, his committing "crimes against the Jewish people" and "crimes against humanity," do not differ so much in magnitude, but their difference is to be understood as the distinction between a crime in the proper legal sense of the term and something that altogether exceeds the notion of crime. The Eichmann trial, then, seeks to pronounce on acts that have not only wounded the body politic and threatened the laws that protects it but have damaged the very possibility of the law—what lies at the basis of the law yet cannot be *codified* in strictly legal terms. This opposition raises the question: How can this new crime (which exceeds the definition of a crime) against a community (which is not quite a community) be staged within the framework of a trial? Furthermore, how can the human community, if it is indeed wounded by the Nazi crimes, be repaired through a verdict? Using the speech-act terms I employed earlier, the question may be reformulated as to how the performative aims of the trial—its attempt to (re)constitute the community that is damaged by the crime—can be felicitous, when this community is, according to Arendt, one of an "altogether different nature." In what type of theatrical scene can this healing take place, if, as Jaspers suggests, our coming to terms with "metaphysical guilt," the breach of a basic human solidarity, cannot take place in a theatrical event, but requires a "different scene"?[30]

Conclusion: Pronouncing a Verdict
in the Name of Humanity

Unique to *Eichmann in Jerusalem*, I feel, is the way Arendt's deals with these questions in philosophical or legal terms as much as performatively. By opening the book with the exclamation of the usher, "*Beth Hamispath*," which symbolically raised the curtain onto the legal scene, rendered in the original Hebrew as if to preserve its illocutionary force as a "magic formula," she (implicitly) suggests that her own *report* on the trial opens up a *literary* house of justice, comparable to the one in Jerusalem. In a similar gesture, she ends her report on the trial with a three-page speech addressed to Eichmann. In fact, by addressing him, she turns away from her readers and pronounces her own verdict. Arendt's report thus mimics the structure of a trial and thereby proposes an alternative, fictional space in which she can judge Eichmann. Arendt ends her epilogue with the following words:

And just as you supported and carried out a policy of not wanting to share the earth with the Jewish people and the people of a number of other nations—as though you and your superiors had any right to determine who should and who should not inhabit the world—we find that no one, that is, no member of the human race, can be expected to want to share the earth with you. This is the reason, and the only reason, you must hang. (279)

Arendt's book doesn't merely present a *report* on the trial. Through an act of writing, she is able to construct her own "scene" of justice, in which she pronounces her own verdict, which is not delivered in the name of the law but instead uttered in the first-person plural of the "we" who inhabit Earth. At this moment, when her report repeats the dramatic scene of the trial by slightly displacing it, restaging it in the imagination, and rearticulating its verdict in the name of a different community, it becomes a *supplement* to the trial, rather than a mere description of it. As such, it points to something that was not fully resolved in the original trial, something she has not covered in her report but that nonetheless emerges in her book.

Arendt shifts registers as much as positions: Starting off as a journalist reporting on the trial, she becomes a writer of a semifictional speechact addressed to a man who must die. Arendt's shifting registers can be understood as attempts to *invent* a new scene of justice, in which a new set of judgments can be made and, as a result, a different type of community can be healed. In the next chapter, I will show how the writings of poet Charlotte Delbo attempt to stage a similar scene of justice, giving voice to a community that differs profoundly from the one that can be reconstituted by legal speech acts. Rather than understanding her texts as responses to certain legal phenomena, as was the case in Arendt's report, I see her poetry as an artistic attempt to stage that which escapes the legal theater, to try to fill a breach that cannot be mended by legal means.

3

A Cry for Justice

CHARLOTTE DELBO'S *AUSCHWITZ AND AFTER*
AND *DAYS AND MEMORY*

> Lamentations . . . are what we owe the dead ones precisely because we go on living.
> —Hannah Arendt

> Is it not derisory, naive and downright childish to come before the dead and to ask for their forgiveness? Is there any meaning in this? Unless it is origin of meaning itself? An origin in the scene you would make in front of others who observe you and who also play off the dead?
> —Jacques Derrida

In Chapter 2, we saw how Arendt's report on the Eichmann case emphasized that the two indictments for which Eichmann stood trial in Jerusalem—that is, of having committed crimes against the Jewish people and of having committed crimes against humanity—should not be understood as possessing simply a difference in magnitude but rather as expressing the distinction between a crime in the proper legal sense of the term, as a breaking of the laws of a juridico-political community and something that exceeds the legal definition of a trial, a wounding of an altogether different, perhaps more primordial community, namely humanity itself. The question of the relation between these two indictments is raised in the book's postscript but is also, I suggested, more poignantly invoked in its final paragraph, in which Arendt delivers her own verdict of Eichmann, pronounced, as she puts it, in the name of "the inhabitants of the Earth." These words constitute a shift in discursive mode that transforms Arendt's book from a constative act of reportage about a trial into a performative repetition of the scene of the trial. I concluded that this shift implicitly broaches the question of the mise-en-scène in which a "call for justice" in the name of humanity can be uttered. Can a "crime against humanity" be prosecuted within the confines of a legal trial, or do we need, in order to articulate its indictment, to construct a different theatrical space?

Central to the present chapter are related but slightly different questions, namely: How can one prosecute crimes in the name of the dead? How does one speak for the dead and demand for justice in their name? These questions were implicitly raised during the Eichmann trial when prosecutor Gideon Hausner opened his address to the Israeli court with the remarkable words:

When I stand before you, judges of Israel, in this court, to accuse Adolf Eichmann, I do not stand alone. Here with me at this moment stand six million prosecutors. But alas, they cannot rise to level of the finger of accusation in the direction of the glass dock and cry out *J'accuse* against the man who sits there. . . . Their blood cries to Heaven, but their voice cannot be heard. Thus it falls to me to be their mouthpiece and to deliver the heinous accusation in their name.[1]

Hausner utters these words at a crucial moment in the trial, occurring just before he formulates the official complaint filed against Eichmann. This introductory speech should therefore be understood as a clarification of the position from which he will make his accusation. The many deictic terms (such as "When I stand before you"; "in this court"; "here, with me at this moment") announce that his speech will be of a particular order; they indicate that a special event is going to happen. He is preparing to make an accusation in the name of the dead. And when he pronounces this accusation, Hausner claims that he speaks not in his own voice but that his voice is a stand-in for those of the six million Jews who perished in the camps and whose silent j'accuse haunts the courtroom.

In light of my previous chapter, Hausner's claim is remarkable because as a prosecutor he is supposed to speak in the name of *"the people,"* a community of citizens whose relations to one another are mediated by the law. Declaring that the prosecution is being mounted in the name of the *dead*—a quite different entity—inevitably leads to the question whether this accusation falls within the narrow framework of a criminal trial. Indeed, in *Eichmann in Jerusalem*, Arendt takes precisely these words to reveal that Hausner lost sight of his proper role as a prosecutor during the proceedings. Citing Telford Taylor's remark in *The New York Times Magazine* that "a crime is not committed only against the victim, but primarily against the community whose law is broken,"[2] Arendt reminds her readers that in a criminal trial "the wrongdoer is brought to justice because his act has disturbed and gravely endangered the community as a whole and not because, as in civil suits, damage has been done to individuals who are entitled to reparation" (261). For Arendt, Hausner's words suggest that he spoke for the *victims*, not for the legal community that he, as a prosecutor in a criminal case, should have represented.

Although Arendt's criticism is relevant from a legal point of view, I do not think it does justice to the full complexity of Hausner's speech. His accusation "in the name of the dead" cannot simply be reduced to the claim that the dead, as victims, are "entitled to reparation." Indeed, what sort of reparation can the dead demand from the living? I would propose that something more radical happened when Hausner addressed the court. At this precise moment, his discourse shifts into a mode that is no longer entirely legalistic. The pathos of phrases such as "their blood cries to Heaven" and "alas, they cannot rise" signals a switch in genre. They stand out as locutions alien to the legal sphere; they more properly belong to a poetic or a religious discourse. Another idiom seems to be at work in his speech, one that empties out his legal discourse because, as Hausner states, when he slips into this mode, his words no longer seem to be his own. He merely lends his voice to a demand for justice coming from beyond the community of the living: "Their blood cries to Heaven, but their voice cannot be heard. Thus it falls to me to be their *mouthpiece*" (260, emphasis mine).[3] Furthermore, as Hausner's words make plain, this demand for justice takes a peculiar form: It is both silent—"their voice cannot be heard"—and of the order of a *cry*, a scream for justice that is not articulated in language but somehow speaks through the discourse of the official prosecutor, redoubling his voice into an instrument that at once makes a legal demand and channels a mute cry for justice that seems to come from beyond the law. Under the impact of Hausner's words the courtroom itself seems to split: The official legal tribunal is joined by its haunting double, in which a different cry for justice reverberates.

This disruption of the prosecutor's legalistic speech by an accusation in the name of the dead is hardly unique to the Eichmann trial. In fact, this sort of rupture is a recurrent feature of trials concerning crimes against humanity. The hearings of South Africa's Truth and Reconciliation Commission, for example, also included moments in which victims raised their voices to demand justice on behalf of those no longer there.[4] These remarkable scenes, in which a witness or a prosecutor becomes a medium for a demand for justice that seems to come from elsewhere, have, of course, a paradoxical status within legal discourse—at least within the confined goals that a trial sets itself, which I have outlined in my previous chapter. They raise questions about both justice (what would "doing justice to the dead" entail?) and the nature of the community that is to be repaired through the ritual of the trial. Indeed, what is the relation between a community that includes the dead as well as the living and a political community bound by laws? Can a demand for justice for the dead be articulated in a juridical vocabulary? What sort of language do we need to give voice to the dead so that they may address us with their demand for justice? The precise wording of Hausner's accusation in the name of the dead suggests that the call for justice of the dead is situated on the threshold of speech because it is both silent and comparable to a cry.

*

This chapter offers reflections on the questions posed above through an analysis of the literary writings of poet, playwright, and Auschwitz survivor Charlotte Delbo. Delbo is the author of a small oeuvre that consists of poetry, drama, and prose, a large part of which is autobiographical in nature and concerns her experience surviving the camps. In recent years Delbo's writings, and in particular her autobiographical trilogy *Auschwitz et après* (*Auschwitz and After*, 1965–1971), have become classics (if I may use the term) in Holocaust studies.[5] Critics such as Geoffrey Hartman, Lawrence Langer, and Ernst van Alphen have regarded her unique mode of writing, in which she mingles poems with small vignettelike prose fragments that evoke life in the camps, often rendered in a present tense that avoids a retrospective perspective, as typical of the discourse of the traumatized survivor who is not in full possession of her life story but for whom the past returns in flashbacks.[6] These critics have informed my understanding of Delbo's writings, but I depart from their approaches by emphasizing a different aspect of her work. As I will demonstrate, Delbo's literary oeuvre is driven not only by a desire to give testimony about her particular traumatic experiences. Her writings also show a recurring fascination with the figure of the survivor who, on the threshold between the dead and the living, seeks to address the living in name of the dead and at times gives voice to the dead's silent j'accuse.[7]

I will examine Delbo's theme of calling for justice for the dead in close readings of two of her long poems, "Les folles de mai" ("The Madwomen of May") and "Kalavrita des mille Antigone," ("Kalavrita of the

Thousand Antigones") published shortly after Delbo died in 1985 in her final work *La mémoire et les jours* (*Days and Memory*).[8] Consisting of both poetry and prose and written in a style that resembles *Auschwitz et Après*, *La mémoire et les jours* differs from her earlier books in that it combines personal memoirs with texts of a more political nature, discussing atrocities that she has not witnessed herself, such as torture in Algeria. It therefore situates her own gesture of witnessing in a context that raises the question of justice more explicitly than in her earlier works. Within the architecture of the book, "Kalavrita" and "Les folles" are grouped together to form a diptych of poems in which each describes a specific historic event: a massacre in Greece during the Nazi occupation and the disappearance of thousands of political prisoners during Argentina's dirty war. The poems focus on the surviving family members of the victims, those who, years after the atrocities, are still tied to their dead loved ones and demand justice in their names.

I will argue that both poems, read together, shed light on Delbo's autobiographical writings, whose gesture of publicly testifying her attachment to the dead can, within the context of her oeuvre, be read as a call for justice for the dead, perhaps even as a channeling of a silent cry for such justice, comparable to the silent cry that reverberates through the courtroom in Jerusalem. In the discussion that follows I will first analyze "Les folles de mai" and "Kalavrita des mille Antigone," then proceed to use these poems to guide my reading of the second volume of *Auschwitz et après*.

A Cry for Justice

"Les folles de mai" concerns the Argentinean "mothers of the disappeared" (*madres de los desaparecidos*) who gathered every Thursday afternoon at 3:30 to march in circles on the Plaza de Mayo, the central square of Buenos Aires, to protest the disappearance of their family members during the period known as the "dirty war" (1976–1983).[9] In this period the military regime of Argentina made as many as 30,000 left-wing intellectuals and other civilians accused of terrorism and other (dubious) charges "disappear."[10] Beginning in 1977, the mothers and wives of these victims sought to find out what had happened to their children and husbands.[11] Initially started as an unorganized event, this demand for information gradually took on the characteristics of a very strict ritual, or rather, as Diana Taylor calls it, a performance, a piece of street theater during which the participants wore white scarves on their heads and carried large photographs of their *desaparecido* family members.[12] In silence, this group marched in circles on the square, sometimes carrying placards that posed the question, "When will justice be done?"

Written in 1979, at the height of the dirty war, Delbo's eight-page poem evokes this performance on the Plaza de Mayo in which the mothers both mourn and commemorate the disappeared as well as protest the injustice done to them. Delbo's language seems to mimic the movements of the mothers on the square. The poem opens:

> Round and round they go
> mad women
> round the plaza they go
> the madwomen of May
> round the Plaza de Mayo
> round they go (79)[13]

These lines return six times in the poem to form a chorus that alternates with passages that describe the gathering of the women at the square. Interspersed with these descriptive passages are bits of dialogue between the mothers in which they refer to their particular losses. These shreds of dialogue are rendered without quotation marks and form a patchwork of voices in which each voice elliptically alludes to a disappearance, often only in brief deictic terms such as "my husband, last night" (80) or "My son, last night" (80). Despite its length, "les folles de mai" does not read as a narrative poem. Refusing to embed the activism of the mothers in a story about their lives that develops over time, the poem focuses exclusively on the here-and-now of their gathering on the Plaza de Mayo. The consistent use of the present tense throughout the poem, and the repetition of the phrase "they turn" seems furthermore to indicate that the circles in which the mothers go round on the square are symptomatic of their being stuck in time. This reading is suggested by a pun that plays a central role in the poem. The signifier "mai" of the poem's title refers, of course, to the *place* on which they gather, the Plaza de Mayo, but at various points its meaning as the name of a month is used to suggest that, temporally speaking, the mothers are also caught in a loop:

> Round and round they go
> the madwomen of May
> upon the Plaza de Mayo

go round in June and September
in winter and summer
they circle and they cry (84)[14]

Each mother's march seems to consist of an endlessly repeated circling around the same empty spot: the nonevent of a disappearance.[15] This event seems to have disrupted the experience of time as a linear succession of months or seasons. During their demonstrations, the mothers made one recurring demand: that the government return the corpses of the disappeared to their families for proper burial: "Give them back to us / that we may bury them":

Give us at least his torn body
give us his broken limbs
give us his crushed hands
give them back to us
so that we may know
give them back to us
so that we may bury them (81)[16]

The repetitive, rhythmic, chantlike tone in which the demand "that we may bury them" is phrased throughout the poem indicates that the mothers utter it in a trancelike state; their insistence is not so much determined by their strong "will power" but instead has a rather mechanical character, giving the impression that something has taken possession of their will. The poem's title suggests furthermore that the women, in the machinelike, robotic persistence with which they demand the corpses of their family members, have moved beyond what society considers reasonable or sane. They are "*folles de mai*," mad mothers who cannot detach themselves from their dead children and continue to act out of a bond they cannot sever.

*

In *La mémoire et les jours* (1985), "Les folles de mai" is grouped with the poem "Kalavrita des mille Antigone," to form a diptych with a common theme: the impossibility of leaving behind the bodies of executed loved ones. "Kalavrita des mille Antigone" is a twenty-one-page prose poem based on events that took place in the Greek village of Kalavrita, nearly all of whose adult male population of some 1,300 were executed by German soldiers on the night of December 13, 1943, as a reprisal for an ambush of Greek partisans.[17] The Kalavrita case became notorious, as it was one of the few cases that the prosecution during the Nuremberg trials discussed in detail as an example of the atrocities committed by the German army during their occupation of Greece.

Delbo's poem focuses, as does "Les folles de mai," on the survivors of the massacre: the village's women, who were locked up in a school during the shootings and who return the following day with the almost impossible task of rendering to the massive number of dead the duty they owe each of them, namely, to provide the men with a funeral. Compared to the preceding poem, "Kalavrita des mille Antigone" contains more narrative, as it tells of the executions and the burials in gruesome detail. Yet, as in "Les folles de mai," the poem eschews the retrospective gaze that usually comes with narration. Written as an address to a traveler or tourist who happens to walk by the monument commemorating the events of 1943, it opens with the words "Right here. Here it is. This is the path they took" (87), and contains many demonstrative pronouns (such as "There, up there, on the hill" and "there, in that ravine on the side of the hill" [87]) and admonitions to look that link the events of the past both to the present in which the past is evoked and to the particular places in which the events took place. The poem's final stanza, furthermore, suggests that place itself has become an index of an event that seems to have been cut loose from the linear order of time:

> Farewell, traveler.
> When you walk through the village to get back to the road and
>   head homeward,
>   look at the clock on the public square. The time the clock shows
>   is the time it happened that day. Something in the clock's
>   mechanism broke with the first salvo. We haven't had it
>   repaired.
> It's the time it was that day. (108)[18]

Delbo stresses that for the survivors of Kalavrita the massacre is not "over." Just as the lives of the *folles de mai* continue to circle around the disappearance of their family members, Delbo describes how the women of Kalavrita experience the executions of their husbands not as a past "event" after which their lives continued but rather as something that they continue to endure. The women of the village live *with* instead of *after* the killings. The shock of the violence of the executions has interrupted a continuous experience of time. The clock on the central square, frozen at the exact moment of the first shots, forces them to live their collective life, literally, *next* to their trauma,[19] as if their "memory" has materialized and has come to exist as a nonprocessed, not-understood "empty spot" around which their community is woven.

*

Both poems, then, tell of traumatic events that continue to hold the lives of their survivors in their grip. Central to the poems, however, is not so much the violence of the events themselves but the violent unexpectedness of the *loss* of a loved one from which the survivors are unable to recover. Neither the mothers nor the women of Kalavrita are capable of detaching themselves from their lost loved ones in order to continue on with their lives. The executed husbands and the disappeared children still occupy the center of their existence. We could call this situation, in classical Freudian terms, the result of a "pathological mourning process." In his essay "Mourning and Melancholia" (1917), Freud describes how one characteristic of such a failed mourning process is a state of melancholia, a "turning away from any activity that is not connected with thoughts of [the dead],"[20] which usually results in a withdrawal from reality and life in general.[21] The mad mothers as well as the women from Kalavrita are depicted as ghostlike figures who live not so much a life as an afterlife.

Delbo's poems, however, seem to go beyond a mere reflection on mourning. The juxtaposition of the poems in the context of *La mémoire et les jours* emphasizes the political nature of the women's melancholic attachment to their loved ones. Grieving for the dead is in both poems an act with political implications because it takes place within a context in which grief is made impossible—or at least difficult—by the state. The stubborn refusal of the mad mothers to let go of the dead, which their ostentatiously silent "street theater" flaunts, is explicitly staged as a protest against an injustice done to the corpses of the disappeared. Similarly, when the widows of Kalavrita bury the dead side by side in one collective grave, the gesture reads as an act of defiance toward the ruling powers, as the victims' grave becomes a monument that testifies to the injustice done to the dead. Furthermore, the insistence on the importance of burying the dead, which plays a key role in both poems, is presented not as a product of the individual survivors' emotional need for a ritual that would bring closure to their mourning process but rather as a moral obligation toward the deceased that they must carry out. Mourning is in both poems inextricably linked to the desire to do justice to the dead.

The political dimension of the acts of the Argentine mothers and the women of Kalavrita is further emphasized by the title of the second poem, "Kalavrita des mille Antigone," which likens the persistence with which both sets of women insist on their duty toward the dead to the decision of the eponymous heroine of Sophokles' *Antigone* to bury her brother Polynices in defiance of the edict of Kreon, king of Thebes. Kreon had declared that the corpse of Polynices, a traitor in his eyes, be left outside the city walls so as to be eaten by vultures and dogs. Like the women in Delbo's poems, Antigone claims to be acting out of her moral obligation to her deceased brother because, as she puts it in Fitts and Fitzgerald's translation, "it is the dead, not the living who make the longest demands."[22] Because, when Kreon confronts her, she acknowledges her act publicly and refuses to deny it, Sophokles' play presents Antigone's grieving for her brother as an explicit challenge to Kreon's authority.[23] Mourning, as Judith Butler stated in her essay on the play, is in *Antigone* an act of defiance toward the state.[24]

By evoking the figure of Antigone, Delbo's poems place themselves in a long tradition of literary texts that regard the Greek heroine as an exemplar of a heroic, principled, ethical stance against the injustices committed by the state.[25] I would argue, however, that the evocation of Antigone serves not primarily to highlight that the heroines of Delbo's poems are at odds with the ruling powers (though of course they are) but rather, more precisely, that their demand for justice for the dead stems from somewhere beyond the law and can perhaps not even be phrased in legal terms. From Hegel's reading of the play onward, as George Steiner reminds us, *Antigone* has been understood as a drama about a conflict between the law, represented by Kreon, and a different type of legality—the *dike* (invoked by Antigone)—that is not codified in legal-political terms.[26] Hegel understands this as a conflict between the demand for justice stemming from a natural community—or the *family*—on the one hand and the law of the political community of the *state* on the other.[27] In his influential reading of the *Phenomenology of Spirit*, Alexandre Kojève states that Hegel's distinction between these two different communities pertains to the two modes in which humanity exists, namely as a universal and as a particular being.[28] Kojève explains this difference by comparing it to the grammatical distinction between definite and indefinite articles. The state recognizes only the universal element in humanity because a citizen is always *a* citizen and never *the* citizen. Only in the sphere of the family is one's *particularity* recognized. Kojève writes:

In the bosom of his Family, Man is not just another Master, just another Citizen, just another warrior. He is father, husband, son; and he is *this* father, *this* husband: *such a one*, a "particular." (60)

One's particularity—or, in Hegel's and Kojève's idiom, one's "being"—should not, however, be understood as the sum of individual character traits. For Hegel and Kojeve, one's being is precisely empty of characteristics. It is simply the "left over" that cannot be reduced to one's identity as a member of a symbolic community; it is that which *remains* after we have subtracted all character traits of a person.[29] To recognize someone's particularity without taking character traits or actions into consideration is to love someone. Kojève continues:

[T]o attribute an absolute value to a being not in relation to what he *does*, to his acts, but simply because he *is*, because of the simple fact of his *Sein*, his *Being*—is to love him. (61)

Love is always aimed at this empty particularity; in fact, Kojève claims that one loves a person as a *corpse*: "Since love does not depend on the *acts*, on the *activity* of the loved one, it cannot be ended by his very *death*. By loving man in his *inaction*, one considers him *as* if he were dead" (61: emphasis in original). Death—the return to a form of "pure being"[30]—should therefore coincide with a return from the polis to the family, a realm in which this particularity is recognized.[31] Kojève argues that this was indeed the case in the ancient polis because funeral rites usually took place within the institution of the family. The drama of Sophocles' *Antigone* lies, in this perspective, in Kreon's prohibiting the return of Polynices' body to his family. Through this interdiction, Kreon *extends* the laws of the polis to a *corpse*. By forbidding the corpse its burial, he punishes the "particularity" of Polynices' body. Antigone protests against this punishment because it is precisely the dead who should not be subjected to the law. Her castigation of a society that makes her brother's funeral impossible is thus *not* a legal indictment. She protests against an injustice that cannot be brought to justice in a criminal court because the court is an instrument of the state, the community of citizens; she speaks as a *family member* who loves the particularity of her brother and in the name of this love demands justice for him.

Judith Butler, in her reading of the play, goes one step further by raising the question whether the principle on which Antigone demands justice for her brother's corpse follows the logic of a law at all. Pointing to an infamous passage in which Antigone states that her act is precipitated not because of her faithfulness to her family per se but rather out of loyalty to *this* particular brother (who is irreplaceable because their parents are deceased), Butler writes that Antigone seems to be acting on the basis of some sort of law, but "her law appears to have but one instance of application," namely her brother Polynices.[32] Antigone's act of defiance toward the state is therefore not only illegal because it goes against the edicts of Kreon, but it is also nonlegal because the principle on which she acts cannot be universalized. She acts on the basis of something that Butler labels "the law of the instant and, hence, a law with no generality and no transposability, one mired in the very circumstances to which it is applied, a law formulated precisely through the singular instance of its application and, therefore, no law at all in any ordinary, generalizable sense."[33] Yet the fact that Antigone utters her singular claim to justice *publicly* has, according to Butler, the surprising effect of performatively constituting the space in which this claim can be articulated as a political demand. Antigone's defiance of the law of the state should therefore not be understood as a prepolitical act, as Hegel and Kojève effectively regard it when they claim that she represents the laws of the family, but rather as a claim made on the threshold of the political. Implicit in her demand for justice for her brother is a call for us to reimagine which utterances are readable as political claims.

*

In light of these reflections, the codified nature of the performance of the mothers on the Plaza de Mayo as described by Taylor—the wearing of the plain white head scarves as well as the carrying of the photographs of the disappeared on their bodies—serves to indicate that their demand for justice comes as well from beyond the legal sphere. The simple, silent gesture of displaying photographs, which expose the *particularity* of the disappeared bodies to the public, has the force of a demand for justice without referring to a universal law. Likewise, the head scarf, associated with household labor and work in the domestic sphere, signals that their demand is not articulated within a legal framework by a prosecutor who speaks in the name of "the people," a symbolic community bound by a law, but is uttered by a group of *mad mothers* who are still madly attached to the particularity of their unburied family members.[34] They call for justice as family members having a *loving* relationship to the dead, and it is this love that obligates them to the disappeared. A similar love condemns Antigone, who insists that she cannot continue to live without betraying the dead and so becomes herself a living corpse when, at the end of the play, she is sentenced to be entombed alive.[35] This love forces the mothers to return to the same spot day after day, to circle like ghosts on the Plaza de Mayo and to repeat, with mechanical insistence, the demand: "When will justice be done?"[36]

Delbo's poem further suggests that the mothers' insistence on justice not only falls outside the legal sphere but pushes the mothers beyond the threshold of speech itself. The disappearance of their loved ones has literally struck the mothers dumb:

> So anguish-stricken they cannot cry out
> cannot cry out
> for the knot in their throat
> for the pain
> which grips their whole body
> so strong
> they cannot cry forth
> for the dry terror in their heart (79)[37]

During their demonstrations on the Plaza de Mayo they somehow manage to release, out of this very muteness, a *silent cry*. "Their tight-locked mouths shriek . . . a blank shout," Delbo writes later in the poem (80); they scream in silence. She suggests that to be heard this silent cry needs a particular "mouthpiece," namely that of the silent performance of a group of mad mothers, who return, with stubborn persistence, week after week to the Plaza de Mayo, the most public of public squares in Argentina.[38]

*

Delbo wrote most of the poems in the posthumously published *La mémoire et les jours* at the end of her life. It is therefore tempting to read these poems as an "afterword" to her oeuvre that may offer clues to understanding the position she assumes as a writer who seeks to bear witness. We could read Delbo's book *Le convoi du 24 janvier* (1965), for example, which consists of a series of meticulously researched miniature biographies of all 230 women with whom Delbo was sent to Auschwitz, as a "monument" for those who vanished in the camps (only forty-nine survived), a literary tombstone on which Delbo commemorates those who remain unburied. Delbo's simple gesture of narrating the particular life stories of those who disappeared can be likened to the showing of the photographs of the disappeared by the mothers, a gesture that has the force of a moral outcry, an "accusation" made in the name of the dead.[39]

This implies that Delbo, at least in *Convoi*, did not so much write as a "victim," as Lawrence Langer suggests,[40] but as a *prosecutor for the dead*. Her work aims to find a voice or a genre in which this demand for justice can be made. The stylistic oscillation from poetry to storytelling to essay, characteristic of both *La mémoire et les jours* and *Auschwitz et après*, is thus symptomatic of her search for a mode of speaking—lyric, narrative, or argumentative—to assert this demand for justice, a search for an "I" who could evoke the situation, narrate the story, or argue the case. If her literary project is indeed an attempt to find a voice for such a prosecution, which could supplement the legal cases of her era, "Les folles de mai" would be a central poem; its mise en abyme serves as an allegory of Delbo's very attempt to find a voice for a similar silent "cry for justice."

In the following section I will propose a reading of Delbo's autobiographical writings that is attentive to the way in which her work searches for precisely this voice. I will take "Les folles de mai" as programmatic for this dimension of her work, not only because Delbo's writings testify to an attachment to the dead that reminds one of that of the "folles de mai" but also because the poem provides us with a figure that plays a key role in her autobiographical writings, namely, the date. The date—or more specifically *a* date in May—plays such a crucial role in Delbo's autobiography that I would like to suggest that it forms the center around which her writings circle. Just as *les folles* obsessively return to the Plaza de Mayo or May Square, a geographical place but in Delbo's treatment also a symptom of their being stuck in time, the word *May* recurs in Delbo's autobiographical texts both as an event in time and as a "place" from which she, as a survivor, cannot depart without betraying the dead.

My reading will concentrate on the second volume of Delbo's autobiographical trilogy, *Auschwitz et après*, entitled *Une connaissance inutile* (*Useless Knowledge*). Whereas volume 1, *Aucun de nous reviendra* (*None of Us Will Return*) describes life in the camps, and volume 3, *La mesure de nos jours* (*The Measure of Our Days*), focuses on life after liberation, *Useless Knowledge* is concerned mainly with the experience of survival itself, which is depicted in the book through a series of departures, arrivals, and farewells. As in the other volumes, the different scenes of survival are not narrated chronologically. The volumes consist of a series of short, vignettelike chapters, organized along thematic lines that juxtapose different experiences of survival to touch on the nature of the experience of survival itself. The chapters are very diverse, using various idioms (such as the essay and first-, second- and third-person narratives), and include poems as well as prose.

A Return to Life

Useless Knowledge opens with a chapter entitled "The Men," which describes the relations between men and women in the camps, and then contains an untitled poem that recounts two key motifs of *Auschwitz and After*, Delbo's love for Georges Dudach and his execution by the Gestapo in a French prison. Delbo and Dudach were members of the French resistance who were both arrested when the Gestapo discovered anti-German leaflets in their apartment in March 1942. Dudach was executed by firing squad on May 23, 1942. Delbo was incarcerated in several prisons before being deported to Auschwitz with a convoy of other female French resistance fighters in January 1943. The experiences of love and death are brought together in the fourth stanza of the poem:

> I used to call him
> month of May lover
> of childhood days
> happy because
> I let him
> when no one watched
> be
> my month of May lover
> even in December
> . . .
> He spoke the words
>   words uttered by month of May lovers.
> I alone heard them
> One does not heed these words
> Why
> One listens to the throbbing heart
> Believing these tender words
> will sound a lifetime
> So many months of May
> throughout the lifetime
> of two who love.
>
> One month of May
> they shot him (124–125)[41]

The word *May*, so often repeated in this poem, refers to two different things. First it stands for her *love* for Dudach, whom she calls "my month of May lover." This appellation may be read as simply a reference to the

month in which they met, but the poem also enriches it with various met-
aphorical meanings: It stands for spring, youth, and a feeling of happiness that seems to fall outside calendar time, as it can also be experienced
in the winter month of December. In this light, "the words spoken by
month of May lovers," which the lovers believe will sound for a lifetime
of "so many months of May," may be a declaration of love, perhaps a
promise to be faithful, but, because they can only be heard by the lovers, they may represent a promise that is not articulated in language but
remains implicit in the experience of love itself as an unspoken promise
that lovers take for granted because they can hear it in the throbbing of
their hearts.

At the same time, May is the month of Dudach's execution, which,
as the subsequent chapters make plain, coincided with Delbo's separation
from him and her deportation to Auschwitz.

Hence two different stories are knotted together in the poem by one
signifier, a date: a story of love (and perhaps the promise implicit in the
experience of love) and a story about death, survival, and departure. The
entanglement of these stories raises questions that are at the heart of *Useless Knowledge*: What is the relation between love and survival? In what
way are the stories of survival and of love implicated in one another?[42]
And what, then, is the meaning of the "words uttered by a month of May
lover?" Is the speech-act of a lover—a "declaration of love"—similar to a
symbolically articulated contract—say, the marriage vow "till death do
us part"—or do such acts promise something more? Do they establish
obligations *beyond death*?

*

If the word *May* is already dense with significance in this poem,
later passages in *Useless Knowledge* complicate it even further. Toward the
end of the book, Delbo describes how she and her comrades are impris-
oned in the concentration camp at Ravensbrück, where they have been
sent after having spent a few months at Auschwitz. They know they will
be set free and anxiously await the Swedish Red Cross. When the arrival
of the Red Cross is postponed over a few consecutive days and as a result
one of Delbo's exhausted comrades is getting desperate, Delbo decides to
invent a date of departure to reassure her friend: "Finally, exasperated by
these questions which I could not answer, I decided to say 'Yes, yes, we're
going to leave. We'll leave on the 23rd'" (205):

Why did I say we'd be leaving on the 23rd? I'm not superstitious. Was it impatience? Charity? Was it because I could no longer bear those eyes begging for a ray of hope, a crumb of conviction? And since I was stating with the firm self-confidence of an accomplished actress, "We're leaving on the 23rd," they went off comforted. We left on the 23rd, the 23rd of April.

If Mado weren't alive to attest to this fact, I wouldn't dare recall my prophecy. (206)

What makes her prophecy so very daring is the fact that this date, the 23rd, the date of the departure from the camps, is the same date as the execution of Dudach, albeit not in April but in May. "It was also on a 23rd," the chapter continues, "May 23rd, that I was called to his cell at the prison of Santé, where I was also incarcerated. They were taking me to him for a last farewell" (206).

Again, one signifier, "the 23rd," refers to two different experiences: departing from Dudach and leaving the camps. Because departing from the camps implies leaving behind those who died there, the same date also points to two different experiences of survival. The textual organization of the book, furthermore, presents these as parallel stories, as the final four chapters (with poems interlarded between them), entitled "Departure," "The Farewell," "The Final Night," and "The Morning of Our Freedom,"[43] recount in turn the final meeting with Dudach and the last days in Ravensbrück.

These very different stories of survival and departure, the meaning of which the book tries to grasp, are in *Useless Knowledge* condensed in one *date*: the 23rd. It is significant that a date comes to stand for these events because a date *marks* a singular, unique moment without *signifying* it. "The 23rd" dates two survivals and departures but reveals nothing about their *meaning*.[44] Yet it functions as the "knot" that ties together the different story lines of *Useless Knowledge* and so is at the very core of the enigma of survival to which the book is devoted.

*

At the center of these various interlinked stories of survival and departure is a scene of farewell—or rather a scene in which the word *farewell* is uttered. It is hard to tell whether it was cruel or merciful on the part of the Germans; but, on the day of Dudach's execution, Delbo was permitted to see her lover one last time. The chapter "The Farewell," describes how during this final meeting Delbo and Dudach are at first at a loss for words, not having enough time to tell each other what needed to be told.[45] When the time comes to utter her "adieu," Delbo knows that words— in contrast to those spoken between "month of May lovers"—effectively imply a betrayal. When the guard knocks on the door of the cell for the third time, to indicate that the time of departure has come, Delbo knows that she is destined to forget Dudach. Evoking the figure of Ondine, hero- ine of one of Jean Giraudoux's plays, she writes:

They led me to a cell with the door open. Leaning against the wall, Georges was expecting me . . . We hardly had enough time to tell one another everything we wanted to say. A soldier called out, "Madame!" in that same tone which cast a mortal meaning on each word. I gestured: Wait. One more minute. Let us have another minute, another second. He called me again, but I would not let go of Georges's hand. The third time he called, I had to go, just like Giraudoux's On- dine whom the King of the Sylphs had to call thrice while she was bidding fare- well to the Chevalier who was about to die. After the third call, Ondine would forget her mortal existence and return to the underwater realm. (207)

Giraudoux's *Ondine* tells the story of a water nymph who falls in love with a human being, Hans, and becomes mortal to be with him. Hans betrays her and is sentenced to death by Ondine's father, the king of the Sylphs.[46] In the final scene of the play, Ondine, like Delbo, is given the chance to see her beloved one last time before his execution, on the condition that she return to the water realm after Hans's death. On her return, she will experience total amnesia of her mortal existence. In Giraudoux's play, Hans states that what is unbearable to him is not so much his death but his being forgotten. His tragedy lies in his having no widow to mourn him: "I am the last of my house. I shall leave no trace behind me. There will be only an Ondine, and she will have forgotten."[47] The adieu between Ondine and Hans, then, is a "real" adieu, as Hans puts it in Giraudoux's play:

It's a real farewell, [*un vrai adieu*] you understand! Not like those lovers who part on the threshold of death, but who are destined to meet in the future, and to continue to affect one another, because they are shadows in the same realm. They part only in order to never part again. But Ondine and I will remain on differ- ent sides for eternity [*Ondine et moi partons chacun de notre bord pour l'éternité*]. On one side nothingness, on the other forgetting. [*A bâbord le néant, a tribord l'oubli*].[48]

If the "adieu" between two lovers usually implies a promise to remember, as Hans suggests—a promise to mourn someone, in short to *not fully depart* from someone—then Ondine's departure from Hans is a *real* one. Hans's fate, in fact, is worse than death: Not only will he die, but he will be forgotten, and so will die what Lacan calls a "second death": His biological death will be followed, when the memory of him is erased from Ondine's mind, by a symbolic death of total annihilation: "On one side nothingness, on the other forgetting."

Ondine knows there is nothing she can do about it, and during their final meeting she asks for forgiveness, "Forgive me, Hans . . . I will lose my memory." Delbo claims that her own departure from Dudach is also a real farewell: "I knew that, like Ondine, I would also forget," Delbo continues in the chapter "The Farewell," "since to go on breathing is to forget, and to continue remembering is also to forget" (207). Survival itself means forgetting, she states, because to continue living is an act of forgetting, and even the act of *remembering* someone itself implies a forgetting on a different level because, as she reflects elsewhere, it means translating the experience of physical intimacy into images, words, or stories that effectively efface that which is not expressible in words. Again referring to Ondine, she writes:

I call forgetting this faculty of rejecting into insensitivity the memory of a sensation, warm and alive, to transform into images which have lost their ecstatic or frightful power the memory of a living love, a love of flesh and warmth. And Ondine reappeared then at that moment in my life when destiny was playing itself out—the farewell—where everything was set in such a way that nothing could alter the course of it. Hans was going to die and I would live on.[49]

If, as Hans puts it, the "adieu" between lovers usually implies a promise to remember, to be faithful to the dead, this is, according to Delbo, an impossible promise. The survivor, departing from the one who will die, "crosses over" to the side of the living and, at the moment of this crossing, she forgets.

*

A similar experience of forgetting characterizes two other scenes of survival, placed in the middle of *Useless Knowledge*. In two consecutive chapters, entitled "Boire" ("Drinking," translated by Lamont as "Thirst") and "The Stream," Delbo recounts how unexpected contact with water in Ravensbrück was a lifesaving experience, giving her the opportunity to drink and to wash. The opening paragraphs of "Thirst" describe the devastating thirst Delbo suffered in the camps. This almost fatal thirst changed her into a "zombie," one of the *living dead, une folle*, a madwoman, blind, deaf, mute, and insane; having an open mouth, yet unable to utter words:

I'd been thirsty for days and days, thirsty to the point of losing my mind, to the point of being unable to eat since there was no saliva in my mouth, so thirsty, I couldn't speak, because you're unable to speak when there's no saliva in your mouth. My parched lips were splitting, my gums swollen, my tongue a piece of wood. My swollen gums and tongue kept me from closing my mouth, which stayed open like that of a madwoman with dilated pupils in her haggard eyes. (142)

The experience of excruciating thirst had not only turned her into a mute, staggering along with an open mouth that was incapable of speech; it also made her semiblind, or at least that is what her comrades believed. She continues:

At least, that is what the others told me, later. They thought I'd lost my mind. I couldn't hear anything, see anything. They thought I had gone blind. It took me a long time later on to explain that, without being blind I saw nothing. All my senses had been abolished by thirst. (142)

The experience of extreme thirst, then, seems to preclude witnessing. Because thirst involves both blindness and (literal) speechlessness, it is impossible to testify to one's experience while suffering from it. In this light, it is significant that, even though the chapter is narrated in the first person, it is explicitly presented as a recovered memory based on descriptions from others ("At least, that is what others told me, later.")

The second and largest part of the chapter describes an unexpected opportunity to drink a bucket full of water, which is depicted not only as a life*saving* experience but as a sudden return of life, or perhaps a return *to* life, that takes place *unexpectedly*:

Suddenly, I felt life returning to me. It was as if I were regaining consciousness of my blood circulating through my body, of my lungs breathing, of my heart beating. I was alive, I lived. (145)

A similar experience of "returning to life" is described in the chapter "The Stream," which narrates how Delbo and her comrades, when working outside the camp, come across a little stream, which gives them the chance to wash themselves. The moment of cleansing—which she calls "the forgotten contact of water on one's skin" (151)—is experienced as magical and radically new: "The sensation of water on my face was so new, so wonderful" (151).

Although neither chapter mentions *Ondine* explicitly, I would argue that Giraudoux's play is evoked here, and not only because in both cases stories of survival are associated with water. More importantly, they are told as stories of "crossing over" from the realm of the dead to that of the living, an event that in both cases involve an experience of amnesia. "The Stream" begins with a sentence that emphatically states that the episode to be related has not been fully remembered: "Strange, but I don't recall anything about that day. Nothing but the stream" (147). It ends: "It must have happened like this, but I have no memory of it. I only recall the stream" (153). The chapter has as its central paragraph:

So, on that day, at the stream, I must have thought of the last shower, and also of the pleasure of immersing one's body in gentle, warm water. Or perhaps I thought of all the ones who had died since our arrival without having been able to splash some water on their faces. All of this is but reported remembrances. Actually I thought of nothing except the stream. (152)

In this dense fragment, imagery of bathing—which usually has connotations of rebirth and baptism and thus the *beginning* of life—is linked to the "the last shower." In the context of *Useless Knowledge* this refers both to the last shower taken before deportation *and* to the last shower the camp inmates take before their deaths—an association confirmed by the evocation of "the ones who had died since our arrival" in the following sentence. Yet this association is denied as soon as it is established, as she continues by reflecting: "Actually, I thought of nothing except the stream." Going into the stream—the experience of survival—was an act that *should have* made her think about those who went to the last shower, but *in fact* it brought amnesia. In "Thirst," the same element, water, which would give her saliva necessary for speaking or fluid her eyes need to see—which would, in short, enable her to testify—brings with it a forgetting, as she writes, "I knelt near the pail and drank like a horse . . . I can't remember whether the water was cold . . . I felt neither the cold nor the wetness . . . I drank and drank breathlessly . . . I drank with no thought of any kind" (144).

*

To return to life, then, implies a departure from the dead that involves a radical forgetting. When time has come to bid Dudach farewell, she states that the difference between life and death is unbridgeable: "The distance between life and death is far greater than the one between earth and the waters to which Ondine had to return in order to forget" (207). The "adieu" between the living and the dying, which is central to the experience of survival in *Useless Knowledge*, is always a *real adieu*. It implies a promise to remember that cannot be kept. During their farewell at the French prison, Dudach and Delbo decide to remain silent:

His voice [was] darkened by advancing shadows. Should we speak to one another, or embrace in silence? We chose to speak first. Soon, however, I measured the uselessness of speech of me, at such a time. What could I say to the one who was about to disappear? (20)

In Giraudoux's play, Ondine, knowing she will forget, similarly decides to remain silent at the moment of departure: "Je me tais," I remain silent.

A silence also overwhelms the Ravensbrück survivors after they have been liberated. Knowing they are about to leave the place from which no one was meant to return, and preparing themselves to depart the site where so many of their comrades have been left dead, they are overtaken by a sudden speechlessness:

Then, the voice of one of us rises. "Comrades! Think of those we are leaving here. Let's have a moment of silence for them." And this voice asking for silence actually breaks the silence. (223)

The "adieu" uttered by the person who departs from the dead already *is* the departure. It is articulated from the side of the living, and, as such, it breaks its implied promise to be faithful. Like the voice asking for silence that breaks the silence it asks for, the utterance of "adieu" shatters the silent bond that links the survivor to the dead.

*

A Cry Stuck in the Throat

I would claim that this silent "adieu," which implies both a departure from the dead and the impossible promise to remain at their side, lies at the heart of the experience of survival as depicted in *Useless Knowledge*. The date—the 23rd—around which the book circles refers to an obligation to remember that cannot be fulfilled. Yet even though this date stands for a "real adieu" and a "real departure," it is an "adieu" that leaves a *mark* on the one who departs, albeit not in the form of a conscious "memory" accessible to the survivor herself. When the moment of farewell comes, Ondine explains to Hans that although she will survive without remembering him, the movements of her body will nonetheless testify to his death:

And now, in the depths of the Rhine, even without memory, I cannot but repeat the movements that I made when I was with you. The plunge that took me to the grotto will now take me from my table to my window. The gesture I used to turn a shell on the beach will be one I use eating my pastry.[50]

Although her *mind* will bear no trace of the memory of her dead lover, her *body* will repeat the movements it once made. Her forgotten past will return to her in the form of empty, meaningless movements and habits, compulsively repeated, that have lost their utility. Despite her amnesia, the past will still form the *core* of her being, unconsciously organizing her "afterlife."

Similarly, the lives of the *folles de mai* circle around the mark left by the disappearance of their loved ones. And, again, this mark exists in the first place as a *bodily* symptom. According to Delbo's poem, the sorrow over the loss of family members who remain unburied *squeezes their throats* and makes it impossible to speak, they are so "anguish-stricken they cannot cry out."[51] They are marked by a "cry" over a loss that is literally stuck in their throats. It marks their bodies with speechlessness. They cannot articulate this cry as a "message" conveyed consciously and articulated in language; but during their performance on the Plaza de Mayo they manage to give voice to it and make it audible as a *silent cry*.[52] Furthermore, their performance imbues it with the force of a cry for justice, which "roars" from their silent throats. Delbo writes:

Round and round and their whole being shrieks
their tight-locked mouths shriek
a shriek that won't come forth
a blank shout (80)[53]

In contrast to the voice asking for silence at Ravensbrück, which broke the very silence it asked for, the performance of the mothers on the Plaza de Mayo, in its very inarticulateness, makes a screaming silence audible. Moreover, the mothers manage to give this silence the force of an address to the living, asking, *"When will justice be done?"*

*

Useless Knowledge concludes with a poem entitled "Prière aux vivants pour leur pardonner d'être vivants" (189–191), in which the dead address the living and this time ask whether the living could ever be forgiven by the dead:

> You who are passing by
> well dressed in all your muscles . . .
> how can we forgive you
> that all are dead
> You are walking by and drinking in cafés
> you are happy she loves you
> or moody worried about money
> how how
> Forgive you for being alive
> How how
> will you ever be forgiven
> by those who died
> (229–230, translation modified)[54]

By raising the question of forgiveness, this final poem, which immediately follows the chapters on the departure from Auschwitz and the farewell with Dudach, echoes a phrase used on the book's opening page, set shortly after Delbo's arrival in Auschwitz (which, in the course of the book, comes to stand for her departure from Dudach), which describes the indifference she feels looking over the barbed-wire fence at the prisoners in the men's camp:

Deep inside me [*au secret de moi*] there was a terrible indifference that comes from a heart reduced to ashes . . . I resented all the living. *I had not yet found inside me* [au fond de moi] *a prayer of forgiveness for the living.* (117, emphasis mine)

Useless Knowledge frames its stories about survival between these two fragments: an admission that she has not *yet* found a prayer to forgive the living for being alive and a poem that asks whether such forgiveness is possible *at all*. This framing suggests that the problem of survival may lie in a search for a prayer of forgiveness, which might very well be impossible to reach. Being a survivor means being marked by an obligation to remember the dead. "To forget would be atrocious," a survivor named Mado explains in *Mesure de nos jours*: "Our loyalty to the comrades we left back there is all we have" (266). Yet, she adds, this exacts an enormous price:

To live in the past is not to live. It is to cut oneself off from the living. But what shall we do to cross over to their shore, to stop remaining paralyzed on the other side [*sur l'autre rive*]? (264)

"How do we *cross over* to the side of the living, without betraying the dead?" is the problem of the survivor, according to *The Measure of Our Days*. How does one stay loyal to the dead, without being cut off from the living? And vice versa: Is it possible to be "alive" without being deaf to the demands of the dead?[55]

"It is the dead, not the living who make the longest demands" (188), Antigone tells her sister Ismene as she explains her decision to bury Polynices. Ismene makes a different choice, claiming that it is beyond her capacity to follow her brother's demands; she chooses to follow the laws of the polis to stay alive. She begs the dead for forgiveness:

> The law is strong, we must give in to the law
> in this thing and in worse. *I beg the Dead*
> *To forgive me*, but I am helpless (188, emphasis mine)

If the living need to be forgiven by the dead it is not only *because* they chose life (like Ismene) but also, in a sense, because they did so *to survive*, to exist among the living and not to look at them from the other side of the fence with a "heart reduced to ashes," condemned to exist, like Antigone, as one of the living dead. Yet, as the poem emphatically states, it is never clear whether this forgiveness is possible at all.

*

Delbo's "Prayer to the Living to Forgive Them for Being Alive" suggests, however, that not only the survivors need forgiveness to remain alive but that the *living in general*—the *quelconque* addressed by the poem—must be forgiven by the dead:

> You who are passing by
> Full of tumultuous life within your arteries
> Glued to your skeleton
> As you walk with a sprightly step
> athletic awkward
> Laughing sullenly, you are so handsome
> So commonplace
> So commonplacely like everyone else (229)[56]

The figure of speech used throughout the poem—the figure in which the dead address the living as "you, who are passing by"—is known, since Paul de Man's "Autobiography as De-Facement," as *prosopopeia*, the figure in which "the dead are made to have a *face* and a *voice*."[57] But the *voice* of the dead, which Delbo's poem makes audible, addresses the living with the question: "How can we ever forgive you?" In this, her poem resembles the gesture of the mothers on the Plaza de Mayo who, by showing the photographs of the disappeared, confront us with the *face* of the dead, asking in their name: "When will justice be done?" As Delbo's poem suggests, this question concerns us not as citizens of a nation that may (or may not) have been implicated in a history of violence but rather as singular, living human beings, inhabiting mortal bodies that consist of bones, veins, and muscles.

Conclusion: A Cry Inscribed in the Sky

I would argue that this poem, placed strategically at the end of the book, is crucial to our understanding of the position that Delbo assumes as a witness. *Useless Knowledge*, which depicts the experience of survival as a series of departures, crossings, and returns, exposes to its readers the marks left on the survivor by her departure from the dead. It thereby confronts us with the bond that still obligates the survivor to the dead. Delbo's gesture of publicly exposing this secret bond gives her published works a particular force that may be compared to that of the performance of the mothers on the Plaza de Mayo. By publicly demonstrating their unconditional faithfulness to the dead, the mothers address the living and give voice to the dead. As Delbo's poem suggests, the silent cry for justice made audible in the demonstrations of the mothers is not completely their *own*. As Delbo's poem puts it, *it simply happens to resonate in their empty throats*—in that part of the body from where a shriek won't come forth— "*d'où le cri ne sort pas*." In their demonstrations, then, they give voice to the silent cry for justice *of* the dead, which resonates in the community of survivors. This cry coming from the dead—which crosses over from the side of the dead—reaches us, the living, through the silent and speechless figure of the survivor, and it confronts us with a gaze that cannot forgive us.

In *Auschwitz et après*, Delbo sketches an image that serves as the perfect (but horrible) allegory of this "silent cry," when she describes the unburied bodies piled up outside the barracks in the camps, then writes:

For eternity, these shaven heads, squeezed against one another, bursting with shouts, mouths twisted by cries we do not hear, hands waving in a mute cry.

The cry remains inscribed upon the blue of the sky. (xvii)

This mute cry, which issues from the open mouths of the unburied, will continue to haunt the realm of the living. Although the cry roaring from their throats cannot be heard, it is nevertheless "written in the sky." That is, although this demand cannot be articulated in strictly legal terms and resists integration into public memory, it is nevertheless inscribed in the very reality of the sky under which we live and the bodies we inhabit. It returns to haunt us, not so much as citizens living under the rule of law, but as living human beings.

Gideon Hausner may have had a similar cry in mind when he evoked the silent j'accuse of the six million in his opening address during the Eichmann trial, but the framework in which he gave voice to it differs profoundly from Delbo's literary staging of this cry. Whereas Hausner evokes the dead in the context of a trial, which inevitably seeks for closure, completion, and a departure from the past, Delbo's writings emphasize that the cry for justice of the dead is bound to continue for eternity.

"Les folles de mai" ends with an address to the mothers, encouraging them to keep marching, not for eternity, but until the ghosts of the disappeared awaken and their accusing gaze makes the world explode from shame:

> Go round madwomen of May
> round and round on the Plaza de Mayo
> cry women of Buenos Aires
> cry till the ghosts of your tortured rise
> like so many staring eyes
> staring into ours and accusing us
> incandescent stares that burn
> burning the skin from our souls
> and causing us to scream from your pain
> cry until the world
> bursts from shame (86)[58]

"Kalavrita des mille Antigone" ends its address to the passerby with an "adieu voyageur": It continues to state that a full departure may be impossible, as the time on the clock still indicates the time of the mass executions. The time on the clock, frozen under the impact of the shocking events of December 1943, is here a date, in the precise, double meaning that Derrida gives it in his essay on Paul Celan. It marks a singular, unique event that the linear progression of time will never erase, and it similarly obliges the witnesses of this event to the past. The survivor still has a date with the past, as it were, and by exhibiting this "datedness" to us—the readers, the living, the passersby—we are confronted with an injustice that continues to haunt us. Through her writings, then, Delbo lets her own "date" with the past speak to us, giving it the force to *call* on us, a call that comes from the past but that is channeled through the silences in the discourse of the survivor. If Delbo's voicing of a demand for justice for the dead resembles Hausner's voicing a silent cry for justice for the dead during the Eichmann trial, it does so with a major difference: It knows that it cannot be articulated on a legal stage but needs an altogether different theater, a literary theater of justice.

4

Brecht on Trial

THE COURTROOM, THE THEATER,
AND *THE MEASURES TAKEN*

Brecht, in the course of yesterday's conversation: "I often imagine being inter-
rogated by a tribunal. 'Now tell us, Mr. Brecht, are you completely serious?' I
would have to admit that no, I'm not completely serious. I think too much about
artistic problems, you know, about what is good for the theater to be completely
serious. But having said 'no' to that important question, I would add something
still more important: namely that my attitude is entirely legitimate."
—Walter Benjamin

The aims of the epic theater can be defined more easily in terms of the stage
than of a new drama. Epic theater allows for a circumstance which has been too
little noticed. It may be called the filling in of the orchestra pit. The abyss which
separates the players from the audience, as it does the dead from the living; the
abyss whose silence in a play heightens the sublimity, whose resonance in an
opera heightens the intoxication—this abyss, of all elements of the theater the
one that bears the most indelible traces of its ritual origin, has steadily decreased
in significance.
—Walter Benjamin

Brecht on Trials: The Theater as Courtroom

In 1932, during one of his visits to Moscow, Brecht informed his
friend and colleague, the Russian futurist playwright Sergej Tretiakov, of
a plan to organize in Berlin a series of theatrical performances that would
reenact the most interesting trials in the history of humanity. Possible trials to be staged included those of Socrates and of George Grosz's alleged
blasphemy for his cartoon "Christ in a Gasmask," as well as the trial of
Karl Marx's *Neue Rheinische Zeitung* and a medieval witch trial. Tretiakov

had probably met Brecht in 1930 or 1931 when he visited Berlin on the occasion of the staging of his piece *Roar China* by the Meyerhold Company, and thereafter the two writers began an intensive correspondence on the nature of the theater.[1] In his introductory essay to the Russian translation of three of Brecht's *Lehrstücke* (learning plays, or didactic plays), Tretiakov recounts his conversation with Brecht regarding this plan.[2] The theater would function like a courtroom, Brecht explained, in which several trials were to be reenacted during one evening's performance.[3] Tretiakov describes how Brecht is carried away by his enthusiasm for this plan when the German playwright begins to elaborate:

Let us suppose that the trial of Socrates is over. We organize a short witch's trial where the judges are armored knights who condemn the witch to the stake. Then the trial of Georg Grosz begins, but we forget to remove the knights from the stage. When the indignant prosecutor storms at the artist for having insulted our mild and compassionate God a terrific racket breaks loose, as though two dozen five-gallon samovars were applauding. The noise is caused by the knights who are moved to applause by the defender of the defenseless god. (23)

Brecht's desire to create a "legal theater" was developed in a period when he was in the process of radically transforming (*Umfunktionierung*) the traditional Aristotelian theatrical apparatus, an aim that Tretiakov shared.[4] Both writers believed that a formal restructuring of the theatrical space, and the relation between audience and stage, would open up new possibilities for a political theater. As Tretiakov points out in his introductory essay, Brecht's plays characteristically address the audience in a new way. They do not evoke feelings of compassion and pity in the audience, as in Aristotelian theater, nor do they leave the audience purged; their aim is to teach the audience so that each member leaves the theater a changed person. The theater must make the spectators "ready for political action."[5] Brecht and Tretiakov were suspicious of left-leaning authors who included revolutionary themes in their plays without truly revolutionizing their audience. This type of theatrical performance, as Benjamin has argued in an essay that discusses both Brecht and Tretiakov, makes the depiction of human misery as well as the struggle against it into "an object of consumption."[6] The characteristic feature of this literature, Benjamin writes, is that it is watched by a passive audience and evokes feelings of left-wing melancholia: "The effect is that the political issues put on stage cease to be a compelling motive for an *Entscheidung*," which has the dual meaning of both decision and verdict.[7]

Trained as a lawyer before he started writing, Tretiakov expresses an interest in the "legal structure" of Brecht's *Lehrstücke*. The *Lehrstücke*, didactic pieces that Brecht wrote between 1928 and 1932, were meant to be performed by amateurs such as schoolchildren and workers. When performed, the pieces would be instructive for the actors as well as for the audience.[8] The *"Umfunktionering"* of the traditional stage into a didactic theater, Tretiakov explains, often occurs in Brecht's plays because Brecht models his theater on the dramatic structure of the trial; the audience is asked to watch the events on stage in order to judge them. He quotes Brecht:

The main thing is to teach the spectator to reach a verdict . . . this trains the mind. Any fool knows how to feel sad and to share suffering, and not only fools. You should see the salty tears swindlers can shed when they are moved. (22)

"In Brecht," Tretiakov notes, "we see the transition from the theater into the tribunal. . . . [Brecht transforms] the spectator's chair into that of the judge" (22). Tretiakov refers here to an expression of Osip Brik illuminating this transition: "Brecht's plays are usually in the form of court proceedings." "This is true," Tretiakov concludes, "Brecht the playwright is an able and resourceful casuist" (21).[9]

*

Of the three pieces Tretiakov translated, *Die Maßnahme* (*The Measures Taken*, 1930) fully embodies this "transition from stage to tribunal."[10] An oratorio written by Brecht in collaboration with Hanns Eisler, *Die Maßnahme*, is literally structured like a trial.[11] In the play, four agitators have returned to Moscow from a propaganda mission to Mukden, China, and must make a report to the Communist Party. During their trip they had killed one of their comrades, whose mistakes had imperiled the mission. In order not to interrupt their mission, they disposed of the young comrade's body by throwing it into a lime pit. Having fulfilled their duties toward the Party, they ask for a verdict on their fateful decision. The play consists of the four surviving comrades reenacting for the Party officials, played by the chorus (who at the same time represents the audience) and the series of events that had brought them to their decision to execute their fifth member and concludes with an reenactment of the moment of his death and the destruction of his corpse.

The play is thus composed of a range of embedded moments of decision and verdicts. The young comrade's behavior is judged by the four agitators who decide to kill him. The agitators ask the Party to judge their actions, and the audience, in turn, is invited to make a third verdict, judging the other two verdicts. By being solicited to hand down a sentence of their own, the audience is written into the play as participants. In fact, the play's reception by the audience is a continuation of the structure of the scenes put on stage. The contribution elicited from the public fulfills what according to Brecht is essential to his learning plays, namely that the opposition between actors and audience is *aufgehoben*, or sublated.[12] This sublation takes place exactly when the audience pronounces its verdict, and it is in this moment of enunciation that the public is transformed from a passive spectator into an active participant in the play.[13]

Brecht on Trial: Framing *Die Maßnahme*

In an ironic twist of history, this play, with its set of embedded trials and verdicts, itself became part of a very different form of "legal theater." In 1947, when Brecht was summoned to appear before the House Un-American Activities Committee (HUAC) during its investigation of alleged communist infiltration into the film industry, he was questioned about *Die Maßnahme*.[14]

The hearing opened with the now notorious question of whether Brecht was, or had ever been, a member of the Communist Party. Already planning to return to Europe when the McCarthy hearings began, Brecht had prepared a written statement that he had hoped to read to the committee. But when asked the question for the second time he answered: "No. I am not and have not been a member of the communist party of this country or any other country."[15] Brecht's answer came as a surprise to the audience, not so much because of its content—although many believed he was lying—but because he actually answered the question. Brecht was the eleventh of the nineteen "unfriendly" witnesses. The witnesses before him, who later became known as the Hollywood Ten, had all refused to answer the question, which they regarded as a violation of their constitutional rights. On the audio recordings and the film clips that are available of the hearings, one can hear a murmur of surprise in the chamber after Brecht spoke. Even the chairman seemed to have been taken off-guard, as he repeats the question:

> CHAIRMAN: Your answer is, then, that you have never been a member of the Communist Party?

BRECHT: That is correct.
STRIPLING: You were not a member of the Communist Party in Germany?
BRECHT: No, I was not.[16]

After a short silence the chief investigator, Robert Stripling, takes a re-markable step. Rather than cross-examining Brecht on his political activi-ties, Stripling questions him on his literary production: "Mr. Brecht, is it true that you have written a number of very revolutionary poems, plays and other writings?" Brecht answers, speaking with a torturous slowness that seems deliberate:

I have written . . . a number . . . of poems, songs and plays . . . in the fight . . . Against Hitler, and, I of course . . . they can be considered, therefore, as revo-lutionary . . . as I was . . . of course . . . for the overthrow of that government. [Laughter]

The chairman responds with irritation: "NO, NO, NO. Mr. Stripling, we are not interested in any words he might have written for the overthrow of Germany, and the government there!"

The remainder of the hearing turns into a literary debate in which Stripling asks Brecht to engage in an exercise of close reading his own work and invites him to discuss his plays' themes and to give an interpre-tation of their titles, to establish what he calls "the revolutionary content" of Brecht's work. Sidestepping Stripling's ploy, Brecht decides to quarrel about the translations of his work provided by the HUAC. He argues that some of the translations brought into the courtroom weren't authorized by him and, in fact, missed the point of the text. When Stripling rattles off an English translation of Brecht's "Solidaritätslied" ("Forward, We've Not Forgotten") in a particularly inelegant way and turns to Brecht with the question, "Mr. Brecht, did you write this poem?" Brecht replies: "No. I wrote a German poem, but that sounded quite different." The audience roars with laughter.

After a discussion of Brecht's poetry, Stripling brings in what he thinks is his most damning piece of evidence of Brecht's subversiveness: the play *Die Maßnahme*. He proceeds to read large parts of it. Brecht, of course, debates the translation of the title, which Stripling wants to render as the "punitive measure." He explains that *Die Maßnahme* does not mean a punitive measure, as indeed, the young comrade is not punished for his behavior, nor is he murdered: "You will find it when you read it carefully," he explains. A rather detailed discussion follows in which Brecht points to the source of the play in Noh theater.

Like in the old Japanese play where other ideas were at stake, this young man who died was convinced that he had done damage to the mission he believed in and he agreed to that and he was about ready to die in order not to make greater such damage. So, he asks his comrades to help him, and all of them together help him to die. He jumps into an abyss and they lead him tenderly to that abyss, that is the story.[17]

Brecht tries to explain that the play addresses a rather abstract philosophical issue but gets stuck when he tries to find an English word to summarize the theme of the play and mumbles something in German. Stripling, exhausted, then asks: "Mr. Brecht, may I interrupt you? Would you say that the play is pro-communist, anticommunist or that it remains neutral regarding communism?" This question effectively turns the question of whether Brecht's work has a revolutionary content into a multiple-choice examination.

*

Brecht's quarrel with the translation is, of course, evasive and, as the laughter of the audience indicates, gently mocking. The struggle over the translation, however, points to a question that lies at the heart of the hearing. Brecht was initially put under Federal Bureau of Investigation (FBI) surveillance as part of the program of "Alien Enemy Control," which aimed at controlling so-called radical elements who had fled to the United States from Nazi Germany. The slightly xenophobic question at the heart of the HUAC hearing was concerned not only with our understanding of these leftist authors' works but also with how their work fits in an American context. Are these authors, who had been allies in the fight against Hitler, subversive and un-American in the new political climate of the Cold War? Brecht attempts to circumvent this question by embedding his writing in the struggle against Hitler.[18]

In a broader sense the conflict over translation dramatizes the central conflict between law and literature that lies at the heart of the hearing. Stripling attempts to "frame" Brecht's work in both senses of the word: He tries to pin down the content of his work in political terms. With regard to communism, a literary work has to be unambiguously pro, contra, or neutral toward it. Stripling also hopes to frame the author legally and to put him behind bars—at least figuratively. Brecht, with his sense of irony, proves to be as elusive as literary language itself; he seems to escape the attempts to frame his work in straightforward political terms. Furthermore, in keeping with his own poetics, he emphasizes the performative dimension of his writings. Its political nature cannot be reduced to subject matter; rather, it has to be understood within the specific context in which it hopes to intervene.

*

The specific role of *Die Maßnahme* in this debate, however, is remarkable. The HUAC investigated the motion picture industry to test its grip on American popular culture, but *Die Maßnahme* was not a film and could barely have been less popular in German-speaking countries, let alone in the United States. The play was written seventeen years before the hearings; it was never performed in the United States, nor were there plans for a staging there at the time of the hearing.[19] In fact, after the two performances in Germany, the play was never again performed with Brecht's permission and it was not until 1999, after the collapse of the German Democratic Republic (GDR), that the play was revived.

And yet it was this Brecht play that received the most attention during the hearing.[20] The play was translated specially for the occasion by Elizabeth Hanunian, a freelance translator working for the HUAC.[21] This was, furthermore, the second "official" translation of the play. An earlier one had been provided by the FBI, the agency that had kept a 427-page file documenting Brecht's stay in the United States between 1941 and 1947 under the program of "Alien Enemy Control."[22] The first available entry, that of March 3, 1943, is a detailed summary of the play, describing it as a "self styled educational play which advocates Communist World Revolution by Violent Means."[23] *Die Maßnahme* is the only Brecht play to receive such scrutiny by the FBI.[24]

The particular interest of both the FBI and the HUAC can, of course, partly be explained by the play's concern with communism. It is one of the few plays of Brecht that explicitly deals with the Communist Party and its internal politics. The German performances were sponsored by the German Communist Party, and the play contains some of Brecht and Eisler's most powerful communist hymns: "Praise of the Party," "Praise of the USSR," and "Praise of Illegal Work." The play, furthermore, already had a "criminal record." As the FBI file indicates, it had been banned by the Weimar government, which gave it the dubious honor of being the only play of Brecht's that was already outlawed when Hitler came to power.[25]

A closer look at the FBI file on Brecht, however, reveals perhaps a more specific reason for the institution's interest in this play. The play was taken to be a justification for another legal event: the Moscow show trials of 1936–1939, which were held years after Brecht wrote his play. Among the newspaper clippings in the FBI file is an article that, published about a year and a half after the HUAC hearing, attempts to establish this link:

In the "punitive measure," written five years before the Moscow trials, Brecht anticipated its methods and motivations. At this play's climax a young Communist is killed when he revolts against the party line. . . . Such a blind willingness to destroy others and oneself at the behest of a party hierarchy can destroy the humanistic values of art, literature, science and mankind itself.[26]

The title of the article, "Bertolt Brecht, Songbird of the GPU," repeats a phrase used in ex-communist Ruth Fischer's book *Stalin and German Communism*, in which Fischer (notably, Hanns Eisler's sister) virulently attacks Brecht.[27] She calls Brecht the main apologist for Stalinism among German writers and singles out *Die Maßnahme* to prove her point.[28] Fischer may have been the main source of information on Brecht for both the HUAC and the FBI, as Bruce Cook claims.[29] It is, indeed, revealing that her book cites the same passages from both *Die Maßnahme* and Brecht's poetry as those referred to by Stripling during the hearing: "In Praise of Learning" and "Forward, We've Not Forgotten." Furthermore, Fischer also mistranslates *Die Maßnahme* as "The Punitive Measure." She writes:

The one didactic play of this series by Brecht that best digests all the terroristic features into a mirror of the totalitarian party and its elite guard, the NKVD is *The Punitive Measure*, written under the impact of the defeat of Chinese Communism. The accompanying music was written by Hanns Eisler, whose brother, Gerhart, had been sent to China at the end of 1929 to liquidate opposition to the Russian Politburo. The play, a parable on the annihilation of the party opposition, is a preview of the Moscow trials. With a sensitivity to Stalinist methods that denotes his genius, Brecht was able to write in 1931 a play about the show trials his master would produce five years later.[30]

References to the Moscow trials are a recurring theme of the play's reception. In this respect, Fischer's reading of the trial is typical. In particular, the decision of the young comrade to consent to his death and to acknowledge his mistakes as an obstacle in the progress of the revolution are often compared to the rituals of self-accusation made during the Stalinist show trials, in which the defendants confessed to all sorts of betrayals.[31] Martin Esslin, for example, explains that the play expresses the logic of "self-sacrifice" that would be central to the Moscow trials:

Die Maßnahme, written in 1930, is an exact and horrifying anticipation of the great confession trials of the Stalinist era. Many years before Bukharin consented

to his own execution in front of his judges, Brecht had given that act of self sacrifice its great tragic expression.[32]

Other authors, such as Rainer Friedrich, describe the Moscow trials as an
"extension of what one sees in the didactic play, only on a larger scale and
with intensified horror."[33] Hannah Arendt suggests that the play points to
an "inner logic" of the Communist Party, which found its natural ful-
fillment in the Moscow trials.[34] The negative response of critics, such as
Kurella, involved with the Communist Party could be explained, according to Arendt, by the possibility that Brecht exposed something of the
inherent logic of the Party's operations, which had to remain hidden.

More recently, Slavoj Žižek has turned to the play in his investigation
of the logic of "revolutionary self-sacrifice" in the Stalin era.[35] He calls the
play a "literary counterpart" to the Stalinist show trials.[36] He aptly points
to the fact, often overlooked by critics, that the young comrade consents
not only to his death but to the disappearance of his corpse. Žižek points
out that the identification with the revolution implies consent to one's
total annihilation. Thus, according to Žižek, it is not so much that the
young comrade at the end of the play understands his mistakes and consents to his own death but rather that he accepts his "total annihilation,"
an act of willingly endorsing one's radical self-erasure that is thus linked
to the Stalinist purges.[37]

*

If Brecht's play is itself structured as a complex sets of trials and verdicts,
its historical reception embeds it in an even more complex network of
trials, verdicts, and judgments. In the following discussion I aim to dis-
entangle this web of judgments, verdicts, and trials, which are historical,
fictional, and legal. I will argue that these various judgments circle around
an empty spot that lies at their heart: The unburied body of the young
comrade that, in a key scene in the play, is thrown into a lime pit. Hence
not only does the play raise the question of the relation between the (didactic potential of the) theater and the trial, but it does so in a story about
a body that remains unburied. As I hope to demonstrate, this unburied
body is the central "traumatic kernel" around which this tapestry of trials
and judgments is woven.

In the first part of this chapter I will analyze the dramatic structure
of the play, suggesting that it consists of the staging of the tension between
an individual's ethical sense of responsibility and the political need to

subjugate oneself to a collective (the Party) held together by a set of rules, which the play calls an "ABC of Communism." I will then reflect on the implications of the fact that this drama finds its climax in a scene in which a dead body is disposed of. What does it mean that, in *Die Maßnahme*, the conflict between ethics and politics is dramatized in a story about a funeral that does not take place? As I will argue, this raises a question similar to the one that played a key role in my previous chapter: Namely, what kind of justice do we owe the dead? Or: What is the relation between the responsibilities we have toward the living and those we owe the dead? Furthermore, the play's theatrical structure implicitly raises the question of how these two responsibilities can be staged in a "legal theater," one that invites us to make a judgment.

In the final part of the chapter I will relate the play's story of the disappearance of the young comrade's body to the disappearance of an actual body during Stalin's purges, namely the body of Sergej Tretiakov, Brecht's occasional translator, friend, and perhaps main source of inspiration—Brecht later called him "my teacher."[38] I will argue that Tretiakov's disappearance is inscribed in the history of the reception of the play, albeit—again—as an erasure, something that literally remains illegible. Yet it is precisely this erasure that *dates* the play, in the double sense that Derrida gives to the term in his aforementioned essay on Paul Celan: It marks the incision of a singular historic event into the texture of the play and thereby turns the play into a testimony of a unique event that calls on us, the living, to remind us that we still have a *date* with the past.

Die Maßnahme as Legal Theater

When Brecht appeared before HUAC in 1947, it must indeed have been hard to "translate" the play into the situation of postwar America. His experiments with a didactic theater were firmly embedded in the context of Weimar Germany, a period of hopes, fears, and utopian ideals that seemed at odds with the moods of the postwar era. The latter half of the 1920s had seen a growing political awareness on the part of German workers; Brecht's plays assumed a key role in the radical worker's movement and the culture epitomized by the amateur-theater workers' choruses that disappeared in the Nazi years and did not return after the war ended.[39]

In the interwar period, when *Die Maßnahme* was conceived, Brecht became increasingly less interested in producing theater pieces for traditional theatrical venues and instead experimented with the theatrical apparatus, its social and institutional structure. He was inspired by the communist agitprop troupes that were performing in factories, beer houses, and on the streets of Berlin from 1927 onward, ensembles whose activity became more intense with the approach of Reichstag elections in 1930.[40] Agitprop troupes staged short, didactic theatrical events aimed at raising the political consciousness of German workers, and Brecht was especially interested in its attempt to directly affect and influence its audience. Part of his knowledge of agitprop came from Hanns Eisler, who wrote the music for *Die Maßnahme* and had been involved in the agitprop movement as the musical director of one of the many popular workers' choirs. Eisler had also composed songs for troupes, such as the popular "Rote Wedding" and had conducted the proletarian choruses "Karl Liebknecht" and "Stahlklang," all of which had been influenced by the "Moskauer Blauen Blusen," which toured Germany in 1927.[41]

Eisler had discovered Brecht's work at one of the "Neue Musik" festivals organized by Paul Hindemith, who had been experimenting with "*gebrauchsmusik.*" Although Brecht had written two didactic pieces with Hindemith, it was in particular *Der Jasager*, a *Schuloper* written with Kurt Weill, that attracted Eisler's attention. *Der Jasager*, a short piece, is an adaptation of the fifteenth-century Japanese Noh play *Taniko*, initially translated into German from Arthur Waley's English version by Brecht's collaborator Elisabeth Hauptmann.[42] The play narrates the story of a young boy who joins a dangerous expedition that must climb a mountain to retrieve medicine for his dying mother. In the course of the expedition the boy falls ill, and so, according to the *Brauch*—the custom—he has to accept that he must die so as not to imperil the expedition. The dramatic high point that gives the piece its title comes when the young comrade is asked whether he is willing to comply with the tradition. Even though his answer does not matter—he will be killed anyway— the *Brauch* gives him a chance to say "yes" and assume his destiny as his own. At the climax of the piece, when the boy accepts his fate, the music falls silent, and the boy utters a monotone "*ja.*" This moment is rendered as an antiaria, devoid of musical pathos.

Eisler was impressed by the structure of the play and its music but took offense at what he called the "moronic feudal content of the story."[43] He proposed that Brecht rewrite *Der Jasager* as a political piece. Around February 1930 Brecht and Eisler started working on what was first entitled "Der Jasager 2: Konkretisierung," which gradually grew into *Die*

Maßnahme.[44] *Die Maßnahme* took its basic ingredients from *Der Jasager.* Its central theme is *"Einverständnis"* (agreement), embodied in the moment when the hero consents to his own death.[45] However, *Die Maßnahme* translates the mythical story into political terms: The "expedition" is now a political mission undertaken by five communist agitators who travel to China to spread propaganda for the communist cause and to bring to the Chinese workers, as the play puts it, "the teachings of the classic writers and the propagandists, the ABC of communism; to the ignorant, instruction about their condition; to the oppressed, class consciousness; and to the class conscious, the experience of the revolution" (79/14). The youngest member threatens the operation not by some accidental illness but by a series of political mistakes. When he consents to his own death, he does not die for an abstract *Brauch* but for the cause of the revolution. The young comrade's last words proclaim: "In the interests of Communism / Agreeing to [Einverstanden mit] the advance of the proletarian masses of all lands / Saying Yes to the revolutionizing of the world" (107/82). The story also adds the episode of the disposal of the young comrade's corpse, which has to disappear because its discovery would endanger the operation. Hence the *"ja"* of the young comrade is not a *"ja"* simply to his death but to his complete disappearance.

*

Structurally, the most important difference between *Der Jasager* and *Die Maßnahme* is the legal frame-narrative of the latter. The play opens with a prologue in which the four returning comrades explain their situation and ask the Party for a "verdict" (*"wir fordern euer Urteil"*) (10). After the introductory scene and one in which the four comrades reenact for the control chorus their mission's departure, the play unfolds as a series of short vignettes in which the four comrades *demonstrate* (*zeigen*) the attitude (*Haltung*) of the young comrade in various political situations to the judging gaze of the Party/control chorus/audience. The effect of the legal frame-narrative is that the events of the story are not staged in a naturalistic, direct way; they are merely *demonstrated* by the four surviving comrades. As a result, the audience, alienated from the events on stage, is invited to watch the events in a rational way rather than with empathy. This alienation effect is enhanced by the fact that the four comrades take turns playing the young comrade, with the other three playing various other roles, introducing themselves with phrases such as "I am the Overseer"

(85/28) or "We are the coolies and we pull the rice barge up the river" (84/26). The roles played on stage are not to be understood as characters with psychological depth; they are merely functions, demonstrations of certain types so that the audience does not conflate the actor with a character and to ensure that the actors do not themselves fall into the trap of identification: The young one should not be treated as a "person" or a "character" but rather as the embodiment of a set of actions. The episodes are separated by titles and scenes of "analysis and commentary" in which the political implications of the reported actions are spelled out.

A further effect of the legal structure of the play is that the young comrade, the central character of the story, is absent from the stage. He is literally only *cited* before the tribunal because his words and actions are present on stage only insofar as they are repeated by the surviving comrades.[46] The young comrade's absence in the play's dramaturgy reinforces the central lesson he has to learn: As a Party member, he has to subject himself to the Party rules. Or, rather, becoming a Party member entails an act of subjectivation: By joining the Party one inscribes oneself into the larger structure of the Party. This act means that one must discard one's private identity and assume a new identity.

This theme is announced in the first scene reenacted by the four surviving members of the expedition, the scene of their departure entitled "The Blotting Out" ("Die Auslöschung"). Before the comrades set off for Mukden, they meet with the "Head of the Party House" to receive their instructions. They are told that because of the political situation in Mukden it is of the utmost importance that they remain anonymous. They are asked to wear masks. By putting on the masks they accept their anonymity, and they also demonstrate their consent to the instructions of the Party; they become the "dramatis personae" and adopt their roles in the progress of the revolution. Four times, the Party asks them for their agreement, and each time they answer "*ja*" in one monotone voice.

Wearing masks is, of course, a convention Brecht's theater borrowed from Chinese theater. Within the context of the play's legal drama, it has special connotations. As Hannah Arendt points out in *On Revolution*, the word *persona* was adopted in ancient Roman legal terminology to describe the distinction between a private individual and the Roman citizen; the roman citizen had "a *persona*, a legal personality, as we would say; it was as though the law had affixed to him the part he was expected to play on the public scene."[47] By wearing masks the comrades turn into revolutionary *personae,* and their adoption of these roles takes on an almost religious connotation when it is followed by something that can be called a "negative baptism into anonymity." After the five signal their assent to their instructions, the Head of the Party House declares them beings without names:

Then you are yourselves no longer. You are not Karl Schmitt from Berlin, you are not Anna Kjersk from Kazan, and you are not Peter Sawitch from Moscow. One and all of you are nameless and motherless [*ohne Namen und Mutter*], blank pages on which the revolution writes its instructions. (81–82/18–20)

This moment of "*Einverständnis,*" or of "confirmation," in a quasi-Christian sense, is—of course—a moment in which they express consent to the project; it also implies a radical transformation of their symbolic identities, now collapsed into a single, collective identity. When they utter their "yes," they inscribe themselves in a particular history and destiny—or rather, as the play puts it, they allow the revolution to inscribe itself on them. Thus, this moment of confirmation is paradoxically an effacement of their identities. Rather than taking on a positive symbolic identity, they *lose* their names and become "empty pages." The putting-on of their masks is similarly described as an *erasure* of their faces. As the four agitators explain, "But the work in Mukden was illegal, so, before we crossed the frontier, we had to blot out [*auslöschen*] our faces." (81/18) And they submit to yet a third erasure when they agree to sacrifice their relationships with their families. The Head of the Party House explains that they have to become *motherless* ("One and all of you are nameless and motherless, blank pages on which the revolution writes its instructions [*leere Blätter, auf welche die Revolution ihre Anweisung schreibt*]" (82/20). Thus these three erasures strip the four of their relations to family (no mother), self-image (no face), and, most crucially, their "name." The marker that inscribes them into the symbolic is annihilated.

The three mistakes of the young comrade involve three different betrayals of this first yes: when his individual senses of compassion (scene 3: "The Stone"), justice (scene 4: "Justice" ["*Gerechtigkeit*"]), and honor (scene 5: "What Is a Human Being Actually?") get in the way of his mission. In each case, rather than fulfilling the Party's instructions, he responds to the events as an individual human being. The final mistake, played out in a scene entitled "The Rebellion against the Teaching" ("*Empörung gegen die Lehre*") (1930) /"The Betrayal" ("Die Verrat") (1931) occurs when the young comrade takes off his mask and tears it apart, effectively betraying his first "yes."

In the next two sections I will analyze the four mistakes of the young comrade, as well as the central moment in the play, which is again an instance in which the young comrade says "*ja*." However, this time he consents to a final, definitive erasure of his body.

The Lessons of *Die Maßnahme*:
Spelling Out the ABC of Communism

The young comrade's first mistake is demonstrated in a scene entitled "The Stone." On his first mission, he is sent to a group of horribly treated coolies who drag a rice barge along the slippery banks of a river near Mukden. The young comrade is sent to incite them to organize and collectively demand shoes, which would make their work more bearable. Uttering this demand would also prepare them for later political action. Before he goes, his more experienced comrades warn him not to fall prey to pity at the sight of the coolies' suffering. But when the young comrade first appears by the river, he hears the coolies sing the beautiful, sorrowful "Song of the Rice Barge Coolies." In their reenactment of this scene, one of the four agitators interrupts the song to remind the audience that the song's beauty hides the torment of their work, which is repulsive ("It is repulsive to hear how the torture of these men's labor is masked by beauty") (85/28). The young comrade, however, is moved to pity by the song, and when one coolie collapses he exclaims, "I can't keep going" (85/30). He feels obliged to help by putting stones on the slippery ground so as to keep the coolie from falling. While doing so he asks the overseer, "Aren't you even human?"—which immediately draws the suspicion of another overseer, who recognizes him as an "inciter" seeking to "stir up the people." As a result the young comrade is chased around the city of Mukden for a week before he escapes to safety.

According to the discussion that follows the scene, the young comrade mistakenly followed his feelings rather than his reason.[48] He regarded the suffering of the coolies and their exclamations of pain as personal appeals for help, thereby forgetting the political nature of his mission. The young comrade mistakenly thought himself the addressee of the coolies' song of suffering and acted precipitately in response to its implicit appeal for help. His position as agitator should rather have been that of a translator: He should *rephrase* their song of pain into a collective demand for better shoes to *politicize* them. He needed to teach them to articulate their suffering as political demands. As his older comrades explain, the goal of the mission was not to act with compassion but rather to change the circumstances that make compassion necessary.

The inclusion of the "Song of the Rice Barge Coolies," not coincidentally the first one Brecht and Eisler wrote,[49] furthermore contains an implicit theatrical lesson. It shows that a song expressing suffering that moves the audience to pity is not necessarily a first step toward political transformation. It only evokes, in Benjamin's words, "*linke Melancholie*," an emotional response that can keep people from organizing politically. The compassion and compassionate acts elicited by the song are not so much threats to the political system as they are the oil that keeps the system running smoothly. As one of the overseers remarks in a fragment added in the 1931 version of the play, he would not mind it if each coolie were accompanied by a compassionate fellow who puts stones in front of their feet, as long as it doesn't cost him extra.[50]

The effect of the legal frame-narrative is to invite the audience to look at this scene without making the young comrade's mistake, that is, without falling prey to empathy or pity. Because the audience is put in the position of the judge, it is asked to watch the events on stage with the cool, rational eyes of the "control chorus" ready to deliver its verdict. They are asked not to empathize with him and to understand his acts in a psychological way.[51]

*

The second and third mistakes of the young comrade also result from his tendency to understand his mission in personal terms, thereby forgetting the larger political goal of the operation. In the following scene, entitled "Justice" (88–92/38–46), the young comrade is sent to distribute leaflets to factory workers to build solidarity with an ongoing strike. When another worker is wrongfully accused of distributing the flyers, the young comrade's personal sense of justice forces him to admit to being the distributor, again with disastrous results. In the next scene ("What Is a Human Being Actually? (93–97/48–56), he is dispatched to persuade a merchant to arm the coolies, under the pretext of assisting him in his fight against the British. However, he is so offended by the dehumanizing terms in which the merchant speaks about the workers that his sense of moral dignity makes it impossible for him to sit down and share a meal with the person he despises. The result is that the coolies do not get their weapons.

"But isn't it right [*richtig*] to place honor before everything else?" (96/54), the control chorus asks. "No," the four answer, and sing the chorale "Change the World: It Needs It" (96–97/54–56). The song explains that the revolution has no use for people who consider themselves too righteous to get their hands dirty. "With whom would the right-minded man not sit / to help justice? / What medicine would taste too bad / to a dying man? // What baseness would you not commit / To root out baseness? / If, finally, you could change the world / What task would you be too good for?" (96, translation modified/54–56). The chorale ends with a direct address to the audience: "Sink down in the filth / embrace the butcher, but / change the world: it needs it! / Who are you? / Stinking, be gone from / The room that has been cleaned! Would that / you were the last of the filth which / you had to remove!" (96–97/56). This chorale summarizes the lesson implicit in the three scenes: Becoming a revolutionary does not entail participating in acts from which one grows as a moral being. It entails the opposite: One has to sacrifice one's honor, one's compassion, and one's sense of righteousness. One has to learn to "sink in filth," if that is what is required. Being a revolutionary is not necessarily an "honorable" pursuit; as the older comrades had explained: "Who fights for communism has only one of all the virtues: that he fights for communism" (82/20).

*

The young comrade—and the audience—must learn that to become a revolutionary one must sacrifice one's own sense of ethics—one's compassion, one's feeling of personal responsibility, one's righteousness— for something that the play describes as "the teachings of communism," "the classics," or the "ABC of communism."[52] The young comrade has to learn that his personal sense of injustice needs to be articulated through a specific revolutionary program. What the play "teaches" or offers for our reflection is the relation between ethics and the specific politics of a (Leninist) Party, an organization that strives for justice. Accepting this "lesson" requires in the first place an act of distancing oneself from one's personal sense of ethics.

The play teaches this lesson in the form of a chorale, which the audience is asked to join; in the collective voice, the voices of individuals are dissolved. The chorale is contrasted to another type of song that is included in this scene: the song of the Merchant, the play's only solo performance and the only song sung by a tenor in a free tempo,[53] thus "expressing" the true character of the bourgeois in the narcissistic sense of self-importance that is best illustrated when he asks the young comrade: "Why do I get everything cheaper than an other [*als ein anderer*]? And why would a coolie work for me almost without pay?" (94, translation modified/50). "Because," he continues to explain, "I am bright." ("*Weil ich ein kluger Mann bin*") (94/50). The Merchant's song is included in the play as comic relief, delivered as it is with the narcissism of someone who enjoys hearing his own voice.[54] Repeatedly interrupted by the young comrade, who impatiently asks him whether he will arm the coolies, the Merchant answers each time with an irritated "I'll tell you later," only to pick up the song in which he celebrates his success as a merchant. The Merchant's self-love illustrates the particular nature of the bourgeoisie's misunderstanding of its actual situation. The Merchant regards his success in business as a reward for an inherent quality he possesses, namely his *intelligence*. The narcissism of such an attitude can be detected in the pleasure with which this "intelligence" is compared to the lesser abilities of an imaginary businessman who is not as successful as he is ("why do I get everything cheaper *as an other*," he sings (94/50). The Merchant is oblivious to the real cause of his wealth, which can be found in the property relations under capitalism that allow him to profit from the coolies' labor. The piece, then, presents ideological differences as differences in the use of the voice: The expressive singing of the Merchant and the coolies is opposed to the collective voice of the chorus. The unsentimental choruses that praise the collectivity and anonymity—"Praise of the USSR," "Praise of Illegal Work," and "Praise of the Party"—are set in contrast to both the Merchant's individualistic singing and the coolies' lament.

The scene with the Merchant is meant as a comic intermezzo; the joke lies in the gap between the bourgeois's self-understanding and the "truth" of his symbolic position. Yet the laughter it provokes teaches us the same lesson that the young comrade has to learn: Your role in this world, whether as merchant or revolutionary, is determined by your position in a larger system that is beyond your control.[55] Thinking that your role is dictated by your intelligence or moral dignity is a form of self-deception. It forms a farcical version of the tragic lesson the young comrade learns, namely that his moral rightness does not depend on his compassion, nor even on the justice of his actions, but rather on his contributions to the larger historical development of the revolution. It is a lesson, however, that escapes the young comrade because, as the others explain, "neither threats or laughter could bring him to eat with a man he despised" (96/54).

"Man Cries Out!" Resisting the Lessons

The conflict between the young comrade's sense of justice—based on his compassion, righteousness, and honor—and the Party's political program culminates in the sixth scene of the play, entitled "Rebellion against the Teaching" (98–102/58–64), in which the young comrade decides to break with the Party by taking off his mask and following his own sense of justice. Unlike the previous scenes, which are demonstrations of the young comrade's mistakes, this scene consists of a debate between the young comrade and the older comrades. This debate contrasts two different conceptions of justice, and as such it dramatizes the conflict at the heart of the play.

The scene opens with the young comrade explaining his decision to support the spontaneous uprising of the unemployed by calling for a general strike, even though his more experienced comrades point out that the time is not yet ripe for this sort of action.[56] He counters that the unemployed can wait no longer, and their suffering needs an immediate response.[57] Moreover, *he* can wait no longer. As he explains to them, he has seen too much; The sight of suffering has become unbearable for him. In keeping with the previous lessons, the others suggest that the young comrade has to learn to watch human suffering not with his own two eyes but rather from the detached point of view of the Party. A true Communist, they explain, does not watch the suffering of fellow human beings with compassionate eyes but analyzes it with an unsentimental, rational gaze. They erupt into the chorale "In Praise of the Party," which praises this abstract, suprahuman point of view with which the Party understands things. Unlike the individual, who has only two eyes, the Party has a thousand eyes; whereas the individual is mortal and has a limited time on Earth, the Party cannot die, and thus watches the events from an abstract vantage point, outside of a specific place and time.

The young comrade, however, explains that the suffering he witnesses makes an unconditional demand to which he must immediately respond, regardless of the long-term consequences. Shortly before he takes off his mask, he tears up the leaflets that contain the teachings of communism and shouts: "man, living man, cries out. His misery tears down the dikes of instruction. And that is why I'm going into action—right now, this minute. For I cry out too. I tear down [*zerreiße*] the dikes of the teaching!" (100/64). The human cry of suffering cuts through every lesson spelled out in the ABC of the Party. It pierces through the protective layer of the young comrade's identity as a communist and wounds him, as he says, *as a human being*. It forces him to break with the network of agreements and commitments that formerly defined his identity. "I throw away all that was good yesterday, I reject every agreement with everybody and do what alone is human" ("*das allein Menschliche*") (101/68). Finally he takes off his mask, rejects his role as a revolutionary, and cries: "We have come to help you! We come from Moscow!" (102/70). With this gesture he exposes his human face and voice, and he falls out of his role. The taking off the mask also breaks with the theatrical structure of the text. Rather than citing, or reenacting this scene dramatically, the surviving comrades describe this moment in the third person. They turn to the audience and say: "And we saw him and in the twilight saw / His naked face, human, open, guileless. / He had torn up his mask" (102/70).

This scene, then, does not so much cite yet another mistake of the young comrade but is a rupture in the play's textual organization. It dramatizes a clash between two incommensurable understandings of justice. On the one hand, the Party's strategies and procedures are articulated and codified in a set of teachings, rules, and classic texts. On the other hand, the young comrade's sense of justice—which is foremost a response to the things he witnesses—is not uttered in agreement with a doctrine or a program but is, as he calls it, "purely human." The play shows these two conceptions of justice to be inextricably linked and yet in irresolvable tension with each other. On the one hand, the party strives for a politicization of the human response to suffering; Indignation at the sight of suffering makes up the moral ground on which its political program rests. On the other hand, the play demonstrates that the transposition of these moral feelings into a successful political program requires that it is precisely those feelings that one must give up. The young comrade, therefore, finds himself bound by two mutually exclusive obligations. He feels himself addressed by the appeal of the Coolie, yet his responding to this appeal entails putting the expedition in peril. It would therefore be an act of irresponsibility with regard to the Party. His obligations to the Party, however, demand that he betray the Coolie, whose appeal he experiences as unconditional, "shredding" all bonds and promises that he had been bound by.[58]

The young comrade's predicament is repeated on the level of the play's reception. The legal frame-narrative positions the audience as a spectator-judge, asking it to make a political judgment of the situation and thereby to adopt the logic of the Party. At the same time, the play's pathos derives from its confronting the audience with the young comrade's *cry* for justice, which is presented as something that breaks through the legal framework set up so carefully in and by the play. The youth's cry "We come from Moscow" coincides with his taking off his mask, a gesture by which he not only betrays the Party but also steps out of the theatrical frame of the play because he effectively loses his legal "persona" and becomes someone more than a man "cited" before the law.

In the dramaturgy of the play, this opposition is, again, depicted as a difference between two uses of the voice. The Party's response to the situation is sung in the collective voice of the chorales, whereas the youth's reaction is described as a *cry* for justice, an inarticulate promise to help, in which he discloses himself as a human being.[59] This cry, furthermore, is not presented as being fully his own. It is merely a response—perhaps a reverberation of—another cry that he feels makes a call on him and to which he feels obliged to testify. The play leaves its audience with the question of the relation between this cry for justice and the Party's ABC. What is the relation between this primordial cry and an ABC that seeks to codify it into a set of rules, procedures, and structures? Does it follow that the Party *must* stifle this cry?[60]

"To Die, but Hide Death": The Sacrifice of the Young Comrade

He loses his face, to use a Chinese expression
—Hanns Eisler

[justice] awaits the voices that will recall, to the judgments of the judges and statesmen, the human face, dissimulated beneath the identities of citizens
—Emmanuel Levinas

The conflict between the youth's sense of justice and that of the Party—which is also, I repeat, a confrontation between ethics as entailing an individual obligation to respond to another human being's call and politics as comprising a collective endeavor that seeks justice in the future—is both heightened and resolved in the play's next scene, in which the young comrade consents to his own death. His cry "We come from Moscow" and his deliberate removal of his mask had betrayed their mission, forcing the agitators to flee as a result. Because the young comrade is wounded, he demands care—but they cannot take him back to Moscow without aborting their mission. Because they also must prevent the Chinese authorities from finding the young comrade's body, which had become identifiable without the mask, they conclude that they will have to destroy his body completely:

We decided: Then he must disappear [*verschwinden*], and totally. For we must return to our work and cannot take him with us and cannot leave him behind. We must therefore shoot him and throw him in the lime pit. For the lime will burn him. (106/78)

Although they are resolved to do this, they decide to ask the young comrade for his agreement before they proceed—though even if he were to refuse, the other four would act on their decision. The young comrade is asked not so much to approve or to make a decision but rather to take upon himself what was already decided, a historical necessity.

After the young comrade has consented to his murder and his body's annihilation in the lime pit, he asks the other four comrades to help him die. The killing of the comrade is depicted not as something violent but as something tender, as the others ask him to lay his head on their arms and to close his eyes as they carry him to his death: "We said: lean your head on our arms / Close your eyes / We will carry you" (107/82). In this tableau, which evokes the Christian *pieta*, the young comrade disappears, repeating the words of the leader of the Party House who initiated the mission: "In the interests of communism / Agreeing to [*einverstanden mit*] the advance of the proletarian masses of all lands / Saying Yes to the revolutionizing of the world" (107/82).[61]

Thus, with this final "*ja*," the young comrade reiterates the "*ja*" uttered when he accepted his mission to Mukden, an affirmation subsequently betrayed by the removal of his mask. This "*ja*" completes the set of erasures consented to earlier in the play, when he severed his relations to family (he became motherless), self-image (his face was erased), and identity (he lost his name) so as to become an empty page on which the revolution can inscribe itself. The young comrade now agrees with the erasures of his physical existence (he loses his life) and his corpse, which will be annihilated after it is thrown in the lime pit. This final effacement thus radicalizes the earlier set of erasures. Whereas his first "yes" confirmed his transformation from a private person (with name, face, and family) into a functionary of the Party, the young comrade's agreement to have his corpse thrown into a lime pit gives consent to his complete disappearance. After his execution—no grave or other symbolic marker will memorialize his former existence—there will be no trace left of him. The young comrade dies what Lacan calls "a second death," a symbolic annihilation.[62]

By submitting to such utter effacement he becomes the type of hero that is praised earlier in the play, in the chorale "Praise of Illegal Work." The song summons the comrades, as they depart on their illegal mission to Mukden, to "speak / But conceal the speaker / To win victory / But to conceal the victor / to die / but hide the death" (83/22). According to the song, a revolutionary hero differs from other heroes in that his actions do not disclose his identity.[63] The effect of his achievements, in fact, causes his disappearance. After the right words are spoken, the importance of the person who utters them is eclipsed; the victory cannot be claimed by the person who achieved it; and, finally, in illegal work the person loses that which may be the most intimate feature of identity: his or her own death. The song concludes with a question: "Who would not do much for fame? / But who would do it for silence?" ("*für das Schweigen*") (83/22).

By sacrificing himself not for fame but for silence, the young comrade resembles the type of communist hero analyzed by Ernst Bloch in *Das Prinzip Hoffnung* (*The Principle of Hope*, 1956). According to Bloch, the "red hero" differs from heroes in the literature of earlier periods in that he does not want to distinguish himself from others because, under communism, the individual's relation to his death has changed. The communist hero does not invest much in his own ego, and he identifies completely with the communist cause. Bloch writes:

This means that he had already ceased to take his ego so seriously, he had class consciousness. Personal consciousness is so absorbed into class consciousness that to the person it is not even decisive whether he is remembered or not on the way to victory, on the day of victory. . . . And this certainty of class consciousness, cancelling out individual survival, is indeed a Novum against death.[64]

Thus the communist hero's attitude to his own death is different because it is viewed from a particular perspective: that of a moment of future victory. It does not matter whether one's personal contribution to this victory will be remembered. To describe what is new about the communist attitude toward death, Bloch employs a word that is close to one that Brecht uses, namely *absorbed* (*aufgenommen*)—the communist hero is immersed into the larger collective. The communist's sacrifice, then, is to be understood not as an act of personal greatness but of heroic disappearance, a "dissolution" through an act of solidarity.[65] It is furthermore a moment with a strange temporality: a future anterior. The revolutionary hero understands his own death in relation to a future moment of justice in which his death *will have been dissolved* into the collective.[66]

Similarly, the meaning of the young comrade's death depends on a future moment of redemption. His *Einverständnis* is in the first place an agreement with the *progress* of the revolution and thus points to a moment in the future. The scene of the sacrifice implies a communist eschatology; its beauty can only be seen by the light of a future moment of justice, into which all the struggles and sacrifices will have been dissolved, or with the thousand eyes of the party, who stands outside time. Thus, whereas the first part of the play teaches a lesson about the relation between the individual and the collective, its final scene goes further. This can be understood as a difference between the two *ja*'s in the play. Whereas the first *ja* reduces the person to his legal persona, his position in a symbolic network, the second *ja* effects an erasure out of this very network and performs an absolution into the collective.

The events on stage, then, are not only given over to a political judgment; this judgment has to be made from a particular point in time. It is from this (utopian) position of future redemption that the audience is asked to judge the events; it is called to assume the position of the Party, with its thousand eyes, which judges the events in this world in relation to a moment of justice yet to come. Similarly, the stage is not simply a legal stage in which a judgment is made and the party is performatively constructed. It opens to an altogether different community in which the relation between the dead and the living is restructured. At this precise moment, when the youth utters his final "*ja*," the play accomplishes something that exceeds the teaching of revolutionary strategy. It stages a celebration of a future moment of justice in which the tensions between ethics and politics, and between the individual and the collective, will be overcome. The allegorical figure that encapsulates this future moment of redemption is the unburied body of the youth that will be "resurrected" as it is dissolved into the collective.

As many critics have pointed out, the scene of the young comrade's death has religious overtones. Not only does his killing evoke the image of a *pieta* but the scene in which the young comrade disappears into the lime pit is ironically entitled "*Die Grablegung*," which has been inaccurately rendered in English as "the interment." Unlike *Begräbnis*, the more common German word for burial, *Grablegung* has strictly religious connotations. It is often used in the phrase "*die Grablegung Christi*," the entombment of Christ. And just as the death and resurrection of Christ point to a future moment of redemption, the disappearance of the young comrade points to a future moment of justice. The resemblance of the play, with its choruses, recitative, and dialogue, to a Bach cantata has often been pointed out: The play has been called a "Stalinist passion play" by Marcel Reich-Ranicki[67] and a "counterreligious oratorio" by Eric Bentley.[68] Peter Demetz has compared *Die Maßnahme* to a medieval mystery play.[69] This indicates that we have departed from the legal theater and witness a "different scene," an *umfunktionierung* of the theatrical space of the passion play.

The play, then, teaches that the dilemma of justice that it had staged earlier as a conflict between the individual's sense of ethics and the political strategies of the party can be reconciled in a sublime moment of what it calls "*Einverständnis*," a term that connotes not only political agreement but also a sense of harmony, or, as I propose to call it, "justice-as-harmony." It no longer addresses the audience as a group of individual judge-spectators but demands from it something different: a "harmonizing" with the collective, which requires, in Antony Tatlow's words, a leap of faith.[70]

*

In the next section I will briefly look at the role of the figure of the unburied body in Brecht's poetry. Far from being an isolated image, the unburied body is a recurring topos in Brecht's writings. Its meaning, however, changed fundamentally in the years following the writing of *Die Maßnahme*.

"Why Should My Name Be Mentioned?":
Brecht's Anti-Epitaphs

Auch die Todesfurcht ist mehr als Folge des Zustandes
des Gemeinwesens zu betrachten
—Bertolt Brecht

Not being ritually buried and thus not having a tombstone is a recurring theme in Brecht's poetry during the period in which *Die Maßnahme* was written. Many of Brecht's poems take the shape of an epitaph, only to break with the conventions of the form. Sigrid Thielking has pointed to an evolution in Brecht's poetry in this regard during the late 1920s.[71] Brecht's interest in anonymity and depersonalization expresses itself, as Thielking writes, in his changing attitude toward epitaphs. Whereas his earlier work shows his fascination with the romantic notion of the epitaph, in the late 1920s his epitaphs demonstrate a longing for disappearance, along with a sudden awareness that the dead do not necessarily have to be remembered. In 1927, Brecht wrote a poem that reads as a traditional epitaph, entitled "Inscription on a Gravestone That Has Not Been Picked Up" ("*Inschrift auf einem nicht abgeholten Grabstein*"), which opens with the lines "Traveler, when you pass / know / I was happy."[72] Two years later, however, Brecht's changing perspective is visible in "The Four Proposals for Epitaph" ("*Die vier Vorschläge für Grabschrift, immerfort korrigiert*"). Written one year before the first performance of *Die Maßnahme*, the poem concludes: "Do not write anything on the gravestone / Except the name // I forgot the name / can be left out."[73]

An autobiographical poem written in the 1930s, not discussed by Thielking, testifies to this same attitude. It is entitled "Why Should My Name Be Mentioned?" ("*Warum soll mein Name genannt werden?*"), and it expresses the acceptance—or *Einverständnis*, as the poem calls it—of being forgotten and not having a tombstone:

> Once I thought, in distant times
> When the buildings have collapsed in which I live
> And the ships have rotted in which I traveled
> my name will still be mentioned
> With others. . . . I thought my name would still be mentioned
> on a stone . . . But today
> I accept that I will be forgotten.
>
> Why
> Should the baker be asked for if there is enough bread?
> Why
> Should the snow be praised that has melted
> If new snowfalls are impending
> Why should there be a past
> if there is a future?[74]

If there is a future moment of justice, the poem suggests, there is no need to commemorate the past because all past struggles—like the bread of the baker that is digested completely and the melted snow that is replaced with new snow—will have been dissolved. Similarly, if one learns to look at one's life from the standpoint of this future moment, one understands and accepts the memory of one's name not as something that outlives the physical existence of the person—inscribed on a gravestone or recorded in history books—but as something that melts away.

One of Brecht's most famous *In Memoriams* concerns Lenin and is entitled "The Carpet-Weavers of Kuyan-Bulak Honour Lenin" (*"Die Teppichweber von Kujan-Bulak ehren Lenin"*) (1929).[75] This narrative poem describes how the inhabitants of a small impoverished village plagued by a fever decide to honor Lenin not by erecting a monument or holding a commemorative service but by collecting money from their meager incomes to buy petroleum to fight the mosquitoes carrying the infection. This act is done in honor of the "dead but never to be forgotten comrade Lenin." Brecht explains in the poem's conclusion that this act of commemoration is the best possible tribute to Lenin because the villagers sought to preserve the lesson at the heart of Lenin's teaching rather than the man himself: "So they helped themselves by honoring Lenin, and / Honored him by helping themselves, and thus / had understood them well."[76]

The act of the carpet weavers furthermore fulfilled the will of Lenin himself as it was posthumously expressed by his widow Nadezhda Krupskaya, who claimed to speak for Lenin, shortly after his death: "I have a great request to make of you: do not allow your grief for Illich to express itself in the external veneration of his person. Do not build memorials for him. . . . If you want to honor the name of Vladimir Illich—build day care centers, kindergartens, homes, schools."[77]

In an essay published in 1934, Sergej Tretiakov praises Brecht's poem as an example of a communist *In Memoriam* that refuses the cultic-static monumental style of bourgeois commemorations for deceased leaders.[78] Instead of praising Lenin's unique personality, the poem emphasizes the importance of remembering Lenin's lesson, which is not the same as commemorating the person. Brecht's epitaphs, then, are characteristic of what Boris Groys, in various writings, has called a new attitude toward the dead that emerged during the first decades of the Soviet Union, one that no longer mourned the passing of the individual but celebrated his or her accomplishments, looking back from a future moment in time.[79]

What If the People Are Wrong?
Traces of an Erasure

The connotation of the words *Auflösung* and *Auslösung* changed in the decade followed the staging of *Die Maßnahme*. With Stalin's purges and the Nazis' rise to power, the disappearance without a trace of large groups of people achieved a political actuality that Brecht could not have predicted. In his commentary on Brecht's poetry written in 1939, Walter Benjamin points out that Brecht's interest in the unburied body had taken on an uncanny new actuality. Benjamin cites a poem from *A Reader for Those Who Live in Cities* (*Lesebuch für Städtebewohner*), written shortly before *Die Maßnahme*, which praises illegal work in terms that recall the play. The play urges communists to take care to erase all traces of their work, as the Head of the Party House had done in *Die Maßnahme*. The poem ends by insisting:

> See when you come to think of dying
> That no gravestone stands and betrays where you lie
> With a clear inscription to denounce you
> And the year of your death to give you away.
> Once again:
> Cover your tracks.[80]

Benjamin remarks that anonymity had received a new importance and urgency in Nazi Germany. The recommendation to do away with one's grave has become superfluous: "The underground political workers have been relieved of this worry by Hitler and his thugs."[81] In a similar fashion, Benjamin considers the third poem of the cycle, which contains the lines: "And you must vanish like smoke in the sky / Which no one holds back"[82] and "You must not have been"[83] eerily prophetic of the fate of the Jews in Germany.[84] Remarkable in this last sentence—but overlooked by Benjamin—is the use of grammatical tense. The future anterior of the phrase "you must not have been" expresses not only a desire to murder someone but to erase the very memory of someone's former existence.

In the conversation with Tretiakov cited above, Brecht explains that under Hitler Germany had changed from the country of *Denker und Dichter* to the country of *Denker und Henker*—thinkers and hangmen, or rather (and he corrects himself), the country of *Denkes und Henker*. The criminal Karl Denke, he explains to Tretiakov, had become exemplary of the new German spirit. Denke killed people to use their corpses; he canned his victims' flesh and made soap from their fat, buttons from their bones, and purses from their skins. After his arrest, he explained in court that he thought his acts had been completely legitimate. "Why should the judges, prosecutors and lawyers make such a show of indignation?" Denke asks in Brecht's paraphrase, "he had put his corpses to good practical uses;

and he had utilized only second-grade people, human ballast, so to speak. He had never made a brief case of a general's hide, or soap from the paunch of a factory owner or buttons from the skull of journalist." "I contend," Brecht adds sarcastically,

that the best people of Germany, those who condemned Denke, failed to recognize the qualities of true German genius which the fellow displayed, namely: method, conscientiousness, cold-bloodedness and the ability to base one's very act on a firm philosophical foundation. They should not have executed him; they should have made him a Ph.D. with *honoris causa*.[85]

The conversation between Brecht and Tretiakov was published in 1937. In that same year Tretiakov was arrested.[86] His art, deemed formalist, was no longer ideologically correct. He was executed in Russia between 1937 and 1939—all records of his execution have disappeared. Tretiakov's last letter to Brecht is dated May 3, 1937. On July 1, 1938, Benjamin wrote in his journal: "Very skeptical answers are elicited whenever I touch on conditions in Russia. When I inquired recently whether Ottwald was still in prison, the answer was: if he's still alive, he's in prison. Yesterday Steffin said she doubted whether Tretiakov were still alive."[87] In 1939 Brecht wrote in his *Arbeitsjournal*: "Nobody knows anything about Tretiakov . . . nobody knows anything about Neher . . . Meyerhold has lost his theater . . . literature and art are up the creek, political theory has gone to the dogs, what is left is a thin, bloodless, proletarian humanism propagated by officialdom."[88]

Tretiakov's body was never recovered. He was neither properly buried nor given a grave with his name on it. For twenty years after his death, his name could not be mentioned in Russia. He was considered an "unperson," someone whose name was erased from history.

*

A few months after Tretiakov's death, Brecht wrote a poem about his disappearance, entitled "Is the People Infallible?" ["*Ist das Volk unfehlbar?*"]. The poem, which sets out to memorialize Brecht's friend, colleague, translator, and teacher, begins:

My teacher
Tall and kindly
Has been shot, condemned by a people's court
As a spy. His name is damned.
Talk about him / Is suspect and suppressed

The poem ends with the questions:

> Suppose he is innocent?
> How will he go into his death?[89]

The poem emphasizes that Tretiakov was not simply shot and murdered. His treatment was much more extreme: His name cannot be mentioned anymore. The memory of him is blotted out; he is sentenced to disappear without a trace, like the young comrade in *Die Maßnahme*. The title, however, raises the question that the play had hoped to answer: What if the people are wrong? What if the collective, in which the individual is asked to dissolve, is not infallible?

The poem would remain unpublished until 1964, seven years after Brecht's death. On the manuscript, preserved in the Brecht archive in Berlin, there is a heavily erased word after the word *teacher* in line one—presumably the name Tretiakov.[90] This means that the first line read "My teacher, Tretiakov, tall and kindly, has been shot." Even in the *In Memoriam* Brecht wrote for Tretiakov, his name is erased. It exists only as an illegible spot of ink, something unreadable that is nonetheless at the heart of the poem. As an apt epilogue to his tragic death, Tretiakov's name is crossed out in the very poem that set out to commemorate him, as if he can be remembered only as the trace of an erasure.

*

Tretiakov's name would be mentioned—and spelled—one more time. After questioning Brecht about *Die Maßnahme*, the House committee quoted from Tretiakov's article about his conversation with Brecht, with which this chapter begins—a conversation, I repeat, that exactly concerned itself about the didactic possibilities of a trial:

> STRIPLING: While you were in Moscow, did you meet Sergi Tretyakov, -s-e-r-g-i- -t-r-e-t-y-a-k-o-v?
> BRECHT: Tretyakov; yes. That is a Russian playwright.
> STRIPLING: A writer?
> BRECHT: Yes. He translated some of my poems and, I think one play.
> STRIPLING: Mr. Chairman, International Literature, no. 5, 1937 published by the State Literary Art Publishing House in Moscow had an article by Sergi Tretyakov, leading Soviet Writer [sic] on an interview he had with Mr. Brecht . . . Do you recall that interview Mr. Brecht?[91]

Stripling continues to read excerpts from Tretiakov's essay on Brecht, including Tretiakov's description of *Die Maßnahme* as a play "arranged like a court where the characters try to justify themselves for having killed a comrade, and judges, who at the same time represent the audience, summarize the events and reach a verdict," as well as Brecht's plans to "organize a theater in Berlin which would re-enact the most interesting court trials in the history of mankind."[92] Stripling then repeats the question: "Do you recall that interview, Mr. Brecht?"

> BRECHT: No. [Laughter.] It must have been written twenty years ago
> or so.
> STRIPLING: I will show you the magazine, Mr. Brecht.
> BRECHT: Yes. I do not recall there was an interview. I do not recall—
> Mr. Stripling I do not recall the interview in exact.[93]

In this highly condensed moment, different historical periods, trials, and verdicts come together to reveal various fictional, legal, and autobiographical erasures. First, in its discussion of *Die Maßnahme*, the unburied body of the young comrade is implicitly evoked; second, this corpse is related to those of the victims of the purges—although this link is never made explicit. Finally, by mentioning the name of Tretiakov, the disappearance of the figure whose work may have been the main source of inspiration for *Die Maßnahme* is brought to stage. Thus surprisingly, and perhaps unwittingly, the different "theaters of justice" seem to exist as an intricate web of interrelated scenes of judgment, all woven around an empty center: the case of a person who is erased from history, yet whose annihilated corpse returns to haunt the different tribunals.

This haunting took place in a context that to some extent mirrored both the theatrical structure and didactic-political goals of *Die Maßnahme*. Not simply a series of investigations into the purported influence of communists in the American entertainment industry, the HUAC hearings were widely regarded as show trials that sought to exorcise "un-American" elements and to enforce, through the political and theatrical format of the trial, a harmonious, unified notion of "the American people," safe from the infiltration of "enemy aliens." Second, as I have suggested, reverberating during this particular hearing were echoes of another series of show trials, the Moscow trials, which aimed to purge the Soviet Union of so-called enemies of the people. These trials, furthermore, served a political-didactic, propagandistic role. The proceedings were publicized via newspaper, film, or radio, so that they could instruct a wide audience in a series of political lessons. As Julie Cassiday has convincingly demonstrated, in the choice for the format of the trial as an arena for propaganda and education, the

Moscow trials were typical of a larger interest in the theatricality of court-room proceedings in the Soviet Union, which dates back to the staging of so-called model trials in which traveling agitprop troupes and left-wing theater companies during the first years after the revolution staged po-litical lessons—a practice that may have had a direct influence on Brecht during his writing of *Die Massnahme*.[94] These fictional scenes of legal pro-paganda from the 1920s became the paradigm for the "real" show trials of the 1930s, Cassiday maintains.[95]

By spelling out the proper name *Tretiakov* in this highly charged the-atrical legal setting—a proper name that refers not only to an eliminated, unburied body but also to a singular individual who was a teacher, trans-lator, and friend of Brecht, and therefore someone whom he survived but was perhaps still tied to by the bonds of friendship and indebtedness—the hearing unwittingly reopened the questions that *Die Maßnahme* had tried to solve: namely, how do we reconcile our political striving for unity, justice, and harmony with our obligations to the individual? What do we owe a dead friend, colleague, or comrade who is deemed a public enemy? And, because it was Tretiakov's fate not only to die for what was consid-ered the greater good but to be effaced from history, precisely to make a future moment of redemptive harmony possible, mentioning his name in this context invokes the question raised by Brecht's earlier poem: What, indeed, *if the people are not infallible*? What if there is no future moment of harmonization that annuls our debts to the dead? What if they remain, in a sense, outstanding?

In an unexpected and eerie way, then, the HUAC hearing seems to materialize the intuition that Brecht had presented to Tretiakov in 1932, namely that the juxtaposition of several trials in one theatrical perfor-mance will disclose the repressed political truth of each. By citing *Die Maßnahme* alongside an implicit allusion to the disappearance of Tretia-kov, the HUAC hearing reveals how the dissolution of the young com-rade, which the play stages as a moment of sublime beauty, effectively amounts to an act of violence against an individual. The figure of the "unburied body," furthermore, which in *Die Maßnahme* was an emblem of the individual's harmonious reconciliation with the collective, now re-turns as a specter that reminds us, perhaps, of our unfulfilled obligations vis-à-vis the dead. Because it intrudes into a quasi-legal context and hence into a setting that seeks to determine accountabilities and ascribe respon-sibilities, the question arises whether our responsibilities toward the dead can be captured in legal terms or if they hint at an understanding of the just that remains radically extraneous to the juridico-political sphere.

*

When asked about the theme of *Die Maßnahme* during the hearing, Brecht stumbles. He utters something in German, but he cannot find the right English word. After he returns to his hotel room, he writes in his diary:

For the prosecution Stripling reads from *Die Maßnahme* and has me give an account of the plot. I refer him to the Japanese model, define its content as dedication to an idea, and reject the interpretation that the subject is disciplinary murder by pointing out that it is a question of self-effacement, a *"selbst-Auslöschung."*[96]

I would claim, however, contrary to what Brecht may have believed, that the figure of the "self-effaced body," when recited in the new context of the HUAC hearing, acquires a profoundly different status than it had in *Die Maßnahme*. Grafted onto a new context, the unburied body no longer signals a sense of justice-as-harmony; it becomes a figure for that which precisely resists the accomplishment of such redemptive reconciliation. It embodies what critics such as Rainer Nägele and Hans-Thies Lehmann and Helmut Lethen refer to as a "nondialectizable" core at the heart of Brecht's *lehrstücke*.[97] In otherwise different arguments, writings by both Nägele and Lehmann and Lethen point out that Brecht's *lehrstücke* of 1929–1931, *Das Badener Lehrstück vom Einverständnis, Der Jasager, Der Lindberghflug*, and indeed *Die Maßnahme*, are characterized by sometimes grotesque scenes of violence, as they invariably dramatize stories of death, murder, and dismemberment. The very excess of this violence, they argue, seems to pierce through the dramatic structure of the plays, touching their audiences on a different level. The impression it leaves after the performance forms a remainder that cannot be fully integrated into the political lessons the *Lehrstücke* set out to teach. Lehmann and Lethen even suggest that these violent moments have the effect of splitting the plays into what they call two *levels*, each of which teaches different lessons. Level one insists on the importance of the collective and on what Lethen and Lehmann refer to as the "machinery of dialectics, history or party." Level two, however, highlights the violence to the individual necessarily entailed by a submission to this machinery.[98] This second level forms, in their reading of the plays, a supplement to the first level, but one that effectively undermines the first's political lessons by staging what they call the "mute protest of corporeality."[99] Despite Brecht's claim to be a truly dialectical playwright, the contradiction between these two levels cannot be overcome at a totalizing higher level.

Following Lethen and Lehmann in this regard, but slightly reformulating their terms, I would like to suggest that in the specific case of *Die Maßnahme*, its central scene, that of a "self-effacement," splits the drama—precisely because of the pathos with which it is presented—into two opposed stories that are played off against one another. On the one hand, *Die Maßnahme* dramatizes a story about justice, highlighting the importance of subjecting one's individual sense of justice to the collective. On the other hand, it stages a scene in which an act of violence is done to a corpse. Yet whereas the dramaturgy of the first story aims for a moment of closure in the form of a decision that is rendered as a verdict of the party on stage, something that the spectators in the theater are asked to redouble, the emotional impact of the second story has the effect of reopening that which the first level sought to close.

What strikes me in the *case* of *Die Maßnahme*, however, is that the splitting that Lehmann and Lethen understand in spatial terms, as a division into two levels, here figures as a temporal succession of two different scenes: the play and its reception—a fictional trial and a quasi-legal hearing. That which is erased from the first scene, a dead body, returns to haunt the second scene. This second scene, furthermore, *dates* the play. By bringing the figure of Sergej Tretiakov to the legal stage, the disappearance of a very specific body is brought into relation with the play. This effectively marks the play and turns it retroactively into a surprising testimony of a specific, traumatic event. It is only by being framed by two historical legal trials—at the moment when the echoes of their cases start to reverberate—that this constellation of fictional and historical trials becomes readable as a testimony of a specific historical erasure and, perhaps, even as a call for justice for the unburied.

The case of *Die Maßnahme*, both the play and its "restaging" in the context of the HUAC hearing, reads as a particularly dramatic instance of what Shoshana Felman calls "legal repetition."[100] Felman has coined this phrase to describe the way in which trials unwittingly reenact previous court cases, reopening cases that cannot be closed by a verdict. In Felman's understanding, a trial has the capacity to publicly stage a history of trauma, yet it does so via a specific dramatic structure that works toward a verdict and hence a moment of closure. Because the experience of trauma is precisely characterized by resistance to such moments of closure, historical trials have the paradoxical effect of inaugurating a series of traumatic legal reenactments, in which the very same traumas are, again, brought to the legal stage. The "traumatic core" of a historic court case, then, becomes legible only through what Felman calls a cross-legal reading that juxtaposes two different trials.

Reading *Die Maßnahme* "cross-legally" with the HUAC hearings and (implicitly) with the Moscow trials reveals how the play's textual body is incised by the unique historical erasures that it anticipates and to which it responds. Despite *Die Maßnahme*'s overt political program and its intentional insistence on closure, its historical reception unwittingly brought its "traumatic core" to the fore, exposing something that resists being fully captured by a verdict: an injustice done to a dead body. It is, perhaps, only through its historical reception that the play assumes its full didactic impact and addresses us not as judge-spectators but as witnesses to an injustice done to the dead.

Antigone's Friendliness

Eigentlich habe ich dort keine Freunde. Und die Moskauer selber haben auch keine—wie die Toten.
—Bertolt Brecht

On October 31, 1947, one day after his testimony before the HUAC hearing, Brecht packed his luggage and left the United States for good. A telegram sent to the FBI indicates that he first settled in Switzerland:

BERTOLT EUGEN FRIEDERICH BRECHT, IS R. EXPERIMENTAL THEATER, NYC, ADVISED INFORMANT BRECHT PRESENTLY IN SWITZERLAND. INS RECORDS REFLECT EUGEN BRECHT, REENTRY PERMIT A ONE FOUR THREE SEVEN NINE NINE ONE, LEFT NYC BOUND FOR PARIS, FRANCE, OCT. THIRTY ONE FORTY-SEVEN VIA AIR FRANCE AIRLINES. CUSTOMS STOP PLACED NYC RE SUBJECT RETURN. SUGGEST LA PLACE CUSTOMS STOP NATIONALLY IF DESIRED.[101]

It is hard to tell whether the McCarthy hearing became a site of learning for Brecht in which the repressed "truth" of his own theatrical trials was revealed to him, but the subject matter of his next theatrical production is revealing. A few weeks after leaving the United States, Brecht settled out-side Zürich and started to work on an adaptation of Sophokles' *Antigone*. The play opened in February in Chur, Switzerland, starring Helene Weigel as Antigone.[102] I would hold that Brecht's staging of *Antigone*—a drama about a heroine whose faithfulness to the dead bars her from existing among the living and who insists that our responsibility to our dead loved ones is unconditional—is not only a direct response to the losses he ex-perienced during the dark years of Nazism and Stalinism but, more pre-cisely, an attempt to stage a scene in which the dead—with Antigone as their mouthpiece—can address the living to remind them of their out-standing debts and continuing obligations.

Brecht's version follows Hölderlin's translation of the play rather closely; however, a short prelude has been added, in which Antigone's dilemma is set in the contemporary context of Berlin at the end of the war. The prelude tells of two sisters, who on leaving their air-raid shelter suddenly hear a screaming (*Brülle*) that freezes their blood. Afraid to be seen by the SS, the sisters decide not to listen to the cry that comes from outside: "So we did not go outside the door / and did not see what things were happening out there."[103] When they finally leave their house to go to work, one of them sees the corpse of their brother hanging from a butcher's hook. Attempting to retrieve his corpse, she is confronted by an SS-man who asks them if they know this "traitor to his people." The pro-logue ends with the two sisters looking at each other; one denies knowing her brother, but it remains unclear what the other decides: "Then I looked at my sister. / Should she on pain of death go now / And free our brother who / May be dead or no?"[104]

Whereas in *Die Maßnahme* the young comrade cannot but respond to a similar cry, which ultimately leads to his death, at first the two sisters act as if they have not heard the cry. Brecht emphasizes the sisters' denial by putting most of the sentences describing the sisters' distress after hear-ing the cry into the negative, repeating *Nicht* several times: "*So gingen wir nicht for die Tür under Sahn / Nicht nach den Dingen, die da drauß geschahn*" (11, my emphasis). However, when the SS-man confronts the sisters with the question of whether they know the dead person, one sister denies that she does, but the other refrains from answering.[105] The prelude ends before the audience learns how the second sister responded, leav-ing the spectators with the question of what they would do in a similar situation.

In a poem, simply entitled "Antigone," printed on the first page of the play's program, Brecht salutes Antigone, imploring her to serve as an example to those who, like Brecht and his audience, have recently emerged from the darkness of the war:

> Emerge from the darkness and go
> Before us a while
> Friendly one, with the light step
> Of total certainty, a terror
> To wielders of terror[106]

Remarkably, Antigone is praised neither for her courage nor for her morality but for her *friendliness*. The choice of this word is curious because it goes against the standard interpretation of the Greek heroine. Antigone is usually praised for her strength, persistence, and uncompromising righteousness but rarely for her *friendliness*. More importantly, the word *friendliness* has specific connotations in Brecht's work. Already in 1939, in an essay published in the *Schweizer Zeitung am Sonntag*, Walter Benjamin had suggested that Brecht's poetry implicitly contains a "minimal program" for humanity, centered around the notion of *freundlichkeit*.[107] This friendliness, Benjamin argues, is not an element of a political program but a basic humaneness that should accompany our political decisions. Benjamin finds an example of this kind of friendliness in Brecht's poem about the exile of the Chinese poet Lao Tse, entitled "Legend of the Origin of the Book Tao Te Ching on Lao Tzu's Way into Exile" ("*Legende von der Entstehung des Buches Taoteking auf dem Weg des Laotse in die Emigration*"). The poem tells of Lao Tse, the wise man whose wisdom had brought him in conflict with the reigning powers who eventually sent him into exile. When he is fleeing the country, a guard at the border offers him hospitality and gives him the chance to write down his teachings and thus preserve his legacy. The poem ends praising Lao Tse's wisdom and also the friendliness of his host:

> But not to that wise man alone our praise is due
> Whose name adorns the book *Tao Te Ching.*
> For the wise man's wisdom must be dragged out of him too.
> So the customs man also deserves our thanks for the thing:
> He did the eliciting[108]

Three other acts of friendliness are described in Brecht's earlier poem "Of the Friendliness of the World" ("*Von den Freundlichkeiten der Welt*"): that of a mother who puts diapers on her child, that of a father who takes a boy by his hand, and finally that of a person who throws two handfuls of earth on a man's grave:

> Almost everyone has loved the world
> When he receives two handfuls of earth.[109]

The first two forms of *Freundlichkeit*, Benjamin explains, are what we expect from the world at our most vulnerable moments: not long after our birth, at the time when we are taking our first steps out into the world. The last type of friendliness we receive only after death, when someone else will throw two handfuls of earth on our body, establishing a form of friendship that extends beyond life itself. Although Benjamin refrains from mentioning it, the poem obviously refers to Antigone. "Lastly," Benjamin writes, "apart from the promise and the theory, there is a moral to the poem. Whoever wants to make the hard things give way should miss no opportunity for friendliness."[110] Neither of the order of a law, nor of a political project, nor of an "ABC," this moral of friendliness is only a *minimal* program, supplementary to our behavior and to what Benjamin calls the "harsh verdicts" capitalism asks from us.

*

I propose that we read *Die Maßnahme*—the play as well as its un-anticipated "reframing," by the HUAC hearing of 1947—"with" Brecht's staging of *Antigone* in Switzerland. Both plays revolve around an opposition between two demands for justice: one articulated in a specific political program and the other consisting of a friendliness that, while not being political in and of itself, needs to supplement our political decisions. These two different types of justice involve two different responsibilities, one that we owe to our political community, another that we owe to the dead. The two take different shapes. Whereas the first can be articulated in symbolic terms, captured in a programmatic ABC and enunciated in a legal theater, Antigone's and the young comrade's responses to the suffering they witness are voiced as inarticulate cries for justice, which stem from an unconditional responsibility they feel that comes from somewhere beyond the law.

In the constellation of plays, poems, trials, and hearings that I have analyzed in this chapter, then, the unburied, dissolved body stands out as *both* as a symbol of justice-as-harmony as in *Die Maßnahme and* as a figure that reminds us of an ethical responsibility that remains hetero-geneous to the juridico-political order. The unmourned body summons what Benjamin called an ethical injunction to be friendly, which needs to accompany our political strivings. This supplementary friendliness, how-ever, relies on an ethical logic at odds with the understanding of justice that *Die Maßnahme* presented its audience with. Being "friendly" to the dead—doing justice to them—involves burying and mourning the dead and hence commemorating them in their singularity; in short, protect-ing them from effacement and safeguarding them against a dissolution into the collective. The justice we owe to the dead, then, is precisely what makes justice-as-harmony impossible to reach, because our sense of what is just is not only determined by the future that we aspire to but is also traversed by our outstanding debts to the dead.[111] These debts may not be settled in a courtroom; in fact, as was the case during the HUAC hearing, it is precisely that the dead may return to assert their claims on us when we seek to close the case on the past.

*

Shortly after Brecht's death in 1956 in East Germany, a letter was found that read: "In the event of my death, I don't want to be made to lie in state or be exhibited anywhere. No speeches are to be made at my funeral."[112] His final request was granted. Brecht was buried in the Dor-otheenfriedhof in East Berlin, and no speeches were made during the funeral. His grave is marked by a simple stone inscribed only with his name. When living in exile in Denmark in 1938—the year of the trial of Bukharin, the most infamous of the Moscow cases—Brecht wrote what came to be known as the third part of the poem "To Posterity" (*"An die Nachgeborenen"*), which effectively functions as an epitaph. The poet di-rectly addresses posterity:

> You, who will emerge from the flood
> in which we have gone under
> Remember
> when you speak of our failings
> the dark times too
> which you have escaped. . . .
> Oh we
> who wanted to prepare the ground for friendliness
> could not ourselves be friendly

But you, when the time comes at last
and man is a helper to man
think of us
with forbearance.[113]

From a position beyond his death, Brecht speaks to the generation that will come after him, asking them to be tolerant toward the unfriendliness of himself and his generation. Those who wanted to prepare the soil of the earth for friendliness, Brecht explains, could not overcome their own harshness and fulfill what Benjamin calls Brecht's "Minimal Program of Humaneness"—putting diapers on a baby, taking a toddler by the hand, and burying the dead. Unlike Ismene in the opening scene of *Antigone*, Brecht does not ask for forgiveness for having failed to do justice to the dead—he merely asks posterity for *patience* (*nachsicht*), a benevolent suspension of judgment.

Coda: An Unfriendly Witness

On January 8, 2000, Hungarian-American playwright and director George Tabori fulfilled Brecht's long-held wish, first expressed in his discussion with Tretiakov, to reenact a historical trial in front of a theater audience, when Tabori's play "The Brecht File" ("*Brecht-Akte*") opened in Brecht's former theater in Berlin.[114] The play tells the story of Brecht's life in exile in the United States, culminating in his confrontation with HUAC in 1947. Tabori's script follows the transcript of the HUAC hearings almost verbatim, but in his stage notes he asks the actors to emphasize the comic effects of Brecht's slightly evasive answers. The scene of the hearing reaches its comical climax when the prosecutor asks the playwright: "Mr. Brecht, have you attended any communist party meeting?" Brecht answers: "No, I don't think so."

STRIPLING: You don't think so?
BRECHT: No.
STRIPLING: Well aren't you certain?
BRECHT: Yes. . . . I think so . . . I have not been at any meeting of the communist party.
STRIPLING: Are you certain?
BRECHT: Well, I think I am certain.[115]

Reenacted in a recently reunited Berlin, grafted onto a different political context, performed in front of an altogether different audience, Brecht's testimony during the 1947 HUAC hearings is subjected to yet another set of verdicts, putting him posthumously on trial once more, implicitly raising the question: How do we judge Brecht now, after the Cold War has ended and we can look back at the disasters of the twentieth century? In the context of what history do we understand his work? Is he *only* a representative of "the other Germany," who heroically fought against Hitler, as he himself was keen to suggest in his answers to Stripling? Or can we hear in the evasiveness that characterizes his answers during the HUAC hearings echoes of his reluctance to directly confront the atrocities of Stalinism?[116] To allude to the conversation with Benjamin that is an epigraph to this chapter, how *serious* are Brecht's silences? Was Brecht's attitude of nonseriousness as *legitimate* as he himself thought it was in 1932—according to which laws, and in the eyes of what court?

Hence, the restaging of the HUAC hearings in Berlin reopened what Hannah Arendt had called, in an essay published in 1966, the "case" of Bertolt Brecht.[117] In her essay, Arendt suggests that Brecht's refusal to condemn Stalinism, even though he must have been aware of its atrocities, raises the important question as to what exactly the responsibilities of the writer are with regard to the political events of their times. We tend to be more lenient with writers' dealings with moral and political issues than with those of our fellow citizens, Arendt concedes, and rightly so: A writer's responsibility lies primarily with literature and only secondly with the political situation of his time. Nevertheless, she concludes, Brecht's irresponsible refusal to answer the call that his times made on him may have gone too far. By not bearing witness to that which he undoubtedly must have known was wrong—and by continuing to praise Stalin even as late as the 1950s—Brecht crossed a line. According to Arendt, in Brecht's case this crossing is not just a moral issue but also a literary issue because the undeniable effect of Brecht's complacency with Stalinism is that his later work has lost the power to speak to us. Yet, perhaps surprisingly, Arendt concludes that we should be careful not to dismiss Brecht's work altogether. Even though the times ask us, his readership, to render a harsh verdict on him, within this verdict there should be room for a certain leniency and perhaps even for forgiveness because, as he himself acknowledges in his poem addressed to posterity, Brecht is also marked by the darkness of his time. Exactly because of his inability to assume the friendliness that his work at times calls for, his writing becomes a testimony to the darkness of the period that he lived through. Following Arendt, we may conclude that Brecht remains what he was in 1947, *an unfriendly witness*, whose work testifies to the horrors and disasters of his time without fully being able to assume the responsibilities these disasters asked of him.

*

Die Maßnahme was never again performed during Brecht's lifetime. In 1956, shortly before his death, Brecht imposed an *Aufführungsverbot* that was posthumously maintained by the estate. When Paul Patera in Sweden asked for permission to perform the play, Brecht refused. "Only the actors can learn something from it," he insisted. "In front of an audience it usually just evokes moralistic responses."[118] Shortly thereafter Brecht made one final remark on *Die Maßnahme*:

The author has always refused to give permission to stage *der Maßnahme* in front of an audience, because only the actor playing the young comrade can learn from the play, and only if he has also played one of the agitators and has sung in the Control Chorus.[119]

The play still contains a lesson, Brecht claims, but it is only the young comrade—and not the audience who judges the events on stage—who can learn it. If the play does manage to teach us something, we should receive this lesson not by assuming the role of the judge, or by watching the spectacle from the Party's point of view or even that of the wars' victors, but by adopting the impossible position of someone who is erased from history.

Conclusion

Judging, Staging, and Working Through

I opened this series of reflections by invoking the politically urgent intellectual task that Adorno had prescribed to writers, intellectuals, and pedagogues in the wake of World War II: to conceive of a pedagogical practice that, going beyond the mere conveying of information, would actively work against the many forms of resistance obscuring true insight into what had happened and would thereby contribute toward a process of coming to terms with the past. As I indicated in my introduction, in the decades following the publication of Adorno's essay, his assignment was fulfilled not only by writers, psychologists, and filmmakers in West Germany, where a true cult of so-called *Vergangenheitsbewältigung* emerged, but also by politicians and lawyers within and outside Germany, who discovered in the format of the legal trial a means to stage a national pedagogical scene. A trial, it was believed, has the unique capacity to bring the past to the national stage, and because it culminates in a verdict it could provide—perhaps—a healing moment of closure. The texts I have analyzed by Arendt, Brecht, and Delbo in this book offer reflections on the underlying premises of this conception of the trial as a site of learning and national healing, either by exploring the didactic possibilities of the theatrical setting of the courtroom and investigating the relations between judging and learning or by confronting their readers with a woundedness that forecloses the possibility of (legal) repair and resists being addressed within the confines of the law. Because my readings have been mainly attentive to the singular ways in which the texts of Arendt, Brecht, and

Delbo dramatize moments of learning, mourning, or calling for justice, I will now, by way of a postscript, address more directly the question at the heart of this book: What, indeed, are the relations among the staging, judging, and working through of the past? To what extent does judging the past facilitate what Adorno calls a "serious working through of the past"? To phrase the issue differently: What happens to the subject when he or she pronounces a verdict? As I have suggested in Chapter 2, the verdictive speech act combines the constative act of making a statement about the past and the simultaneous altering of one's relation to this past.[1] What, then, is the didactic or therapeutic nature of this transformation? What type of understanding of the past is enabled by the act of judging?

*

The idea that judging and understanding are mental activities that can easily be aligned is of course not self-evident. In fact, the guiding intuition behind the so-called Law and Literature movement that sought to renew American legal education in the 1970s and 1980s was that the reading of literature could serve as a necessary edifying corrective to legal reasoning, which was taken to be too much concerned with reaching verdicts to truly *understand* the cases on which it seeks to pronounce.[2] In *Poetic Justice*, a book that was published in 1995 but that responds to earlier debates, Martha Nussbaum, for example, argues for the teaching of literature to be an integral part of the curriculum of law schools precisely because reading encourages a mode of understanding that is at odds with the mental attitude that enables one to judge.[3] Asserting that reading novels helps train one to empathize with others, Nussbaum claims that a literature course can serve as a necessary supplement to an educational practice too much concerned with legal technicalities. Because the act of judging—which is arguably at the heart of the legal profession—subsumes particular cases to the generality of a law, it always risks overlooking the uniqueness of each case. Reading literature, which according to Nussbaum familiarizes us with the irreducible singularity of a life story, helps us expand our imaginative capabilities and enlarges our compassion, so that we can come to a judgment that is not only "just," in that it correctly applies the law, but also fair, in that it does justice to a particular case. Nussbaum continues to suggest that the reading of realistic social novels offers especially good training for future legal professionals because this type of literature puts the reader in the position of a judge, albeit a different type of judge than one would usually find in the courtroom. Nussbaum writes how Charles Dickens's novel *Hard Times* "constructs a reader who is a judicious and neutral judge . . . but whose neutrality is different in kind" because it is guided by a sympathetic concern for the novel's characters.[4]

Nussbaum's defense of literature should be seen as part of her argument for the importance of moral sentiments in the public sphere, yet the notion that literature teaches us how to empathize has become a recurring topos in pleas for the importance of reading for legal professionals.[5] To cite just three examples: Paul Gewirtz recommends that his students read because "literature makes its special claims upon us precisely because it nourishes a kind of human understanding not achievable through reason alone."[6] James Boyd White advises law students to engage with Jane Austen's *Emma* because it "trains its reader . . . in a certain sort of kindness . . . This is a training in sympathy and generosity as well as in accuracy of observation."[7] More recently, Markus Dirk Dibber has suggested that our individual and communal senses of justice rely on empathy rather than judgment, pointing, again, to the legal profession's shortcomings in this regard.[8]

*

Arendt's reflections on the Eichmann trial's didactic potential and Brecht's theatrical production of the 1930s can retroactively be construed as interventions into this debate about the relations among judging, understanding, and pedagogy. Both authors agree that judgment should be opposed to empathy, but whereas Nussbaum claims that a judgment not accompanied by empathy is blind,[9] Brecht and Arendt stress the limitations of empathic understanding and explore the educational possibilities of judgment itself, precisely insofar as it *disrupts* our inclination to empathize. As he repeats throughout the theoretical essays that accompanied the staging of *Die Maßnahme*, for Brecht a true moment of learning does not involve empathy, which he associates with passivity and blindness to larger political structures, but rather is centered on the pronouncement of a verdict. His plays therefore put the audience in the position of a judge because only the experience of judging can bring about the revolutionary change in the audience that his theater strives for. Hence, whereas Nussbaum proposes that legal students turn to literature to enhance their empathic sensibilities, Brecht, as a writer of didactic literature, finds inspiration in the theatrical structure of courtroom proceedings because they solicit a judgment from its spectators, which protects them against the temptations of empathy.

Like Brecht, about whom she wrote a short essay prior to the completion of *Eichmann in Jerusalem*, Arendt believes in the value of judgment for pedagogical and political reasons. Her book claims that the didactic potential of the Eichmann trial lies in its confronting the spectators with a past within a theatrical setting that addresses its audience as judge-spectators. In contrast with her contemporaries, who understood the drama mounted in Jerusalem to be a call to empathize with the Nazis' victims, Arendt sees the trial as an occasion to judge the past. Understanding totalitarianism as a closing of the worldly space in which political judgments can be made, she argues that coming to terms with this past—and perhaps repairing the damage it has done to the world—requires judgment, rather than a cathartic moment of compassion. As she claims in *On Revolution*, the overwhelming sentiment of compassion should be resisted in the public sphere because it forms a threat to this sphere as a space that exists between people.

Furthermore, following Kant, Arendt conceives the faculty of judgment to be something that cannot be taught by giving instructions about general principles. One's capacity to judge can be trained only in a confrontation with past judgments as embodied in exemplary cases. Teaching judgment, therefore, requires a theatrical setting in which a spectator is invited to judge examples of past judgments that are dramatized before her gaze, while comparing these judgments with those made by fellow judge-spectators who are also present in the audience. In line with her understanding of the trial's didactic opportunities, Arendt's report about the Eichmann case adopts an "unsympathetic" judgmental tone and ends in a verdict, thereby effectively turning her book into a written reenactment of the trial and inviting her readers to submit the book's judgments to their own individual verdicts.

*

Yet, as I hope to have demonstrated in this study, both *Eichmann in Jerusalem* and *Die Maßnahme* revolve around something that resists being fully captured by a judgment, despite both authors' theoretical insistence on judgment and notwithstanding the theatrical structure of their own texts, each of which culminates in a verdict. Witnessing the proceedings in Jerusalem, Arendt found herself, perhaps to her surprise, stumbling over Eichmann's stupefying banality, in the face of which her judgments fell flat. This experience of stumbling provoked in her a laughter, which does not signal a superior understanding of the situation but should rather be understood as a response to a breakdown of her capacity to understand. This breakdown teaches a lesson, Arendt writes in her book's postscript, but its nature remains radically negative. It cannot be assimilated into a moment of cognition, nor can it be transposed into a theory that one can preserve and transmit because its didactic impact consists precisely in its rupturing of the frameworks on which our judgments and understanding rely. As I have suggested, the performative force of her book—and its continuing to speak to us decades after its publication—relies on its seeking to preserve the scandalous affront to understanding that typifies the Eichmann case. By mimicking the structure of the trial, then, Arendt's book retains the paradoxical didactic nature of this experience of nonunderstanding and confronts her readers with the lasting scandal of incomprehension at the heart of the Eichmann case.

Brecht's play *Die Massnahme* similarly circles around something that resists integration into the legal framework of the play: the unburied, erased body of the young comrade. Whereas the play is structured so that the audience is asked to close the case of the young comrade by pronouncing a verdict on him, the recitation of the play in the context of another quasi-legal setting—that of HUAC's questioning of Brecht in 1947—saw a return of this erased body. In my interpretation of the play and its aftermath, I have proposed that this uncanny return invites us to reread *Die Maßnahme* as a play that stages a conflict between two incommensurable conceptions of justice: one that can be codified in legal terms and transposed into a feasible political program and one that understands justice as a response to the call that the suffering of an individual other makes on us. This call is experienced as unconditional. The play presents it as obliterating all agreements and accords that bind a subject to a political party or a legal community. As I have suggested, this latter responsibility encompasses the dead as well as the living. The sense of justice as responsibility remains not only heterogeneous to the orders of law and politics but implies an understanding of the just that is at odds with the conception of justice-as-harmony (*Einverständnis*) taught explicitly by *Die Maßnahme*. The cry for justice on behalf of a singular individual interrupts the execution of a political program; the dead demand that they be commemorated in their ineffaceable uniqueness, that we do not allow them to be merged into the harmonious unity of the collective. Despite its intentions, then, Brecht's play teaches us that the future community it strives for—if it is to be just—cannot exist in harmony with itself: It will always be traversed by outstanding debts to the dead, to the justice that is owed to them.

*

If we agree with legal scholar Pierre Legendre that a trial's function is to dramatize an act of violence within an institutional framework of the law, and hence to discursify this violence by capturing it in symbolic terms,[10] we can conclude that Arendt's and Brecht's literary "theaters of justice" both stage something that escapes such legal symbolization. Their works confront us with a violation that exceeds legal reparation, a responsibility that cannot be codified in legal terms and a lesson that cannot be articulated in conceptual language. To once again use Arendt's metaphor, their texts revolve around stumbling blocks—*skandala*—that lastingly hinder attempts to reach legal, pedagogical, or emotional closure. For Arendt, such an experience of stumbling occurs when we face Eichmann's scandalous banality and when we contemplate the irreparable consequences of his acts, which have afflicted our community with a wound that exceeds the legal definition of a crime. As crimes against humanity, they cannot be fully addressed in a criminal court because in the face of such crimes all punitive or restorative notions of justice fall short. Eichmann's crime is a *skandalon* in the meaning that the New Testament gives to this word. In a footnote to *The Human Condition*, Arendt explains that the New Testament uses this word to single out crimes that are deemed unforgivable.[11] In contrast to everyday trespasses (*hamartanein*), *skandala* refers to crimes in the face of which the human capacity to forgive breaks down. For Arendt, forgiveness is related to the human experience of time as linear and linked to the human capacity to begin anew by setting up new relationships. We forgive "in order to make it possible for life to go on," and to "put an end to something that without interference could go on endlessly."[12] The unforgivable, then, is something on which time has no hold; it is a scandal that continues to offend and whose wounding force cannot be tempered in a legal setting because, as she has famously put it, "men are unable to forgive what they cannot punish and . . . they are unable to punish what turned out to be unforgivable" (241).[13]

Charlotte Delbo's poems about the massacre in Kalavrita and the mothers of Plaza de Mayo achieve their legal resonance in light of Arendt's reflections on the unforgivable. Both poems are written in response to injustices that either had been or were to be addressed in legal or semi-legal tribunals. The case of Kalavrita was discussed during the Nuremberg trials in 1946, albeit inconclusively.[14] The disappeared were addressed first by the Argentinian truth commissions and later in the trial of the junta in 1985. In contrast to these legal events, which sought to end the suffering of the survivors, Delbo's poems evoke the survivors' irresolvable ties to the dead, connections that exclude them from the living and make it impossible for them to continue with their lives. In Delbo's treatment of both situations, the refusal to depart from the dead is not really to be regarded as a symptom of the survivor's pathological mourning process; through it, Delbo explores how grief, through its public display, can acquire the force of an address to the living. By flaunting their grief, the *madres* and the women from Kalavrita become subjects of a *grievance*, a call for justice on behalf of the dead. As Derrida puts it in a different context, they exhibit a form of "grief in which accusation mingles with mourning to cry out from an infinite wound."[15] This infinite cry for justice, I have argued, can be taken as a metaphor for Delbo's autobiographical writings' structure of address. In her trilogy *Auschwitz et après*, Delbo constructs a counterlegal scene in which the past is staged not to provide closure but to remind us of the call that the dead continue to make on the living. Her writings stage a scene in which we, the living, are addressed by the dead, in whose eyes we are destined to remain unforgiven.

∗

What, then, is the didactic, legal, therapeutic *work* is accomplished by the writings of Brecht, Delbo, and Arendt—if any? As may be clear by now, I contend that, rather than providing a cathartic moment of liberation from the past, their works dramatize how the past cannot be overcome, not even in an act of "clear consciousness" hoped for by Adorno. The three texts that were central to this study each revolve around stumbling blocks to closure in legal (closing a case), therapeutic (finding healing), and pedagogical (reaching a synthetic, positive understanding) senses, which are interminably deferred. *Eichmann in Jerusalem*, *Die Maßnahme*, and Delbo's writings are haunted by a past that remains incomprehensible and unforgivable. We tend to take forgiveness as something that heals, as Paul Ricoeur has suggested, because it seems to signal an endpoint to two types of emotional work, the work of mourning (*trauerarbeit*) and the psychoanalytic working through (*durcharbeitung*).[16] If forgiveness is indeed the endpoint of a "serious working through" of the past, Arendt, Delbo, and Brecht show such an ending to be elusive and the work of mourning to be something that will always remain to be completed.

When Arendt visited Germany in 1959 to accept the Lessing Prize, she suggested that "mastering the past" may indeed be an impossibility. "Perhaps [it] cannot be done with any past, but certainly not with the past of Hitler Germany," she stated in her acceptance speech. "The best that can be achieved is to know precisely what it was, and to endure this knowledge, and then to wait and see what comes of knowing and enduring."[17] Literature may be the best site to set in motion the process of "knowing and enduring" the past, she maintains, as she proceeds to discuss William Faulkner's *A Fable*, a novel about World War I

[in which] very little is described, and nothing at all "mastered"; its end is tears, which the reader also weeps, and what remains beyond that is the "tragic effect" . . . the shattering emotion which makes one able to accept the fact that something like this war could have happened at all.[18]

Literature enables the unique process through which we come to understand and accept reality, not by offering us an explanation of the past, nor by spelling out its lessons, but by evoking a "shattering emotion." It is exactly through this experience of "shattering" that we first start to reconcile ourselves with the past, not as something that we have mastered but as a force in the face of which we are thrown out of joint.[19] Out of this experience of disjointedness arises something different, continues Arendt: There is a *lament*, into which human beings sometimes *erupt* when faced with the ruins of the past (21). These eruptions should not be understood as blind, compulsive impulses, moments of acting-out in which the distinction between the past and the present collapses. But neither do these lamentations heal wounds, nor do they assuage suffering or bring about justice. As Arendt wrote in a letter to Mary McCarthy, "Lamentations are what we owe the dead ones precisely because we go on living."[20]

I would propose that literature, rather than providing closure, is capable of creating a *scene* that is a part of our "real life," yet distinctly different from it. These literary scenes enable us to voice lamentations in which we address the dead and beg them for the forgiveness we need *in order* to continue living without being haunted by the ghosts of the past. This forgiveness may be impossible to obtain—how do we know if the dead have indeed forgiven us? Yet only in being open to its possibility may a true working through of the past begin.

Reference Matter

Notes

1. T. W. Adorno, "Was bedeutet: Aufarbeitung der Vergangenheit?" in *Gesammelte Schriften Vol. 10, pt. 2* (Frankfurt am Main: Suhrkamp Verlag, 1977), 555–572; "What Does Coming to Terms with the Past Mean?" trans. Geoffrey Hartman and Timothy Bahti, in *Bitburg in Moral and Political Perspective*, ed. Geoffrey Hartman (Bloomington: Indiana University Press, 1986), 114–129. References to this text will henceforth appear in parentheses in the body of text.

2. Among the many historical studies of Germany's *Vergangenheitsbewältigung*, see Kathy Harms, Lutz Reuter, and Volker Dürr, eds., *Coping with the Past: Germany and Austria after 1945* (Madison: University of Wisconsin Press, 1990); Charles Maier, *The Unmasterable Past: History, Holocaust and German National Identity* (Cambridge, MA: Harvard University Press, 1988). For psychoanalytic readings of Germany's coping with the past, see Alexander and Margarete Mitscherlich, *Die Unfähigkeit zu trauern: Grundlagen kollektiven Verhaltens* (Munich: Piper, 1977 [1967]); Eric Santner, *Stranded Objects: Mourning, Memory and Film in Postwar Germany* (Ithaca, NY: Cornell University Press, 1993).

3. Adorno's question is not merely theoretical. Soon after the war, both the American and the Soviets embarked on a project of "reeducating" the Germans; the project of "democratization" on an institutional level coincided with a project of public education in which the Germans were taught the values of democracy, and—it was hoped—would be reconstituted as a "demos," a nation ready for democracy. For a brief discussion of the influence on the Allied project of reeducation on the postwar West German intellectual climate, see Anson Rabinbach, "The German as Pariah: Karl Jaspers and the Question of German Guilt," *Radical Philosophy* 75 (January 1996), 15–25.

4. When he returns to these questions in 1966, Adorno's emphasis is slightly different. "The premier demand upon all education is that Auschwitz not happen again," he writes, "The fact that one is so barely conscious of this demand and the questions it raises shows that the monstrosity has not penetrate people's minds deeply, itself a symptom of the continuing potential for its recurrence as far as people's conscious and unconscious is concerned" (Adorno, "Education after

Auschwitz," trans. Henry Pickford, in *Can One Live after Auschwitz? A Philosophical Reader*, ed. Rolf Tiedemann [Stanford, CA: Stanford University Press, 2003], 19). Adorno now turns to Freud's *Civilization and Its Discontents* (1930) and *Group Psychology and the Analysis of the Ego* (1921) to analyze the psychological dynamics that underlay Nazism, arguing that the aim of post-Holocaust education is to teach people to recognize the psychological impulses that had led to Auschwitz.

5. In "Psychoanalysis and Education: Teaching Terminable and Interminable," Shoshana Felman analyzes the relations between pedagogy and psychoanalysis: "Ignorance, in other words, is not a passive state of absence, a simple lack of information: it is an active dynamic of negation, an active refusal of information . . . Teaching, like analysis, has to deal not so much with lack of knowledge as with resistances to knowledge" (Felman, *Jacques Lacan and the Adventure of Insight: Psychoanalysis in Contemporary Culture* [New York: Routledge, 1992], 79).

6. *Aufarbeitung* has different connotations than those of *Durcharbeitung*. In the introduction to the English translation of Adorno's essay, Geoffrey Hartman writes: " 'Aufarbeitung' is colloquially but inadequately translated as 'coming to terms with.' The German phrase has psychoanalytic as well as political connotations and may also allude to the way old materials are 'worked up' into something new, like the fabric of a hand-me-down" (Hartman, *Bitburg*, 114).

7. Sigmund Freud, "Remembering, Repeating and Working-Through (Further Recommendations on the Technique of Psycho-Analysis)," in *The Standard Edition of the Complete Psychological Works of Sigmund Freud, vol. XII*, trans. James Strachey (London: Hogarth and the Institute of Psychoanalysis, 1957), 145–156. References henceforth appear in parenthesis. Laplanche and Pontalis define the concept of working through as follows: "Working-through is taken to be a sort of psychical work which allows the subject to accept certain repressed elements and to free himself from the grip of mechanisms of repetition. It is a constant factor in treatment, but it operates more especially during certain phases were progress seems to have come to a halt and where resistance persists despite its having been interpreted" (J. Laplanche and J. B. Pontalis, *The Language of Psychoanalysis* [London: Karnac Books, 1988], 488). See also Charles Brenner, "Working Through: 1914–1984," *Psychoanalytic Quarterly* LVI (1987): 88–108.

8. As Laplanche and Pontalis put it: "Working through is undoubtedly a repetition albeit one modified by interpretation and—for this reason—liable to facilitate the subject's freeing himself from repetition mechanisms" (Laplache and Pontalis, *The Language of Psychoanalysis*, 488–489).

9. In a series of essays, historian Dominick LaCapra has emphasized this crucial distinction between (a semicontrolled) working through and (a compulsive and blind) acting out, a distinction, he argues, that is often conflated in contemporary debates about trauma. Working through involves some measure of distance, LaCapra insists, and a minimal recognition of the difference between the past and the present. This distance is necessary: "When the past becomes

accessible to recall in memory, and when language functions to provide some measure of conscious control, critical distance, and perspective, one has begun the arduous process of working over and through the trauma in a fashion that may never bring full transcendence of acting out (or being haunted by revenants and reliving the past in its shattering intensity) but which may enable processes of judgment and at least limited liability and ethically responsible agency. These processes are crucial for *laying ghosts to rest*, distancing oneself from haunting revenants, renewing an interest in life, and being able to engage memory in more critically tested senses" (LaCapra, *Writing History, Writing Trauma* [Baltimore: Johns Hopkins University Press, 2001], 90). Working through and acting out are "intimately linked," LaCapra acknowledges, yet "analytically distinguishable processes, and it may be argued that a basis of desirable practice is to create conditions in which working through, while never transcending the force of acting out and the repetition compulsion, may nonetheless counteract or at least mitigate it in order to generate different possibilities" (LaCapra, *Writing History*, 71). See also his *History and Memory after Auschwitz* (Ithaca, NY: Cornell University Press, 1998) and "Conclusion: Acting-Out and Working Through," in *Representing the Holocaust: History, Theory, Trauma* (Ithaca, NY: Cornell University Press, 1994), 205–224.

10. Eichmann had been able to escape the war crimes trials in Nuremberg and had settled in Argentina. Instead of killing him after his hiding place was discovered, the Israeli secret service captured him to put him on trial. The trial opened on April 11, 1961, before a special tribunal of the Jerusalem District Court. The verdict was pronounced on December 11, 1961, and ratified by the Court of Appeal on May 29, 1962. See Moshe Pearlman, *The Capture and Trial of Adolf Eichmann* (New York: Simon and Schuster, 1963).

11. Quoted in Idith Zertal, *Israel's Holocaust and the Politics of Nationhood*, trans. Chaya Galai (Cambridge, UK: Cambridge University Press, 2005), 97.

12. Zertal, *Israel's Holocaust* 92. Zertal calls the Eichmann trial a vehicle for Ben Gurion's "grand national pedagogy" (95). For the extensive literature on the impact of the Eichmann trial on Israel's self-perception, see Tom Segev, *The Seventh Million: The Israelis and the Holocaust* (New York: Hill and Wang, 1993).

13. On the Barbie trial, see Alain Finkielkraut, *La mémoire vaine: du crime contre l'humanité* (Paris: Gallimard, 1989); on Papon, see Nancy Wood, *Vectors of Memory: Legacies of Trauma in Postwar Europe* (Oxford, UK, and New York: Berg, 1999).

14. Historian Le Roy Ladurie, for example, suggests that the trial of Klaus Barbie was intended to provide France with "an enormous national psychodrama, psychotherapy on a nationwide scale" (cited in Henry Rousso, *The Vichy Syndrome: History and Memory in France since 1944*, trans. Arthur Goldhammer [Cambridge, MA: Harvard University Press, 1991], 210). On the Nuremberg trials, see Whitney Harris, *Tyranny on Trial: The Trial of the Major German War Criminals at the End of World War II in Germany, 1954–1946* (Dallas, TX: Southern Methodist University

Press, 1999); and Michael Marrus, ed., *Nuremberg War Crimes Trial, 1945–46: A Documentary History* (Boston: Bedford Books, 1997).

15. Quoted in Guyora Binder, "Representing Nazism: Advocacy and Identity at the Trial of Klaus Barbie," *Yale Law Review* 98 (1989): 1322. In the introduction to the English translation of Alain Finkielkraut's book on the Barbie trial, Alice Yaeger Kaplan describes how "school children in the French system were given lessons about deportation during the Barbie trial. The news papers and magazines were full of references to 'memory,' to 'the lesson of history' to 'an exemplary trial in the service of human consciousness.'" (Alice Yaeger Kaplan, Introduction to *Remembering in Vain*, by Alain Finkielkraut [New York: Columbia University Press, 1992], xvi).

16. Nancy Wood, "Memory on Trial in Contemporary France. The Case of Maurice Papon," *History and Memory* 11, no. 1 (1999): 42, reprinted in Nancy Wood, *Vectors of Memory: Legacies of Trauma in Postwar Europe* (Oxford, UK, and New York: Berg, 1999), 113-114.

17. Mark Osiel, *Mass Atrocity, Collective Memory and the Law* (New Brunswick, NJ: Transaction Books, 1997), 65. Michael Ignatieff notes that these trials create an "official" version of history: "The great virtue of legal proceedings is that its evidentiary rules confer legitimacy on otherwise contestable facts. In this sense, war crimes trials make it more difficult for societies to take refuge in denial; the trials do assist the process of uncovering the truth" (Ignatieff, "Articles of Faith," *Index on Censorship* 5 [1996], 117–118).

18. Osiel, *Mass Atrocity*, 17.

19. The first of the truth commissions was established in Argentina in 1983 by President Raul Alfonsin. Its goal was to investigate the disappearances during the years of the so-called Dirty War. The goal of the Argentinean truth commission was to gather information and to eventually prosecute those who had been responsible. Later truth commissions in Chile and El Salvador were meant as substitutes for criminal proceedings. For a history of the truth commissions, see Priscilla B. Hayner, "Fifteen Truth Commissions—1974–1994: A Comparative Study," *Human Rights Quarterly*, 16, no. 4 (1994), 597–655 and *Unspeakable Truths: Confronting State Terror and Atrocity* (New York: Routledge, 2001). A critical assessment is given by Aryeh Neier in "The Quest for Justice," *New York Review of Books*, March 8, 2001. Stanley Cohen discusses the relation between truth commissions and the construction of a collective memory in "Memory Wars and Peace Commissions," *Index on Censorship* 8, no. 1 (2001): 38–47, and in *States of Denial: Knowing about Atrocities and Suffering* (Cambridge, UK: Polity Press, 2001). For a comparative study, see Audrey Chapman and Patrick Ball, "The Truth of Truth Commissions: Comparative Lessons from Haiti, South Africa and Guatamala," *Human Rights Quarterly* 23, no. 1 (2001): 1–3.

20. For an overview of the extensive literature on the TRC, see David Dyzenhaus, "Survey Article: Justifying the Truth and Reconciliation Commission," *The Journal of Political Philosophy* 8, no. 4 (2000): 470–496.

21. Desmond Tutu, *No Future without Forgiveness* (New York: Doubleday, 1999), 16. The central concern is no longer "justice" but rather "healing." Or, to put it differently, justice is no longer understood in retributive but in "restorative" terms. In the final report, the TRC states its goals in the following terms: "Restorative justice is concerned not so much with punishment, as with correcting an imbalance, restoring broken relationships—with healing, harmony and reconciliation—such justice focuses on the experience of the victims, hence the importance of reparation" (*Truth and Reconciliation Commission of South Africa Report, Vol. 1* [Cape Town: Juta, 1998], 9). On restorative justice, see W. J. Dickey, "Forgiveness and Crime: The Possibilities of Restorative Justice," *Exploring Forgiveness*, ed. R. D. Enright and J. North (Madison: University of Wisconsin Press, 1998), 106–120; Charles Villa-Vicencio, "A Different Kind of Justice: The South African Truth and Reconciliation Commission," *Contemporary Justice Review* 1 (1999): 407–428; and Alex Boraine and Janet Levy, eds. *The Healing of a Nation?* (Cape Town: Justice in Transition, 1995). Mark Amstutz summarizes the distinctions between retributive and restorative justice in the following terms: "Retributive justice, which demands that offenses must be redressed, is expressed through reparations, purges and trials. Restorative justice, the alternative theory, emphasizes the healing and restoration of community relationships through amnesty, forgiveness and truth telling." Retributive justice is "backward looking," whereas restorative justice that strives for healing and reconciliation is forward looking (Mark Amstutz, *The Healing of Nations: The Promise and Limits of Political Forgiveness* [Lanham, MD: Rowman & Littlefield, 2005], 18). Other legal scholars have adopted the term *narrative jurisprudence* to emphasize the healing and reconciling function of storytelling; see James R. Elkins, "On the Emergence of Narrative Jurisprudence: The Humanistic Perspective Finds a New Path," *Legal Studies Forum* 9 (1985): 123–156. In a wide-ranging discussion, Lawrence Douglas defends the exemplary didactic function of war crime trials. Trials can serve both the interest of justice and memory, Douglas insists (Douglas, *The Memory of Judgment: Making Law and History in the Trials of the Holocaust* [New Haven, CT: Yale University Press, 2001]). See also Gerry Simpson, *Law, War and Crime: War Crimes Trials and the Reinvention of International Law* (Cambridge, UK: Polity, 2007). Also important to this discussion is Martha Minow's work, which raises the question: What legal institutions and practices go beyond providing accountability? (Martha Minow, *Breaking the Cycles of Hatred: Memory, Law, and Repair*, ed. Nancy Rosenblum [Princeton, NJ: Princeton University Press, 2002]). For a study on the therapeutic potential of trials, see Martha Minow, *Between Vengeance and Forgiveness. Facing History after Genocide and Mass Violence* (Boston: Beacon Press, 1998); and Graham Hayes, "We Suffer Our Memories: Thinking about the Past, Healing and Reconciliation," *American Imago* 55, no. 1 (1998): 29–50.

22. Shoshana Felman, "Psychoanalysis and Education: Teaching Terminable and Interminable," in *Jacques Lacan and the Adventure of Insight. Psychoanalysis in Contemporary Culture* (Cambridge, MA: Harvard University Press: 1987), 76.

23. As Felman puts it in an essay that explicitly addresses the relation between education and trauma, "Teaching in itself, teaching as such, takes place precisely through a crisis: if teaching does not hit upon some sort of crisis, if it does not encounter either the vulnerability or the explosiveness of a (explicit or implicit) critical and unpredictable dimension, it has perhaps *not truly taught*: it has perhaps passed on some facts, passed on some information and some documents, with which the students or the audience—the recipients—can for instance do what people during the occurrence of the Holocaust precisely did with information that kept coming forth but that no one could *recognize*, and that no one could therefore truly *learn, read* or *put to use*" ("Education and Crisis," in Shoshana Felman and Dori Laub, *Testimony: Crises of Witnessing in Literature, Psychoanalysis and Culture* [New York: Routledge, 1992], 53; emphasis in original).

24. Or, to evoke Dominick LaCapra's question, we need to conceive of an understanding of "working through" "that allows for a critical judgment of the past, and a 'reinvestment in life' but in which 'totalization,' or the illusion of 'mastery' of the past, and finding definitive closure are actively resisted" (LaCapra, *Writing History*, 71, 75).

25. Saul Friedländer, for example, insists that historians seeking to represent the Holocaust adopt narrative modes that "withstand the need for closure" (Friedländer, *Memory, History, and the Extermination of the Jews in Europe* [Bloomington: Indiana University Press, 1993], 132). See also Geoffrey Hartman, "Introduction: On Closure" in *The Longest Shadow: In the Aftermath of the Holocaust* (Bloomington: Indiana University Press, 1996), 1–14. Echoing Friedländer, Dominick LaCapra has pointed to the ethical problems in what he calls "redemptive narratives" about the Holocaust. See LaCapra, *Writing History*, 156–157. Citing Frank Kermode and Northrop Frye, LaCapra suggests that conventional narratives have a strong tendency to work toward "redeeming" endings. Eric Santner coins the term *narrative fetishism* to refer to "the construction and deployment of a narrative consciously or unconsciously designed to expunge the traces of trauma or loss that called the narrative into being in the first place." Santner contrasts this with the Freudian processes of mourning and working through (Santner, "History beyond the Pleasure Principle: Some Thoughts on the Representation of Trauma," in *Probing the Limits of Representation: Nazism and the "Final Solution,"* ed. Saul Friedländer [Cambridge, MA: Harvard University Press, 1992], 144). See, furthermore: Martha Minow, *Between Vengeance and Forgiveness. Facing History after Genocide and Mass Violence* (Boston: Beacon Press, 1998); Cathy Caruth, *Unclaimed Experience: Trauma, Narrative and History* (Baltimore: Johns Hopkins University Press: 1996); Shoshana Felman and Dori Laub, *Testimony*; Lawrence Langer, *Holocaust Testimonies: The Ruins of Memory* (New Haven, CT: Yale University Press, 1991); and Jacques Derrida's reflections on the interminability of mourning in *Mémoires for Paul de Man. Revised Edition*, trans. Cecile Lindsay, Jonathan Culler, and Eduardo Cadava (New York: Columbia University Press, 1989); *Adieu to Emmanuel Levinas*, trans. Pascale-Anne Brault and Michael Naas (Stanford, CA: Stanford

University Press, 1999); and *The Work of Mourning*, ed. and trans. Pascale-Anne Brault and Michael Naas (Chicago: University of Chicago Press, 2001).

26. "Introduction: On Closure," 5, 6. Hartman introduces his notion of "secondary trauma" to point to the effect of televised spectacles of suffering, which, he argues, can lead to a certain desensitization, an indifference or even a coldness on the part of its spectators. The effect of such secondary traumatization is that we understand less, rather than more, about suffering. See "Tele-Suffering and Testimony" in *The Geoffrey Hartman Reader*, edited by Geoffrey Hartman and Daniel O'Hara (New York: Fordham University Press, 2004), 440 ff. See also "Holocaust Testimony, Art, and Trauma" in *The Longest Shadow: In the Aftermath of the Holocaust* (New York: Palgrave Macmillan, 1996), 151–172.

27. Finkielkraut, *La mémoire vaine*.

28. Therefore, Finkielkraut argues, a trial should not be televised. When broadcast into the living rooms of distant spectators, a televised trial effaces the original "cut" of the legal scene. Journalists, politicians, and educators, who argued for televising the Barbie trial to enhance its didactic and therapeutic effect, mistakenly thought that this mediation did not affect the nature of the event. In fact, televising a trial changes its structure in a profound way. "Ce n'est pourtant pas la même chose de suivre un procès dans une salle d'audience, ou chez soi dans son fauteuil. Au tribunal, on ne peut ni téléphoner, ni s'affairer, ni s'affaler, ni aider ses enfants a finir leurs devoirs, ni même grignoter une pomme. 'La Cour': les fonctions corporelles doivent être maîtrisées, la vie doit suspendre son bourdonnement pour que puisse se déployer la cérémonie judiciaire" (118–119).

29. "Il en va d'ailleurs de la justice, comme de la religion, de l'acte théâtral ou de la opération d'enseignement: elle peut être rendue partout (une table suffit) mais à condition de dégager le temps et l'espace des débats de leurs utilisations profanes" (119).

30. See LaCapra, *Writing History*, 153 ff; LaCapra, *Representing the Holocaust*, 171.

31. For a study on the therapeutic potential of trials, see Martha Minow, *Between Vengeance and Forgiveness*; for a defence of "didactic legalism," see Lawrence Douglas, *The Memory of Judgment*. For a collection of essays on the role of trials in the construction of collective memory, see Austin Sarat and Thomas Kearns, eds., *History, Memory and the Law* (Ann Arbor: University of Michigan Press, 2002), and Martha Minow, *Breaking the Cycles of Hatred*. Judith Shklar, *Legalism: Law, Morals, and Political Trials* (Cambridge, MA; Harvard Univerity Press, 1986) is an important study of law as part of a social and political continuum.

32. Ernst van Alphen, "Caught by Images," in *Art in Mind: How Contemporary Images Shape Thought* (Chicago: University of Chicago Press, 2005), 169.

33. Ernst van Alphen, "Giving Voice: Charlotte Salomon and Charlotte Delbo," in *Reading Charlotte Salomon*, ed. Michael Steinberg and Monica Bohm-Duchen (Ithaca, NY: Cornell University Press, 2006), 117.

34. Crucial for the emergence of trauma studies is the pathbreaking collection *Trauma: Explorations in Memory*, ed. Cathy Caruth (Baltimore, MD: Johns Hopkins

University Press, 1995) as well as Caruth, *Unclaimed Experience*. Important
are also Shoshana Felman and Dori Laub, *Testimony*; Dori Laub and Nanette
Auerhahn, "Knowing and Not Knowing Massive Psychic Trauma: Forms of
Traumatic Memory," *International Journal of Psychoanalysis* 74 (1993): 287–302;
Geoffrey Hartman, "On Traumatic Knowledge and Literary Studies," *New Literary History* vol. 26, no. 3 (1995): 537–563; Geoffrey Hartman, "Holocaust Testimony, Art and Trauma," in *The Longest Shadow*, 151–172; Eric Santner, "History
beyond the Pleasure Principle"; Ernst van Alphen, *Caught by History: Holocaust
Effects in Contemporary Art, Literature, and Theory* (Stanford, CA: Stanford Uni-
versity Press, 1997); Ulrich Baer, *Remnants of Song: Trauma and the Experience of
Modernity in Charles Baudelaire and Paul Celan* (Stanford, CA: Stanford University Press, 2000); Jill Bennett, *Empathic Vision: Affect, Trauma and Contemporary
Art* (Stanford, CA: Stanford University Press, 2005); Michael Levine, *The Belated
Witness: Literature, Testimony and the Question of the Holocaust* (Stanford, CA:
Stanford University Press, 2006).

35. Cathy Caruth, "Introduction: The Wound and the Voice," in *Unclaimed
Experience*, 3–4.

36. Arendt, *The Human Condition*, 187 ff.

37. Following Mieke Bal, I understand mise-en-scène in a broad sense as
"the materialization of a text—word and score—in a form accessible for public,
collective reception; a mediation between a play and the multiple public, each
individual in it; an artistic organization of the space in which the play is set; an
arranging of a limited and delimited section of real time and space." This term
can be used as a theoretical concept, Bal holds: "I am maintaining, therefore,
that mise-en-scene, usually conceived of as a theatrical issue of dramaturgy and
performance production, can be taken as a *theoretical concept*, as a tool for the
semiotic analysis of cultural practices outside of theatre and opera" (Mieke Bal,
Travelling Concepts in the Humanities: A Rough Guide [Toronto: University of
Toronto Press, 2002], 97, 109).

38. Shoshana Felman, *The Juridical Unconscious: Trials and Traumas in the
Twentieth Century* (Cambridge, MA: Harvard University Press, 2002), 107.

CHAPTER I

1. Hannah Arendt and Mary McCarthy, *Between Friends: The Correspondence of Hannah Arendt and Mary McCarthy, 1949–1975*, ed. Carol Brightman
(New York: Harcourt Brace, 1995), 168. The letter is dated June 23, 1964.

2. "'What Remains? The Language Remains': A Conversation with Günter
Gaus," in *Essays in Understanding: 1930–1954*, ed. Jerome Kohn (New York:
Schocken, 1994), 16.

3. Arendt, *Eichmann in Jerusalem: A Report on the Banality of Evil* (New York:
Penguin, 1963). All reference to this text will henceforth appear in parentheses
in the body of the text.

4. Gershom Scholem, to cite one example, writes in a letter to Arendt that he was offended by her "heartless, downright malicious tone," the "lighthearted style" and the "English flippancy" she employs: "This is not the way to lay out the true dimensions of this tragedy" (Gershom Scholem, *Gershom Scholem: A Life in Letters, 1914–1982*, ed. and trans. Anthony David and Anthony David Skinner [Cambridge, MA, and London: Harvard University Press, 2002], 395, 396). Looking back on the affair, Walter Lacqueur suggested that "Hannah Arendt was mainly attacked not for *what* she said, but for *how* she said it. She was at once highly intelligent and exceedingly insensitive. . . . She certainly had the intellectual equipment to deal with the subject; but not the temperament . . . The Holocaust is a subject that has to be confronted in a spirit of humility; whatever Mrs. Arendt's many virtues, humility was not among them" (Walter Lacqueur, *America, Europe, and the Soviet Union: Selected Essays* [Piscataway, NJ: Transaction Publishers, 1983], 166–167). For a critical overview of the responses, see Elisabeth Young-Bruehl, "*Cura Posterior: Eichmann in Jerusalem* (1961–1965)," in *Hannah Arendt: For Love of the World* (New Haven, CT: Yale University Press: 2004 [1982]), 328–378.

5. An exception is Deborah Nelson's insightful essay "Suffering and Thinking: The Scandal of Tone in *Eichmann in Jerusalem*," in *Compassion: the Culture and Politics of an Emotion*, ed. Lauren Berlant (New York: Routledge, 2004), 219–244.

6. Karl Jaspers, defending Arendt against critics who had castigated her Eichmann book for the "tone, the irony, this cold soul, this laughter," acknowledges that Arendt, indeed, laughed "not once, but often," only to then suggest that this laughter is grounded in an "extraordinary seriousness." Citing Plato, he writes, "Only a great writer of comedies can be a great writer of tragedies" (Jaspers, cited in Arendt's *Love And Saint Augustine*, edited and with an interpretative essay by Joanna Vecchiarelli Scott and Judith Chelius Stark [Chicago: University of Chicago Press, 1996], 210). Similarly, John Durham Peters feels the need to emphasize that Arendt's laughter does not emerge from a "lack of seriousness— few know the meaning of seriousness as well—but from an acquaintance with folly" (Durham Peters, *Courting the Abyss: Free Speech and the Liberal Tradition* [Chicago: University of Chicago Press, 2005], 277).

7. In "Randall Jarrell: 1914–1965," Arendt writes: "It took me even longer, I must confess, to realize that his marvelous wit, *by which I mean the precision of his laughter . . .*" (Arendt, *Men in Dark Times* [New York: Harcourt Brace, 1968], 266). Jarrell's laughter, she notes, is "exactly right" (Ibid., 267).

8. In his influential essay "Holocaust Laughter," Terence Des Pres suggests that the "comic" depiction of the Holocaust that he finds in the works of Borowski, Epstein, and Spiegelman serves to maintain a certain distance: "Pity and terror are held at a distance, and this is not, finally, a bad thing . . . [because] by setting things at a distance it permits us a tougher, more active response" (Des Pres,

"Holocaust Laughter?" in *Writing and the Holocaust*, ed. Berel Lang [New York: Holmes and Meier, 1988], 232). Referring to Des Pres, Alan Rosen suggests that Arendt's focus on the comic aspects of the trial amounts precisely to such a distancing strategy (Rosen, *Sounds of Defiance: The Holocaust, Multilingualism and the Problem of English* [Lincoln: University of Nebraska Press, 2005], 102). Shoshana Felman argues something similar: "For Arendt, this is a comedy. Pain is translated into laughter. . . . Keeping her distance is crucial for Arendt" (Felman, *The Juridical Unconscious*, 143). Deborah Nelson writes how her ironical stance serves to "hold back the tide of suffering that she felt threatened to overwhelm the trial" (Nelson, "Suffering and Thinking," 226).

9. Jean-Luc Nancy, "Laughter, Presence," in *The Birth To Presence*, trans. Brian Holmes (Stanford, CA: Stanford University Press, 1993), 368–392. As Freud writes, when we laugh, we frequently "do not know . . . what we are laughing at." Glossing on Freud, Shoshana Felman writes that "the comic is comic only in that it does not know its own nature. Jokes achieve, in this way an unsettling effect with regard to knowledge, according to Freud they 'set themselves up against . . . critical judgment" (Felman, *The Claims of Literature: A Shoshana Felman Reader*, ed. Ulrich Baer, Eyal Peretz, and Emily Sun [New York: Fordham University Press, 2007], 123).

10. Arendt, *The Origins of Totalitarianism*.

11. Arendt, *The Life of the Mind. One-volume edition* (New York: Harcourt Brace Jovanovich, 1971/1978), 3, 4. Arendt, in a letter to Mary McCarthy, remarks: "You write that one hesitates to claim the right to define my ideas. As I see it, there are no 'ideas' in this report. There are only facts with a few conclusions" (Arendt, *The Portable Hannah Arendt*, ed. Peter Baehr, [New York: Penguin, 2000], 389).

12. Arendt, "Understanding and Politics (The Difficulties of Understanding)," in *Essays in Understanding: 1930–1954*, 325, n.8.

13. In the preface to the first edition of *The Origins of Totalitarianism* Arendt suggests that the goal of comprehension is always to come to terms with the shock of the new: "Comprehension does not mean denying the outrageous, deducing the unprecedented from precedents, or explaining phenomena by such analogies and generalities that the *impact* of reality and the *shock* of experience are no longer felt. It means, rather, examining and bearing consciously the burden the century has placed on us—neither denying its existence nor submitting to its weight. Comprehension, in short, means the unpremeditated, attentive facing up to, and resisting of, reality—whatever it may be" (viii, emphasis mine).

14. Quoted in Telford Taylor, "Large Questions in the Eichmann Case," *New York Times Magazine*, January 22, 1961.

15. Arendt writes that a "love of showmanship" characterizes the prosecution (4). She praises Moshe Landau, the presiding judge, about whom there is nothing theatrical and who resists the temptation to playact at various occasions (4).

16. Anette Wieviorka argues that the Eichmann trial is characterized as the "coming into being of the witness" (Wieviorka, *The Era of the Witness*, trans.

Jared Stark [Ithaca, NY: Cornell University Press, 2006]). See also her *Procès Eichmann, 1961* (Brussels: Éditions Complexe, 1989). In two pathbreaking essays, Shoshana Felman analyzes the Eichmann trial in relation to the web of stories that was woven out of the individual testimonies. See Felman, *The Juridical Unconscious*, 106–166.

17. Eichmann is "like the hero in a play—and if he suffers, it must be because of what he has done, not for what he has caused others to suffer" (*Eichmann in Jerusalem*, 9).

18. Lawrence Douglas makes this criticism in *The Memory of Judgment*, 2ff. Shoshana Felman speaks of Arendt's focus on the perpetrator instead of the victims as a "conservative legal approach" in *The Juridical Unconscious*, 120, 122, 183.

19. Tom Segev notes that Ben-Gurion believed that "something was required to unite Israeli society—some collective experience one that would be gripping, purifying[:] . . . a national catharsis" (Segev, *The Seventh Million*, 328).

20. Susan Sontag, "Reflections on *The Deputy*," in *The Storm over the Deputy*, ed. Eric Bentley (New York: Grove Press, 1964), 117.

21. Ibid.

22. Ibid., 118.

23. Lionel Abel, *The Intellectual Follies: A Memoir of the Literary Venture in New York* (New York: Norton, 1984), 271. Abel's interpretation of the Eichmann trial is a clear example of what Dominick LaCapra calls a "redemptive, fetishistic narrative that excludes or marginalizes trauma through a teleological story that projectively presents values and wishes" (LaCapra, *Representing the Holocaust*, 192). Citing Tom Segev, LaCapra suggests elsewhere that an (admittedly simplified) Zionist redemptive narrative has had a certain force in Israeli history. LaCapra summarizes this narrative as follows: "The Holocaust is in some sense the necessary culmination of Diaspora, showing the error of stateless wandering, during the Diaspora, and then the foundation of the state of Israel as the redemptive moment." See his *Writing History, Writing Trauma*, 156–157.

24. Arguably, the assumption that the trial ought to have inspired feelings of compassion and pity was so ubiquitous because it reiterated powerful cultural preconceptions about the theater as a site that fosters precisely such feelings. This conception of the theater, which derives from Adam Smith, holds that theater has a social function precisely because it allows for feelings of sympathetic identification with suffering and thereby stimulates the socially important feelings of compassion and pity, feelings which, according to Smith hold society together. See David Marshall, *The Surprising Effects of Sympathy: Marivaux, Diderot, Rousseau and Mary Shelley* (Chicago: University of Chicago Press, 1988). Marshall argues that eighteenth-century understanding of sympathy is inherently bound up with theatricality: "Sympathy itself finally must be seen as a theatrical relation formed between a spectacle and a spectator, enacted in the realm of mimesis and representation . . . the experience of sympathy itself seems to be uncomfortably like the experience of watching a play" (21).

25. See Arendt, "Bertolt Brecht: 1898–1956," in *Men in Dark Times*, 207–249.

26. Nelson, "Suffering," 219–244.

27. Ibid., 221, 226.

28. Regarding Robespierre's sympathy for the poor and destitute, Arendt writes, "the ocean of suffering around him and the turbulent sea of emotion within him . . . drown all specific considerations, the considerations of friendship no les than considerations of statecraft and principle" (Arendt, *On Revolution* [New York: Penguin, 1990], 90).

29. "Because compassion abolishes the distance, the worldly space between men where political matters, the whole realm of human affairs are located it remains, politically speaking, irrelevant and without consequence" (Arendt, *On Revolution*, 86). Arendt differs here from Adam Smith, who had precisely argued that sympathy implies that the difference between self and other is maintained. Explicating Smith, David Marshall writes, "Sympathy must stop short of total identification: if we really changed persons and characters with the people we sympathize with, we might not feel sympathy" (Marshall, *The Figure of the Theatre: Shaftesbury, Defoe, Adam Smith and George Eliot* [New York: Columbia University Press, 1986], 179).

30. Arendt blames ruthlessness and cruelty of the revolutionaries to their having been overwhelmed by feelings of pity: "Since the days of the French Revolution, it has been the boundlessness of their sentiments that made revolutionaries so curiously insensitive to reality in general and to the reality of persons in particular, whom they felt no compunctions in sacrificing to their 'principles' or to the course of history, or to the cause of revolution as such" (90); and "The lawlessness of the 'all is permitted' sprang here still from the sentiments of the heart whose very boundlessness helped in the unleashing of a stream of boundless violence" (92).

31. See Arendt, *The Human Condition*, 63, for a description of Law as *nomos* that "fences in" the realm of the political, separating it from the private sphere. As she writes elsewhere, laws *"establish* the realm of public, political life" ("Understanding and Politics," in *Essays in Understanding*, 315; my emphasis).

32. Hannah Arendt, *The Jew as Pariah: Jewish Identity and Politics in the Modern Age*, ed. Ron H. Feldman (New York: Grove Press, 1978), 248 (my emphasis).

33. Rolf Hochhuth, *Der Stellvertreter*; *The Representative: A Christian Tragedy*, trans. Robert MacDonald (London: Oberon, 1998). For a collection of essays on *Der Stellvertreter* in English, see *The Storm over the Deputy*, ed. Eric Bentley (New York: Grove Press, 1964); in German, *Summa Iniuria: oder Durfte der Pabst schweigen? Hochhuth's "Stellvertreter in der öffentlichen Kritik*, ed. Fritz Raddatz (Reinbek bei Hamburg: Rowohlt, 1963).

34. For a historical overview of German documentary theater and its relation to Brecht and to absurdism, see Hans-Thies Lehmann's chapter "Third Stage: 'Neo-Avantgarde,'" in *Postdramatic Theatre*, trans. Karen Jürs-Munby (London and New York: Routledge, 2006), 52–57. For a general overview see Laureen Nussbaum,

"The German Documentary Theater of the Sixties: A Stereopsis of Contemporary History," *German Studies Review*, Vol. 4, No. 2 (May 1981): 237–255. See also Marvin Carlson, *Theories of the Theatre. A Historical and Critical Survey from the Greeks to the Present* (Ithaca, NY: Cornell University Press, 1993), 426–427. For a critical reading of *Der Stellvertreter* in the context of Germany's *Vergangenheitsbewältigung*, see Andreas Huyssen, "The Politics of Identification: 'Holocaust' and West German Drama," in *After the Great Divide: Modernism, Mass Culture, Postmodernism* (London: MacMillan Press, 1986), 94–114.

35. Erwin Piscator, "Vorwort," in Hochhuth, *Der Stellvertreter*, 7–8; a translation by Clara Mayer is included in Bentley, ed., *The Storm over the Deputy*, 11–15.

36. Piscator in Bentley, ed., *Storm over the Deputy*, 11; "Vorwort," 7.

37. Piscator insists that assuming responsibility for our decisions should be "our point of departure if we wish to master our past" (in Bentley, ed., *The Storm over the Deputy*, 12).

38. Piscator echoes here Hochhuth defense of his play against Adorno, who had argued in an open letter written to Hochhuth in 1965 that his humanist insistence on individual responsibility tends to disregard the power structures that determine human relations. Adorno insists that one could no longer write about individual human beings "as in years past" and that the individual itself is a historical category, stemming from the bourgeois age, which is in decline in industrial society (Theodore Adorno, *Notes to Literature, Volume 2*, ed. Rolf Tiedemann, trans. Sherry Nicholson [New York: Columbia University Press, 1993], 240, 242). In his response to Adorno, Hochhuth emphasizes the political importance of accountability and individual responsibility ("Soll das Theater die heutige Welt darstellen? Antworten auf Fragen der Zeitschrift *Theater Heute*." in *Die Hebamme: Komödie, Erzählungen, Gedichte, Essays*, [Reinbek bei Hamburg: Rowohlt, 1971], 317).

39. Eric Bentley writes in his introduction to *The Storm over the Deputy*: "It is almost certainly the largest storm ever raised by a play in the whole history of the drama," 2.

40. Arendt's essay is republished in Bentley, ed., *The Storm*, 85–94.

41. In the historical appendix to the book, for example, Hochhuth takes issue with a publication in the French Jewish journal *l'Arche*, which claimed that the pope's silence should be understood as an expression of violent anti-Semitism, which it inherited from the Middle Ages (*The Representative*, 358): "Unpopular as this may be at the moment, one of the most essential tasks of the drama is to maintain that man is a responsible being."

42. In "Personal Responsibility under Dictatorship" (1964), Arendt makes a similar argument. Published in *Responsibility and Judgment*, ed. Jerome Kohn (New York: Schocken, 2003), 17–48.

43. The concluding part of *Life of the Mind*, intended to address judgment, was left unfinished when Arendt died. The 1978 edition of *Life of the Mind* collects some of her lecture notes on judgment, which are also available in Hannah Arendt, *Lectures on Kant's Political Philosophy* (Chicago: University of Chicago

Press, 1982). Ronald Beiner 's "Interpretive Essay" in *Lectures on Kant* attempts to reconstruct Arendt's theory of judgment. Richard Bernstein, "Judging the Actor and the Spectator," in *Philosophical Profiles: Essays in a Pragmatic Mode*, contrasts Arendt's earlier understanding of judgment as explained in *The Human Condition* to her later reflections on judgment in *The Life of the Mind* (Cambridge, UK: Polity Press, 1986), 221–238. Majid Yar makes similar points in "From Actor to Spectator: Hannah Arendt's Two Theories of Judgement," *Philosophy and Social Criticism* 26, no 2 (2000): 1–27. On Arendt and Kant, see Paul Ricoeur, "Aesthetic Judgment and Political Judgment According to Hannah Arendt," *The Just*, trans. David Pellauer (Chicago: University of Chicago Press, 2000), 94–108; and Julia Kristeva, "Thinking, Willing and Judging," in *Hannah Arendt*, trans. Ross Guberman (New York: Columbia University Press, 2001), 171–240.

44. Immanuel Kant, *Critique of Judgment*, trans. Werner Pluhar (Indianapolis: Hackett, 1987). Arendt turns in particular to his notion of reflective judgment, as distinguished from determinant judgment. In determinant judgment the universal rule is given, and a judgment subsumes the particular under its determinant. In the case of reflective judgment, only the particular is given, and the universal has to be found. "For Kant determinant judgments were cognitive, while reflective judgments were non-cognitive. Reflective judgment is seen as the capacity to ascend from the particular to the universal without the mediation of determinate concepts given in advance" (Maurizio Passerin D'Entrèves, "Arendt's Theory of Judgment," in *The Cambridge Companion to Hannah Arendt*, ed. Dana Richard Villa, [Cambridge, UK: Cambridge University Press, 2000], 250).

45. In 2000 the German army honored Anton Schmid. See Roger Cohen, "The German Army Hero, Updated," *Sunday New York Times*, May 12, 2000, section 2. Arendt misspells his name as Schmidt.

46. "Philosophical truth can become 'practical' and inspire action without violating the rules of the political realm only when it manages to become manifest in the guise of an example" (Arendt, "Truth and Politics," in *Between Past and Future: Eight Exercises in Political Though* [New York: Penguin, 2006, 247–248. Arendt adds that these examples derive from history and poetry (248).

47. "The exemplar is and remains a particular that in its very particularity reveals the generality that otherwise could not be defined" (Arendt, *Lectures on Kant's Political Philosophy*, 77). Kant's notion of "exemplary validity," then, enables Arendt to think the relation between the universal and the particular. As Maurizio Passerin D'Entrèves writes, to Arendt, "[Examples] permit us to discover the universal in and through the particular, insofar as they embody a universal meaning, while retaining their particularity" (Passerin D'Entrèves, "Arendt's Theory of Judgment," 251).

48. Quoted in Beiner, "Interpretative Essay," in *Lectures on Kant*, 113 (Arendt, "Thinking and Moral Considerations: A Lecture," *Social Research* 38, no. 3 [Autumn 1971]).

49. Karl Jaspers, *The Question of German Guilt*, trans. E. Ashton (New York, Capricorn Books, 1961).

50. Arendt writes in the introduction to *Men in Dark Times* that sometimes only the light of individuals illuminates the darkness of their times: "That even in the darkest of times we have the right to expect some illumination, and that such illumination may well come less from theories and concepts than from the uncertain, flickering and often weak light that some men and women, in their lives and their works, will kindle under almost all circumstances and shed over the time span that was given them on earth-this conviction is the inarticulate background against which these profiles were drawn" (ix).

51. In the same paragraph, she refers to yet another moment of comedy to illustrate Eichmann's banality: the transcripts of the police investigation taken shortly after Eichmann's capture. During the hearings Eichmann lengthily narrates the story of his career path, explaining why he never reached a higher rank within the Nazi hierarchy. All this is narrated in the tone of someone telling a hard-luck story, expecting to find a sympathetic listener. What makes these transcripts farcical is that Eichmann seems to be so absorbed by his own storytelling that he forgets that he is speaking to a Jewish police officer who is, of course, less than sympathetic to Eichmann's career struggles. Again, Eichmann is shown to be capable of telling a story that is completely coherent on the level of narrative, yet is preposterous in the specific situation in which he narrates it. As Arendt writes, "It was precisely this lack of imagination which enabled him to sit for months on end facing a German Jew who was conducting the police interrogation, pouring out his heart to the man and explaining again and again how it was that he reached only the rank of lieutenant colonel in the S.S. and that it had not been his fault that he was not promoted" (287).

52. Arendt, *Life of the Mind*, 4.

53. Commenting on Eichmann's witness-stand testimony, Arendt notes: "When confronted with situations for which such routine procedures did not exist, [Eichmann] was helpless, and his cliché-ridden language produced on the stand, as it had evidently done in his official life, a kind of macabre comedy" (7).

54. Empty speech does not disclose anything about the person: "Speech becomes indeed 'mere talk,' simply one more means toward the end, whether it serves to deceive the enemy or to dazzle everybody with propaganda" (Arendt, *Human Condition*, 180). In the introduction to *Men in Dark Times*, she characterizes the "mere talk"—the chatter—that overtook shortly before the Nazis came to power as "the highly efficient talk and double-talk of nearly all official representatives who, without interruption and in many ingenious variations, explained away unpleasant facts and justified concerns" (viii). This type of speech "does not disclose what is but sweeps it under the carpet, by exhortations, moral and otherwise, that, under the pretext of upholding old truths degrade all truth to meaningless triviality" (viii).

55. Emile Benveniste, "Subjectivity in Language" in *Critical Theory since 1965*, ed. Hazard Adams and Leroy Searle (Tallahassee: University Presses of Florida, 1986), 728–732. See also his "The Nature of Pronouns," in *Problems in General Linguistics*, trans. Mary Elizabeth Meek (Coral Gables, FL: University of Miami Press, 1971), 210–220.

56. Paul de Man gives the following definition: "It designates any grammatical or syntactical discontinuity in which a construction interrupts another before it is completed" (*Allegories of Reading: Figural Language in Rousseau, Nietzsche, Rilke and Proust* [New Haven, CT: Yale University Press, 1979], 289).

57. Arendt, "Truth and Politics," in *Between Past and Future*, 234–235.

58. Arendt, *Origins of Totalitarianism*, 470.

59. Ibid.

60. Ibid., 470–471.

61. Arendt, *Essays in Understanding*, 317.

62. Ibid.

63. Arendt continues to historicize the equation of knowledge to logic: "Only under conditions where the common realm *between* men is destroyed and the only reliability left consists in the meaningless tautologies of the self-evident can this capacity become 'productive,' develop its own lines of thought" (Arendt, "Understanding and Politics," in *Essays in Understanding*, 318).

64. Arendt is here close to Paul de Man's definition of ideology as "the confusion of linguistic with natural reality, of reference with phenomenalism" (Paul de Man, *The Resistance to Theory* [Minneapolis: University of Minnesota Press, 1986], 11.

65. In Paul de Man's formulation, the figure disrupts "a semantic continuum in a manner that lies beyond [hermeneutic] integration" (de Man, *Aesthetic Ideology*, ed. Andrzej Warminski [Minneapolis: University of Minnesota Press, 1996], 61). See also J. Hillis Miller's helpful discussion of this trope in "Three Literary Theorists in Search of o," in *Provocations to Reading: J. Hillis Miller and the Democracy to Come*, ed. Barbara Cohen and Dragan Kujundzic (New York: Fordham University Press, 2005), 223 ff.

66. Arendt, "Social Science Techniques and the Study of Concentration Camps" in *Echoes from the Holocaust: Philosophical Reflections on a Dark Time*, eds. Alan Rosenberg and Gerald E. Myers (Philadelphia: Temple University Press, 1988), 366.

67. Arendt, "Some Questions of Moral Philosophy," quoted in Beiner, "Interpretative Essay," 113.

68. Arendt, *The Jew as Pariah*, 251.

69. See de Man's understanding of irony as "the systematic undoing of understanding," which occurs precisely in relation to the machinelike quality of grammar, its capacity to produce language "prior to any figuration or meaning" (De Man, *Allegories of Reading*, 301, 299). In "The Concept of Irony," de Man notes:

"What is at stake in irony is the possibility of understanding, the possibility of reading, the readability of texts" (*Aesthetic Ideology*, 167).

70. Arendt, "Understanding and Politics," in *Essays in Understanding*, 307–308.

71. " . . . understanding [will never] be the product of questionnaires, interviews, statistics or the scientific evaluation of data" (Ibid., 323, no 1).

72. Ibid., 311.

73. Arendt, "On Humanity in Dark Times: Thoughts about Lessing," in *Men in Dark Times*, 21.

74. Ibid., 21.

75. Ibid., 6.

76. Ibid., 6.

77. Arendt, "A Reply to Eric Voegelin" in *The Portable Hannah Arendt*, 159.

78. Ibid., 159.

79. Mieke Bal, *Double Exposures: The Subject of Cultural Analysis* (New York: Routledge, 1996), p. 2.

CHAPTER 2

1. Dominick LaCapra has rightly argued that one's subjective position toward the past (whether one is, say, a survivor, a relative of a survivors, or a relative of collaborators) structures the particular *form* that one's resistance to the past takes. Writing about historians (but making an observation equally applicable to spectators of a trial), LaCapra suggests that "the Holocaust presents the historian with transference in the most traumatic form conceivable—but *in a form* that will vary with the difference in subject position of the analyst" (LaCapra, "Representing the Holocaust: Reflections on the Historian's Debate," in *Probing the Limits of Representation*, 110 (emphasis mine). The process of working through implies the acknowledgment of differences in subject positions because "working through requires the recognition that we are in involved in transferential relations to the past in ways that vary according to the subject-positions we find ourselves in" (LaCapra, *Representing the Holocaust*, 64).

2. The situation is, of course, more complex because both Hochhuth's play and the Eichmann trial "traveled." *Der Stellvertreter* was performed in different countries, evoking different historical contexts, while the Eichman trial, which was filmed in its entirety, anticipated a future audience both inside and outside Israel.

3. Arendt, *Eichmann in Jerusalem*, 298. All references to this book will henceforth appear in parentheses.

4. Jaspers, *The Question of German Guilt*. All references to this book will henceforth appear in parentheses.

5. See Anson Rabinbach, *In the Shadow of Catastrophe: German Intellectuals between Apocalypse and Enlightenment* (Berkeley: University of California Press, 1997), 122. Rabinbach refers here to Habermas, who claims that Jaspers's text

was the first contribution to the postwar consensus in the Federal Republic, in that it argues that reeducation should aim at establishing a connection between a collective political responsibility (*Verantwortlichkeit*) and a democratic political identity. See Jürgen Habermas, "On the Public Use of History," in *The New Conservatism: Cultural Criticism and the Historians' Debate*, transl. Shierry Weber Nicholsen (Cambridge, MA: MIT Press, 1989), 233. See also Anson Rabinbach, "The German as Pariah: Karl Jaspers's 'The Question of German Guilt,'" in *Shadow of Catastrophe*, 129–165.

6. Political guilt affects not only those whose political office implies responsibility for acts of state but also the citizens of the state because each human being is "co-responsible for the way he is governed" (31).

7. Karl Jaspers, "On *The Deputy*," trans. Salvator Attanasio, in *The Storm over the Deputy*, ed. Eric Bentley (New York: Grove Press, 1964), 99–102. Originally broadcast by Radio Basel, Novermber 23, 1963.

8. Jaspers writes: "He can no longer pray before this awesome God. He can no longer dispute with Him, like Job. He can only entreat him" (Ibid., 100). Although Jaspers admires the play's broaching of this metaphysical question—he finds the monologue of the old man "grippingly true"—he is nonetheless struck by the poverty of the answers provided by Hochhuth's play: "In Hochhuth's play I find a great openness, that is, I do not sense a solidly grounded faith, I do not perceive a position which he aims to defend and assert under all circumstances. Rather, what I see at the center of his concern is the question about God, and this question about God receives no answer through him" (101). Nevertheless, as Jaspers asserts towards the end of his brief essay, the fact that the question of God is left in suspense means precisely that it opens up the space in which this question can be taken seriously. As Jaspers concludes: "Hochhuth demands from us that we be open, and take questions with complete seriousness, in the face of God, of the Transcendent" (102).

9. Pierre Bourdieu argues, in his analysis of the legal field, that a verdict always seeks to proclaim the truth, but because it is spoken from the sovereign perspective of the state, its act of proclaiming is always an act of "instituting" in the same gesture. A verdict does not only confirm the sovereignty of the state. By uttering a verdict, the sovereignty of the state is constituted as well (Pierre Bourdieu, "The Force of Law: Toward a Sociology of the Juridical Field," *Hastings Law Journal* 38 [1987]: 805–853). Pierre Legendre's psychoanalytically informed analysis of the trial argues that the restaging of a crime, in a legal setting, serves to reconstitute the law. See Pierre Legendre, "Id Efficit, Quod Figurat (It Is the Symbol Which Produces Effects): The Social Constitution of Speech and the Development of the Normative Role of Images," *Legal Studies Forum* 20 (1996), 247–263. See also his article "The Other Dimension of Law," in *Law and the Postmodern Mind: Essays on Psychoanalysis and Jurisprudence*, eds. Peter Goodrich and David Carlson (Ann Arbor: University of Michigan Press, 1998), 175–192.

10. In *How to Do Things with Words*, J. L. Austin discusses the "verdictive" as a particular type of illocutionary act, distinct from exercitives, commissives, behabitives, and expositives because it remains a declaration that has a certain "truth value" (Austin, *How to Do Things with Words*, ed. J. O. Urmson and Marina Sbisa [Cambridge, MA: Harvard University Press, 1962], 153 ff). John Searle, in his *Expression and Meaning: Studies in the Theory of Speech Acts* (Cambridge, UK: Cambridge University Press, 1979), subsumes it under the category of "declaration" (24). See also Austin's *Sense and Sensibilia*, reconstructed from the manuscript notes by G. J. Warnock (Oxford, UK: Oxford University Press, 1962), 140–142; Austin, *Philosophical Papers*, edited by J. O. Urmson and G. J. Warnock (Oxford, UK: Oxford University Press, 1970), 62–69.

11. Taylor, "Large Questions," 22.

12. Ibid.

13. Ibid.

14. Ibid.

15. Taylor writes: "There is a generally accepted principle of law that a man is entitled to be tried where his offense is charged to have been committed" (Ibid.).

16. In *The Human Condition*, Arendt argues that the political sphere is one of "distinctions." Arendt's writings of the 1950s and 1960s, the context in which *Eichmann in Jerusalem* should be understood, are investigations into the public sphere. At the heart of her examination is the Aristotelian difference between the *oikos* (the household, the private realm) and the polis (the public, political realm). The law, or *nomos*, is a gesture of separation between these spheres—it is the "fundamental cut" that separates the two spheres and "fences in" a particular domain. This cut separates the private, the sphere of necessity and of the "eternal rounds of consumption," from the public sphere (Arendt, *The Human Condition*, 63).

17. Arendt's criticism of Israel concerns the fact that it sometimes employs religious categories, rather than political ones. In *Eichmann in Jerusalem*, she criticizes the fact that "rabbinical law rules the personal status of Jewish citizens, with the result that no Jew can marry a non-Jew" (7). During and after the war, Arendt published a set of essays on Zionism in *Aufbau*; most of them are collected in *The Jew as Pariah*. On Arendt's ambivalent relation to Zionism, see Richard Wolin, "The Ambivalences of German-Jewish Identity: Hannah Arendt in Jerusalem," *History & Memory* 8, no. 2 (1996): 9–35; and Seyla Benhabib, "Identity, Perspective and Narrative in Hannah Arendt's *Eichmann in Jerusalem*," *History & Memory* 8, no. 2 (1996): 35–60.

18. Arendt, *The Origins of Totalitarianism*, 8. All references will appear henceforth in parentheses.

19. *Eichmann in Jerusalem* similarly notes how "in nearly all countries anti-Jewish action started with stateless persons" (138).

20. Burke, *Reflections on the Revolution in France* (1790). Quoted in Arendt, *The Origins of Totalitarianism*, 299.

21. See Giorgio Agamben's philosophical study on the relations between "naked life" and the law in *Homo Sacer: Sovereign Power and Bare Life*, transl. Daniel Heller-Roazen (Stanford, CA: Stanford University Press, 1998). In an argument that builds on Arendt, Agamben proposes that the refugee and the inmate of a concentration camp are paradigmatic examples of the way power is exercised in contemporary politics. Agamben makes a similar argument in *Means without End* when he writes: "The by now unstoppable decline of the nation-state and the general corrosion of traditional political-juridical categories, the refugee is perhaps the only thinkable figure for the people of our time and the only category in which one may see today . . . the forms and limits of a coming political community" (Agamben, "Beyond Human Rights," in *Means without End: Notes on Politics*, transl. Vincenzo Binetti and Cesare Casarino [Minneapolis: University of Minnesota Press, 2000], 19). Agamben argues that "there is no autonomous space in the political order of the nation-state for something like the pure human in itself" (19). See also Agamben, *Remnants of Auschwitz: The Witness and the Archive*, transl. Daniel Heller-Roazen (New York: Zone Books, 1999). For a critique of Agamben, see Slavoj Žižek, *Welcome to the Desert of the Real* (New York: Wooster Press, 2001).

22. Agamben points to this paradox being already contained in the phrasing of the document: "This is implicit, after all, in the ambiguity of the very title of the 1789 *Déclaration des droits de l'homme et du citoyen*, in which it is unclear whether the two terms are to name to distinct realities, or whether they are to form, instead, a hendiadys in which the first term is actually always already contained in the second" (Agamben, *Means without End*, 19).

23. Arendt, *On Revolution*, 125. All references will henceforth appear in parentheses.

24. Jacques Derrida's analysis of the Declaration of Independence reaches a similar conclusion, although he insists that a "theological moment" lies at the heart of the declaration, when "the good people" of America call *themselves* and declare *themselves* independent at the moment at which they invent (for) themselves a signing identity "they sign in the name of the laws of nature and in the name of God" (Derrida, "Declarations of Independence" in *Negotiations: Interventions and Interviews*, transl. Elizabeth Rottenberg [Stanford, CA: Stanford Universty Press, 2002], 51). See also Derrida's "Force of Law" in *Deconstruction and the Possibility of Justice*, eds. David Carlson, Drucilla Cornell, and Michel Rosenfeld (New York: Routledge, 1992), for a discussion of the theological moment that lies at the center of the establishment of the law. Bonnie Honig gives a comparative analysis of Arendt's and Derrida's readings of the Declaration. She concludes that "for Arendt, then, the problem of politics in modernity is, how do we establish lasting foundations without appealing to gods or an absolute? Can we conceive of institutions possessed of authority without deriving that authority from some law of laws, from some extra-political source?" (Honig, "Arendt's Accounts of Action and Authority," *Political Theory and the Displacement of Politics*

(Ithaca: Cornell University Press, 1993), 97. Claude Lefort points out that the French and American Declarations both insist that the source of rights is to be found in the human utterance of rights (Lefort, "Human Rights and the Welfare State," in *Democracy and Political Theory*, transl. David Macey (Cambridge, UK: Polity, 1988), 37. See also Thomas Keenan, *Fables of Responsibility: Aberrations and Predicaments in Ethics and Politics* (Stanford, CA: Stanford University Press, 1997).

25. As early as 1946, Arendt had already expressed her concern as to whether the Nazi crimes could be understood within the framework of the law. In a famous letter to Karl Jaspers, dated August 17, she writes that the Nazi crimes "explode the limits of the law. And this is exactly what constitutes their monstrousness . . . This guilt, in contrast to all criminal guilt, oversteps and shatters any and all legal systems . . . We are simply not equipped to deal, on a human, political level, with a guilt that is beyond crime" (54). Shortly before the trial, she concedes, however, again in a letter to Jaspers, "It seems to me to be in the nature of this case that we have no tools to hand except legal ones with which we have to judge and pass sentence on something that cannot be adequately represented either in legal terms or in political terms" (417). This concession, however, which insists on the *necessity* of capturing Eichmann's crimes in legal terms, does not necessarily imply that this can be done successfully. Legal tools may be the only ones at hand, yet they can still fail us (*Hannah Arendt and Karl Jaspers: Correspondence 1926–1969*, ed. Lotte Kohler and Hans Saner, transl. Robert Kimber and Rita Kimber [New York: Harcourt Brace, 1992]).

26. Arendt, *Between Past and Future. Eight Exercises in Political Thought* (New York: Penguin, 2006). In her essay on Karl Jaspers, Arendt writes: "A citizen is by definition a citizen among citizens of a country among countries . . . Philosophy may conceive of the earth as the homeland of mankind and of one unwritten law, eternal and valid for all. Politics deals with men, nationals of many countries and heirs to many pasts; its laws are the positively established fences which hedge in, protect and limit the space in which freedom is not a concept, but a living, political reality" (Arendt, "Karl Jaspers: Citizen of the World?" in *Men in Dark Times*, 81–82).

27. Arendt uses the exact same formulation earlier in the book as well: "An international court . . . would have indicted Eichmann, not for crimes 'against the Jewish people,' but for crimes against mankind committed on the body of the Jewish people" (Arendt, *Eichmann in Jerusalem*, 7).

28. Arendt states that the atrocities would be "minimized" before a tribunal representing one nation only (270).

29. Humanity, according to Thomas Keenan, is "the name of that which would precede geographical divisions and political articulations, of that which is by definition essentially unbordered" (Keenan, "Introduction to 'Humanism without Borders: A Dossier on Humanitarianism and Human Rights,'" *Alphabet City* no. 7 (2000): 41).

30. A comparable question is posed by Jacques Derrida in "On Forgiveness." Referring to the South African Truth and Reconciliation Commission, he suggests that the "scenes of repentance, confession, forgiveness, or apology which have multiplied on the geopolitical scene since the last war" should be understood in relation to the "international institution of a juridical concept such as the 'crime against humanity' . . . This sort of transformation structured the theatrical space in which the grand forgiveness, the grand scene of repentance . . . is played." Derrida holds, not unlike Jaspers, that a religious understanding of "humanity" lies at the basis of the notion of a "crime against humanity": "Only a sacredness of the human can, in the last resort, justify this concept . . . if this sacredness finds its meaning . . . in a Jewish but above all Christian interpretation of the 'neighbour' or the 'fellow man' . . . then the 'globalisation' of forgiveness resembles an immense scene of confession in progress . . . a process of Christianisation which has no more need for the Christian Church" (Derrida, *On Cosmopolitanism and Forgiveness*, trans. Richard Kearney [New York: Routledge, 2001], 29–31). I will return to the question of forgiveness in Chapters 3 and 4.

CHAPTER 3

1. Cited in Arendt, *Eichmann in Jerusalem*, 260. All references to this text will henceforth appear in parentheses.

2. Taylor, "Large Questions." Cited in *Eichmann in Jerusalem*, 261.

3. In fact, as historian Idith Zertal notes, Hausner may have lifted the phrase from a editorial in the Israeli newspaper *Ma'Ariv*, which stated: "From the abyss of the Jewish bereavement, from the mounds of ashes of the burned, from all the anonymous, nameless buried, rose the silent cry that shattered Israel: The greatest nations on earth could not catch him. The lads of Israel did" ("The Day of the Great Shock," in *Ma'ariv*, May 24, 1960. Cited in Zertal, *Israel's Holocaust*, 96).

4. Mark Sanders notes how, during TRC hearings, the call for justice for the dead often took the shape of a demand for a restitution of the body or of body parts. See Mark Sanders, "Ambiguities of Mourning: Law, Custom, and Testimony of Women Before South Africa's Truth and Reconciliation Commission," in *Loss: the Politics of Mourning*, ed. David Eng and David Kazanjian (Berkeley: University of California Press, 2003), 80. See also Michael Ignatieff, "Digging Up the Dead," *New Yorker*, November 10, 1997, 84–93. See also Antjie Krog, *Country of My Skull* (London: Jonathan Cape, 1998), 204–205; and Mark Sanders, *Ambiguities of Witnessing: Law and literature in the Time of a Truth Commission* (Stanford, CA: Stanford University Press, 2007).

5. Charlotte Delbo, *Auschwitz et après: Aucun de nous ne reviendra* (Paris: Minuit, 1970); *Une connaissance inutile* (Paris: Minuit, 1970); *La mesure de nos jours* (Paris: Minuit: 1970); *Auschwitz and After*, trans. Rosette Lamont (New Haven, CT: Yale University Press, 1995). References to these texts will henceforth appear in parentheses.

6. Van Alphen, *Art in Mind*, 163–179; Langer, *Holocaust Testimonies: The Ruins of Memory* (New Haven, CT: Yale University Press, 1993); and *Admitting the Holocaust. Collected Essays* (Oxford, UK: Oxford University Press, 1996); Hartman, *The Longest Shadow*. Dominick LaCapra mentions Delbo as a writer who "resisted narrative closure and engaged in hesitant posttraumatic writing" (Lacapra, *Writing History, Writing Trauma*, 70). See also Jill Bennett, "Insides, Outsides: Trauma, Affect, and Art," in *Empathic Vision*, 22–45.

7. As Geoffrey Hartman suggests, this peculiar illocutionary structure may be typical of the discourse of the survivor. "While survivor testimony elicits its own kind of dialogue, it is only partly a dialogue with *us*. The survivors face not only a living audience . . . They also face family members and friends who perished. . . . Though they address the living frontally, often using warnings and admonishments, they also speak (at some point in the testimony this is usually made explicit) for the dead or in their name" (Hartman, *Longest Shadow*, 139).

8. Delbo, *La mémoire et les jours*, translated as *Days and Memory* by Rosette Lamont (Evanston, IL: The Marlboro Press/Northwestern University Press, 2001). References to these texts will henceforth appear in parentheses.

9. For an oral history of the Argentinean mothers, see Jo Fisher, *Mothers of the Disappeared* (Boston, MA: South End Press, 1989). For a "close reading" of the mothers' demonstration that has informed my chapter, see Diana Taylor, "Making a Spectacle: The Mothers of the Plaza de Mayo," in *Radical Street Performance. An International Anthology*, ed. J. Cohen-Cruz (London and New York: Routledge, 1998), 74–85.

10. This is the estimate given by human rights organizations. An "official" count, conducted in 1984, immediately following the end of the military regime, came to 8,960 disappearances. See Fisher, *Mothers of the Disappeared*.

11. "Les folles de mai" was published in 1985, two years after democratic elections marked the end of military rule in Argentina. In 1985, trials were organized against military officials who were responsible for human rights violations during the "dirty war." On December 10, 1985, a civil court sentenced General Jorge Videla, junta chief during the military period and as such ultimately responsible for the disappearances, to life imprisonment. Yet, despite this sentence, which should have closed the case, the mothers continued to march on the Plaza de Mayo until 2006.

12. Diana Taylor, "Trapped in Bad Scripts: The Mothers of Plaza de Mayo," in *Disappearing Acts: Spectacles of Gender and Nationalism in Argentina's "Dirty War"* (Durham, NC: Duke University Press, 1997), 183–222.

13. The French original suggests, more than the English, that the effect of the mother's turning is that they stay *sur place*, that is, "on the spot": "*Elles tournent elles tournent / les folles / Elles tournent sur la place / les folles de mai / sur la place de mai / elles tournent*" (95, emphasis mine).

14. "Elles tournent elles tournent / les folles de mai / sur la place de mai / elles tournent en juin et en septembre / en hiver et été / elles tournent et elles crient" (100)

15. In "The Empty Circle: Children of Survivors and the Limits of Reconstruction" Dori Laub describes a patient who has a recurring dream about an "empty circle." Laub refers to this dream-image as an apt metaphor for trauma. At the heart of a trauma is an empty, nonprocessed event, an "absence," central to the life of the traumatized person but not possessed as a "memory" (Laub, *Journal of the American Psychoanalytic Association*, vol. 46, no.2 [1998], 507–529).

16. "Rendez-nous au moins son corps en lambeaux / rendez-nous ses membres brisés / rendez-nous ses mains écrasées / rendez-nous les / que nous sachions / rendez-nous les / que nous puissions les enterrer" (97)

17. For a historical description, see: Dimitris Kaldiris, *The Drama of Kalavryta* (N.P.: Society of Natives of Kalavryta: 1998); Whitney Harris describes the massacre briefly in *Tyranny on Trial*. The German action was brought up during the Nuremberg trials.

18. "Adieu, voyageur. / Quand vous traverserez le village pour regagner la route et rentrer chez vous, / regardez l'heure à l'horloge de la place. / L'heure que vous lirez au cadran de l'horloge, c'est l'heure de ce jour-là. Le ressort de l'horloge s'est rompu à la première salve. Nous ne l'avons pas réparé. / C'est l'heure de ce jour-là." (124)

19. This formulation alludes to Delbo's description of her life after Auschwitz, made on the opening pages of *Days and Memory*: "I don't live after Auschwitz, I live next to it [*à côté de*]," "Auschwitz is there, unalterable, precise, but enveloped in the skin of memory, an impermeable skin that isolates it from my present self" (2).

20. Sigmund Freud, "Mourning and Melancholia," in *The Standard Edition of the Complete Psychological Works of Sigmund Freud XIV*, trans. James Strachey (London: Hogarth and the Institute of Psychoanalysis, 1957), 244. Freud continues: "It is easy to see that this inhibition and circumscription in the ego is the expression of an exclusive devotion to mourning, which leaves nothing over for other purposes or other interests" (244).

21. "The normal outcome is that deference for reality gains the day" (Freud, "Mourning and Melancholia," 126).

22. Sophocles, *The Oedipus Cycle*, transl. Dudley Fitts and Robert Fitzgerald (New York: Harcourt Brace, 1949), 188.

23. "Creon: You with your head hanging—do you confess this thing? Antigone: I do. I deny nothing" (Sophocles, *Oedipus*, 202).

24. Judith Butler, *Antigones Claim. Kinship between Life and Death* (New York: Columbia University Press, 2000). Butler emphasizes the fact that when Antigone speaks publicly, "she speaks, and speaks in public, precisely when she ought to be sequestered in the private domain" (4). For discussions about the relations between mourning and politics, see Judith Butler, "Violence, Mourning, Politics," in *Precarious Life: the Powers of Mourning and Violence* (London: Verso, 2004), 19–49; Judith Butler, *Frames of War: When Is Life Grievable?* (London: Verso, 2009); and Douglas Crimp, "Mourning and Militancy," *October* 51 (Winter 1989): 3–18.

25. See George Steiner, *Antigones* (Oxford, UK: Clarendon Press, 1984).

26. Jacques Lacan understands this as a conflict between the law as such, represented by Kreon, and a type of legality, the dike, represented by Antigone. This latter type is not exactly legal: "These are no longer laws, nomos, but a certain legality which is a consequence of the laws of the gods that are said to be agrapta, which is translated as 'unwritten' because that is in effect what it means. Involved here is an invocation of something that is, in effect, of the order of law, but which is not developed in any signifying chain or anything else" (Jacques Lacan, *The Seminar of Jacques Lacan, Book VII: The Ethics of Psychoanalysis [1959–60]*, ed. Jacques-Alain Miller, trans. Dennis Porter [New York: Norton & Co., 1992], 278).

27. George Hegel, *The Phenomenology of Spirit*, trans. H. P. Kainz (University Park: Pennsylvania State University Press, 1994).

28. Alexandre Kojève, *Introduction to a Reading of Hegel*, trans. J. H. Nichols (New York: Basic Books, 1965). All references to this text will henceforth appear in parentheses.

29. In "Antigone between Two Deaths," Lacan writes: "It can be seen that Antigone's position represents the radical limit that affirms the unique value of his being without reference to any content, to whatever good or evil Polynices has done, or to whatever he may be subjected to" (Lacan, *The Ethics of Psychoanalysis*, 279).

30. Steiner summarizes Kojève's point as "death is the return from action into being" (Steiner, *Antigones*, 35).

31. In death "the husband, son or brother passes from the dominion of the Polis back into that of the family" (Ibid., 34).

32. Butler, *Antigone's Claim*, 10.

33. Ibid.

34. Their demand for justice comes from the sphere of the *oikos*, the household, by definition lying outside the realm of the public sphere and the law. For a philosophical exploration of the centrality of the difference between the household and the public sphere in the ancient polis, see Arendt, *The Human Condition*, 28–37. Arendt argues that the law (or *nomos*) separates these two spheres, and as such it "fences in" the domain of the political.

35. Antigone herself claims she acts out of love, "But as for me, I will bury the brother I love" (188).

36. Taylor, "Making a Spectacle."

37. "Si angoissées qu'elles ne peuvent crier / ne peuvent pas crier / tant leur gorge est serrée / poignantes d'une douleur /qui tient tout leur corps / si fort / qu'elles ne peuvent crier / tant leur coeur est serré" (95)

38. "Plaza de Mayo is the most public space in Argentina," according to Diana Taylor, "Making a Spectacle," 77.

39. Charlotte Delbo, *Convoy to Auschwitz: Women of the French Resistance* (Boston: Northeastern University Press, 1997).

40. "[Charlotte Delbo] writes not as a heroine, but as a victim" (Lawrence Langer, "Introduction" to *Auschwitz and After*, ix).

41. "Je l'appelais / mon amoureux du mois de mai / des jours qu'il était enfant / heureux tellement / je le lassais / quand personne ne voyait / être / mon

amoureux du mois de mai / même en décembre . . . / il disait les mots / que disent les amoureux du mois de mai / J'étais seule à entendre / On n'écoute pas ces mots-là / Pourquoi / On écoute le cœur qui bat / On croit pouvoir toute la vie les entendre/ ces mots-là tendres / Il y a tant de mois de mai / toute la vie / À deux qui s'aiment // Alors / ils l'ont fusillé un mois de mai" (20–21)

42. On the relation between survival and love, see Cathy Caruth, "Literature and the Enactment of Memory. (Duras, Resnais and Hiroshima mon amour)" in *Unclaimed Experience*, 10–24.

43. These texts are followed by the poem "Prayer to the Living to Forgive Them for Being Alive," which I will discuss in the final section of this chapter.

44. As Derrida suggests in his essay on Paul Celan's poetry, the date may be the trope of witnessing par excellence because it refers to the incommunicable, irreplaceably singular uniqueness of an event, which may be decipherable only by the witness. See Jacques Derrida, "Shibboleth," trans. Joshua Wilner, in *Acts of Literature*, ed. Derek Attridge (London: Routlege, 1992), 370–413.

45. "They led me to a cell with the door open. Leaning against the wall, Georges was expecting me. I'll never forget his smile. We hardly had enough time to tell one another what we wanted to say" (207).

46. Jean Giraudoux, *Ondine* (Paris: Editions Bernard Grasset, 1939); "Ondine," in *Drama in the Modern World*, trans. and ed. by Samuel Abba Weiss (Boston: D. C. Heath, 1964).

47. Ibid., 364.

48. Ibid., 364 (translation modified).

49. Charlotte Delbo, "Phantoms, My Companions," trans. Rosette Lamont, *Massachusetts Review* vol. 12, no.1 (1971): 20–21.

50. Giraudoux, "Ondine," 364 (translation modified).

51. Delbo, "Madwomen," 79.

52. Their "silent cry" is not so much a "coded message" communicated to the state as something much more complex. The mothers refuse to articulate their demand linguistically: They insist on clinging to the particularity of the bodies of their sons and speak "in the name of" this pure particularity by showing photographs of the disappeared. Hence their activism can't be called "civil disobedience," in which the "disobedience" remains a civic act, something communicated to the state. Their protest comes rather from outside the civic community altogether.

53. "Elles tournes et c'est tout d'elles qui crie / leur bouche serrée qui hurle / d'où le cri ne sort pas / crié à blanc" (96)

54. "Vous qui passez / Bien habillés de tous vos muscles / Comment vous par-doner / Ils sont morts tous / Vous passez et vous buvez aux terrasses / Vous êtes heureux elle vous aime / Mauvaise humeur souci d'argent / Comment comment / Vous pardonner d'être vivants / Comment comment / vous ferez-vous pardoner / par ceux-là qui sont morts" (190)

55. Elsewhere in the book Delbo has Mado state: "That's the difference; time does not pass over me, over us. It doesn't undo it. I am not alive. I died in Auschwitz but no one knows it" (267).

56. "Vous qui passez / Animés d'une vie tumultueuse aux artéres / Et bien collée aux squelette / D'un pas alerte sportif lourdaud / Rieurs renfrognés, vous êtes beaux / Si quelconques / Si quelconquement tout le monde" (189)

57. Paul de Man, "Autobiography as De-Facement," in *The Rhetoric of Romanticism* (New York: Columbia University Press, 1984), 122.

58. "Tournez folles de mai / Tournez tournez sur la place de mai / criez femmes de Buenos-Aires / criez juscq'à ce que les spectres de vos suppliciés se lèvent / comme autant de regards / qui nous dévisagent et nous accusent / regards incandescents comme autant de brûlures / qui nous arrachent la peau de l'âme / et nous fassent hurler de vortre douleur / criez jusqu'à ce que le monde / éclate de honte" (102).

CHAPTER 4

1. A selection of Tretiakov's letters to Brecht are published in Sergej Trejakow, *Gesichter der Avantgarde: Porträts—Essays—Briefe* (Berlin and Weimar: Aufbau Verlag, 1985), 402–416. For a short biography of Tretiakov, see Fritz Mierau, "Gesicht und Name," in: *Gesichter der Avantgarde: Porträts—Essays—Briefe* (Berlin and Weimar: Aufbau Verlag, 1985), 447–459.

2. Tretiakov translated *Die Heilige Johanna der Schlachthöfe*, *Die Mutter*, and *Die Maßnahme*. The three plays were collected in *Bert Brecht, Epiceskie dramy* (Moscow–Leningrad: Staatsverlag für künstlerische Literatur, 1934). Tretiakov's introductory essay was reprinted in English as "Bert Brecht" (translator unknown) in *International Literature* (Moscow), May 1937, 60–70. Reprinted in: *Brecht: A Collection of Critical Essays*, ed. Peter Demetz (Englewood Cliffs, N.J.: Prentice-Hall, 1962), 16–29; a longer version was published in German as "Bert Brecht," in Tretjakow, *Gesichter der Avantgarde* (Berlin and Weimar: Aufbau Verlag, 1985),153–185.

3. Sergej Tretiakov, "Bert Brecht," *Brecht: A Collection of Critical Essays*, ed. Peter Demetz (Englewood Cliffs, NJ, Prentice-Hall, 1962), 20. References to this text will henceforth appear in parentheses.

4. Werner Mittenzwei argues that Tretiakov was a key influence on Brecht's *Lehrstücke*. "Es ist sicherlich nicht zu weit gegangen, wenn man darauf hinweist, daß durch Tretjakows Gedanken über die operative Kunst, über den Autor als Produzenten Brecht wesentlichte Anregungen für die Weiterentwicklung seines Lehrstückmodells erhielt und neue aesthetische Lösungen ausprobierte, die sich wesentlich von dem Weg unterscheiden, den er anfangs mit dem 'Ozeanflug' eingeschlagen hatte." See Werner Mittenzwei, "Die Spur der Brechtschen Lehrstück-Theorie Gedanken zur neueren Lehrstück-Interpretation," in *Brechts Modell der Lehrstücke: Zeugnisse, Diskussion, Erfahrungen*, ed. Reiner Steinweg (Frankfurt am Main: Suhrkamp, 1976), 225–254. For other assessments of Tretiakov's influence on Brecht see Henry Glade, "Brecht and the Soviet Theater: A 1971 Overview," in *Brecht Heute/Brecht Today Jahrbuch der Internationalen Brecht Gesellschaft* 2 (1972), 164–173; Marjorie Hoover, "Brecht's Soviet

Connection: Tretiakov," in *Brecht Heute/Brecht Today. Jahrbuch der Internation-alen Brecht Gesellschaft*, 3 (1973), 39–56; Leo Kopelew, "Brecht und die Russische Theaterrevolution," in *Brecht Heute* (1973), 19–38; Robert Leach, "Brecht's Teacher," *Modern Drama* 32, no. 4 (1989), 502–511; Fritz Mierau, "Tatsache und Tendenz: der 'operierende' Schriftsteller Sergej Tretjakow," in Sergej Tretjakow, *Lyrik, Dramatik Prosa* (Leipzig: Verlag Philipp Reclam, 1972), 423–477; Katerine Eaton, "Die Pionierin und Feld-Herren vorm Kreidekreis. Bemerkungen zu Brecht und Tretjakow," in *Brecht Jahrbuch 1979* (Frankfurt am Main: Atheneum Verlag, 1979),19–29; John Fuegi, *Brecht & Company: Sex, Politics and the Mak-ing of the Modern Drama* (New York: Grove Press, 1994); Katerina Clark, *The Author as Producer: Cultural Revolution in Berlin and Moscow* (New Haven, CT: Typescript 2003). On the cultural exchange between Weimar Germany and the Soviet Union, see Karl Schlögel, *Berlin Ostbahnhof Europas. Russen und Deutsche in ihrem Jahrhundert* (Berlin: Siedler Verlag, 1998).

5. "The point is not to leave the spectator purged by a cathartic but to leave him a changed man, or rather, to sow within him the changes *which must be completed outside the theater*" (emphasis added; Tretiakov, "Bert Brecht," 27). In other words, the play is necessarily unfinished; it finds its completion only outside the theater, in the lives of its spectators.

6. Walter Benjamin, "The Author as Producer," *Reflections: Essays, Aphorisms, Autobiographical Writings*, ed. Peter Demetz and trans. Edmund Jephcott (New York: Schocken Books, 1986), 231–232.

7. Benjamin notes that "The transformation of the political struggle from a compulsion to decide [*einem Zwang zur Entscheidung*] into an object of contem-plative enjoyment, from a means of production into a consumer article, is the defining characteristic of this literature" (Benjamin, "The Author as Producer," in *Reflections*, 232; Benjamin, "Der Autor als Produzent" in *Versuche über Brecht*, ed. Rolf Tiedemann [Frankfurt am Main: Suhrkamp Verlag, 1978], 112). *Enschei-dung* carries the specific connotation of a legal verdict, a *"Gerichtsentscheidung."* Katerina Clark notes that Benjamin's essay was written under the influence of his repeated visits to Moscow in 1926 through1932; see Clark, "Author as Producer." In "Moscow," included in *Reflections*, Benjamin describes agitprop pieces that take the shape of trials in which "typical" mistakes, such as alcoholism, hooliganism, prostitution, or fraud, are weighed and judged. Benjamin concludes, "For mobiliz-ing the public on questions of Bolshevik morality in accordance with Party wishes there can be no more effective means [than 'pedagogical theater in the form of legal proceedings']." The austere forms of such educational work are entirely ap-propriate to Soviet life, being precipitates of an existence that requires that a stand be taken a hundred times each day" (Benjamin, *Reflections*, 123–124).

8. The best-known of the learning plays include *Der Lindberghflug/ Der Ozean-flug* (1927, 1929); *Das Badener Lehrstück vom Einverständnis* (1929), *Der Jasager, Der Neinsager* (1930), *Die Maßnahme* (1930–1931). For a thorough study of Brecht's *Lehrstücke*, see Reiner Steinweg, *Das Lehrstück. Brecht's Theorie einer politisch-ästhetischen Erziehung* (Stuttgart: Metzler, 1972); Reiner Steinweg, ed., *Brechts*

Modell der Lehrstücke: Zeugnisse, Diskussion, Erfahrungen (Frankfurt am Main: Suhrkamp, 1976); Reiner Steinweg, ed., *Auf Anregung Bertolt Brechts: Lehrstücke mit Schülern, Arbeitern, Theaterleuten* (Frankfurt am Main: Suhrkamp, 1978); Roswitha Müller, "Learning for a New Society: 'The Lehrstück,'" in *The Cambridge Companion to Brecht*, ed. Peter Thomson and Glendyr Sacks (Cambridge, UK: Cambridge University Press, 1994), 79–95; Andrzej Wirth, "The Lehrstück as Performance," *The Drama Review* 43, no. 4 (1999): 113–121; Rainer Nägele, "Brecht's Theater der Grausamkeit: Lehrstücke und Stückwerke," in *Brechts Dramen*, ed. Walter Hinderer (Stuttgart: Reclam, 1984), 300–315.

9. In *Brecht and Method* (London and New York: Verso, 1998), Frederic Jameson employs André Jolles concept of "casus,"—one of Jolles's basic forms of narration—to characterize Brecht's typical mode of storytelling. By the addition to narrative of the element of judgment, Brecht's plays make the transition from reflection to action. See André Jolles, *Einfache Formen: Legende, Sage, Mythe, Rätsel, Spruch, Kasus, Memorabile, Märchen, Witz* (Leipzig: Halle, 1930).

10. *Die Maßnahme* was first performed in the *Haus der Berliner Philarmonie* on the night of December 13–14,1930, and on January 18, 1931, in the *großes Schauspielhaus*. The libretto was published as volume 4 of *Versuche* (Berlin: Gustav Kiepenheuer Verlag) in September–November 1930. A second, modified edition appeared in 1931. Bertolt Brecht, *Die Maßnahme: Zwei Fassungen*, contains both. Unless otherwise indicated, all quotations in the chapter will be taken from the 1930 version. The English translations are quoted from Bertolt Brecht, *The Jewish Wife and Other Short Plays by Bertolt Brecht*, ed. and trans. Eric Bentley (New York: Grove Press, 1965), 75–108. References to both texts will henceforth appear in parentheses; the first number refers to Bentley's translation, the second to the German 1930 edition, unless indicated otherwise. For a history of the play's production see the "Anmerkungen" in *Die Maßnahme*, 95–108; Werner Hecht, ed., *Brecht Chronik: 1898–1956* (Frankfurt am Main: Suhrkamp, 1997). For documents on the play's production and the *Lehrstücke* in general, see Steinweg, *Brechts Modell der Lehrstücke*.

11. Tretiakov saw the 1931 performance of *Die Maßnahme*. See Steinweg, *Brechts Modell*, 120.

12. Brecht often called the *Lehrstücke* a "theater for the producers"—the audience was not meant to passively gaze at them but to *participate* in the plays. For a collection of Brecht's notes on the *Lehrstücke*, see Steinweg, *Brecht's Modell*. Steinweg argues that the pieces are "formal exercises in the art of the dialectic," a position taken up by Jameson (1998), who suggests that the dramatic structure of "casus" enables him to introduce various positions. Andrzej Wirth ("The Lehrstuck as Performance") calls the pieces "drama therapy": "Drama therapy as pedagogy: Lehrstück texts are therapeutic sound poems" (113).

13. In a theoretical piece, written around the time of the play's production, Brecht points out that the "system Player-Spectator" is sublated at the moment in which both of them become "Studierenden" (Brecht, *Gesammelte Werke*: 21 [Frankfurt am Main: Suhrkamp, 1967], 396). Reiner Steinweg's *Das Lehrstück*

attempts to reconstruct a comprehensive theory of the *Lehrstücke* on the basis of Brecht's notes. Steinweg argues forcefully that Brecht's *Lehrstücke* are not theatrical plays in the traditional sense because they were not to be performed in front of an audience. Steinweg emphasizes the fact the pieces were not meant to be didactic for the audience. As such, they should be understood as "plays without audience." The two performances of *Die Maßnahme* under Brecht's direction, however, *did* take place in front of audiences. Rather than focusing on the absence or presence of a real audience, my reading emphasizes the fact that Brecht's play seeks to overcome the separation between audience and actors. The play seeks to eradicate the imaginary "fourth wall" that traditionally separates the stage from the audience. *Die Maßnahme*, I propose, "deconstructs" the opposition between spectators and actors by creating a new type of theatrical event in which there is no absolute difference between the "scene of production" and the "scene of reception."

14. Having fled the Nazis, Brecht had settled in California in 1941.

15. For a documentation of Brecht's stay in the United States, see James K. Lyon, ed., *Brecht in den USA* (Frankfurt am Main: Suhrkamp, 1994). The book includes official documents, such as Brecht's visas and excerpts from FBI files. Brecht's FBI file is available on the Internet at http://foia.fbi.gov/brecht.htm. See also Eric Bentley, ed., *Thirty Years of Treason: Excerpts from the Hearings before the House Committee on Un-American Activities, 1938–1968* (New York: Viking Press, 1971), 220–223; James Lyon, "Das FBI als Literaturhistoriker. Die Akte Bertolt Brechts," *Akzente* 4 (1980), 362–383; Bruce Cook, *Brecht in Exile* (New York: Holt, Rinehart and Winston, 1982). For documentation on HUAC, see Gordon Kahn, *Hollywood on Trial* (New York: Boni and Gaer, 1948); Larry Ceplair and Steven Englund, *The Inquisition in Hollywood: Politics in the Film Community 1930–1960* (Berkeley: University of California Press, 1983); Jon Lewis, " 'We Do Not Ask You to Condone This.' How the Blacklist Saved Hollywood," *Cinema Journal* 39, no. 2 (2000): 3–30.

16. All quotations are taken from "From the Testimony of Berthold Brecht [sic]—Hearings of the House Committee on Un-American Activities," in *Brecht: A Collection of Essays*, ed. Peter Demetz (Englewood Cliffs, NJ: Prentice-Hall, 1962), 30-42. References will henceforth appear in parentheses.

17. Brecht seems to confuse *Die Maßnahme* with *Der Jasager*. In the latter play the young hero is thrown off a cliff, whereas the hero of the former disappears into a lime pit.

18. Brecht used the same strategy when describing *Die Maßnahme* somewhat later during the hearing: "I tried to express the feelings and the ideas of the German workers who then fought against Hitler." Stripling: "Fighting against Hitler . . . in 1930?" Brecht: "Yes, yes; oh yes. That fight started in 1923" (Demetz, *Brecht: Critical Essays*, 35).

19. This was true not in the least because *Die Maßnahme*, with its two choruses, was too expensive to stage in America, as Brecht explained in an interview with the *New York Times*, included in Lyon, *Brecht in den USA*.

20. In addition to this, the hearing of Hanns Eisler, September 24 through 26, held a few days before Brecht's, also focused on *Die Maßnahme*. See Alexander Stephan, "Enemy Alien. Die Überwachung des exilierten Komponisten Hanns Eisler durch FBI, HUAC und INS," *The Brecht Yearbook* 22 (1997), 181–193.

21. Alexander Stephan, "'. . . Advocates Communist World Revolution by Violent Means.' Brecht, Eisler und The Measures Taken in den Dossiers von FBI und HUAC," in *Massnehmen: Bertolt Brecht/ Hanns Eislers Lehrstück* Die Massnahme. *Theater der Zeit Recherchen* 1 (1998), 116.

22. For Brecht's FBI file, see Alexander Stephan, " . . . Advocates Communist World Revolution"; Alexander Stephan, *Im Visier des FBI. Deutsche Exilschriftsteller in den Akten amerikanischer Geheimdienste* (Stuttgart: Metzler, 1995); and Lyon, *Brecht in den USA*.

23. FBI-Report, Los Angeles (March 30, 1943).

24. Just compare: Hanns Eisler's file consists of 125 pages: 61 pages of questioning of Eisler, 122 documents, and a complete translation of *Die Maßnahme* (Stephan, "Enemy Alien," 187–188).

25. The FBI report includes the remark that *Die Maßnahme* was the only of Brecht's plays in the pre-Hitler period that had been forbidden. In December 1932, the *Landeskriminalpolizei* in Germany made note of the play, noting that "for 'China,' one just has to substitute 'Germany' and the play can be applied to the German situation" (Hecht, *Brecht Chronik*, 447 ff.).

26. Walter R. Storey, "Bert Brecht, GPU Songbird Liked Hollywood Fine," *New Leader*, September 19, 1949, 12; Filed by the FBI on May 2, 1949.

27. Ruth Fischer, *Stalin and German Communism. A Study in the Origins of the State Party* (Cambridge, MA: Harvard University Press, 1948). Fischer uses the phrase "minstrel of the GPU" to describe Brecht on page 615.

28. Characteristic of Brecht's work, according to Fischer, is "the adoration of the discipline and the hierarchical order of the German Communist Party. Hypnotized by its totalitarian and terrorist features he became the most original poet the party ever possessed" (Ibid., 616).

29. Cook, *Brecht in Exile*, 10 and 196.

30. Fischer, *Stalin and German Communism*, 618.

31. For a documentation on the show trials, see J. Arch Getty and Oleg V. Naumov, eds. *The Road to Terror. Stalin and the Self-Destruction of the Bolsheviks, 1932–1939* (New Haven, CT: Yale University Press, 1999). The book contains transcripts, historical documents, and analysis. For an insightful commentary on the book, see Slavoj Žižek, "When the Party Commits Suicide." *New Left Review* 238 (November/December 1999), 26–47.

32. Martin Esslin, *Brecht. A Choice of Evils. A Critical Study of the Man, His Work and His Opinions* (London: Methuen, 1980), 144.

33. Rainer Friedrich, "Brecht and Postmodernism." *Philosophy and Literature* 23, no. 1 (1999), 59.

34. Arendt, "Bertolt Brecht," in *Men in Dark Times*, 241. See also Anthony Tatlow, who remarks: "I cannot approach *Die Maßnahme* without thinking of

the moral destruction of the party under Stalin" (Anthony Tatlow, "Theory and Practice of the Didactic Play," *Brecht Heute/Brecht Today 3. Jahrbuch der Internationalen Brecht Gesellschaft.* 3 (1972), 259).

35. Žižek, "When the Party Commits Suicide," 27.

36. Žižek, *Did Somebody Say Totalitarianism?* (New York, London: Verso, 2001), 174. See also *Enjoy Your Symptom!* (New York: Routledge, 1993), 173–189, for a more elaborate interpretation of *Die Maßnahme*.

37. Žižek notes, "Furthermore the requested sacrifice is not a simple case of the sacrifice for a cause, but far more radical: the subject must 'disappear,' die, yet his sacrifice will not become a myth, it will not be remembered, he will not be inscribed into the register of historical memory as a hero" (Žižek, *Enjoy your Symptom!* 176).

38. There are some similarities between the story of *Die Maßnahme* and Tretiakov's *Roar China*; both stories are set in China and concern the relations between the individual and the collective. Therefore Sheila Delaney notes: "It appears, then, that besides helping familiarize Brecht with avant-garde aesthetic theory, Tretiakov also contributed to the content of *The Measures Taken*." See Sheila Delaney, "The Politics of the Signified in Bertolt Brecht's *The Measures Taken*," *CLIO. A Journal of Literature, History and the Philosophy of History* 16, no.1 (1986), 74.

39. For Brecht's relation to agitprop, see Richard Bodek, *Proletarian Performance: Agitprop, Chorus, and Brecht* (Columbia, SC: Camden House, 1997). According to Werner Hecht, there were more than 200 agitprop troupes active in Germany in 1930 (Werner Hecht, *Brechts Weg zum epischen Theater: Beitrag zur Entwicklung des epischen Theaters 1918 bis 1933* [Berlin: Henschelverlag, 1962], 151).

40. Albrecht Dümling, *Laßt euch nicht verführen: Brecht und die Musik* (Munich: Kindler, 1985), 279.

41. Ibid., 279.

42. Bertolt Brecht, *Der Jasager und der Neinsager: Vorlagen, Fassungen, Materialen*, ed. Peter Szondi (Frankfurt am Main: Suhrkamp, 1978) contains Brecht's plays, as well as Anthony Waley's English translation of *Taniko* and Elisabeth Hauptmann's German translation of Waley.

43. According to Elisabeth Hauptmann's testimony, Eisler called *Der Jasager* "ein Stück mit zwar sehr schöner Musik, aber mit schwachsinnig feudalistischem Text." Quoted in Steinweg, *Brechts Modell*, 66. In an interview given in 1956, Eisler repeats the same words; quoted in Steinweg, *Brechts Modell*, 206.

44. *Die Maßnahme* was rewritten as a piece for workers' choruses and amateur orchestras. Its first performance by the Berliner Philarmonie on December 13–14 was sponsored by the Internationale Tribüne, an organization that promoted revolutionary art and literature. *Die Maßnahme* was directed by Slatan Dudow, while Karl Rankl conducted the orchestra and the three choruses: *Groß Berlin*, the *Fichte*, and the *Schubert Chorus*. The four agitators were played by Helene Weigel, Ernst Busch, Alexander Granach, and the tenor Anton Maria Topitz.

The performance of the play was followed by a discussion with the audience/ participants (Hecht, *Brecht Chronik*, 299–300).

45. *Einverständnis* with one's own death was the central theme of the earlier "Das Badener Lehrstück vom Einverständnis" (1929) in *Gesammelte Werke 2: Stücke 2* (Frankfurt am Main: Suhrkamp Verlag, 1967), 586–612.

46. Rainer Nägele aptly notes that the reduction of the person to his *haltung* is at the heart of Brecht's notion of *Gestus*. *Gestus* is the body "structured by the symbolic code of a specific social situation. The body does not have the identity of its wholeness in itself. It provides the ideal and idol, the *Gestalt*, of wholeness, which it only finds in the distribution along a symbolic chain" (Rainer Nägele, *Reading after Freud: Essays on Goethe, Hölderlin, Habermas, Nietzsche, Brecht, Celan and Freud* [New York: Columbia University Press, 1987], 112–113).

47. Arendt, *On Revolution*, 107. Arendt argues that it is not a natural person who appears before the law but a persona created by the law. The theatrical function of a mask, namely to hide the actor's own face, is metaphorically adopted by Roman law. I would argue that the masks in the context of *Die Maßnahme* maintain their legal connotations.

48. "The Young Comrade perceived that he had put his feelings above his understanding" (87/36).

49. Elisabeth Hauptmann, quoted in Steinweg, *Brechts Modell*, 219.

50. "Ich will euch lieber erlauben, daß euer mitleidiger Kamerad mit einem Stein nebenherläuft und ihn jedem hinlegt, der ausrutscht" (35). (This is not included in Bentley's translation.)

51. Brecht insists, in his instructions to the actors, "Die Dramatische Vorführung muß einfach und nüchtern sein, besonderer Schwung und besonders 'ausdrucksvolles' Spiel sind überflussig. Die Spieler müssen lediglich das jeweilige Verhalten der Vier zeigen, welches zum Verständnis oder zur Beurteilung des Falles gekannt werden muß." Quoted in Steinweg, *Brechts Modell*, 111.

52. "The ABC of Communism" was incidentally the title of a well-known pamphlet written by Nikolai Bukharin and E. Preobrazhensky, first published in 1920, *The ABC of Communism*, trans. Eden and Cedar Paul (Harmondsworth, UK: Penguin, 1969).

53. Dümling, *Latß euch nicht*, 302.

54. Eissler remarked about the song of the Merchant: "Die Musik zu Teil V (was ist eigentlich ein Mensch?) ist die Imitation einer Musik, die die Grundhaltung des Händlers wiederspiegelt . . . Die Brutalität, Dummheit, Souveränität und Selbstverachtung dieses Typus konnte in keiner anderen mulikalischen Form 'gestaltet' werden" (Quoted in Steinweg, *Brecht's Modell*, 110–111).

55. As Benjamin notes about the Brechtian theater: "It sets out, not so much to fill the audience with feelings—albeit possibly feelings of revolt—as to alienate the audience in a lasting manner, through thought, from the conditions in which it lives. Let me remark, by the way, that there is no better starting point for thought than laughter; speaking more precisely, spasms of the diaphragm generally offer

better chances for thought than spasms of the soul" (In "What Is Epic Theater [First Version]" [1931], in *Understanding Brecht*, trans. Anna Bostock [London: Verso, 1983], 100–101).

56. "Your revolution is quickly made and lasts one day," the others tell him, "And is strangled the morning after / But our revolution begins tomorrow. / Conquers and changes the world. / Your revolution stops when you stop. / When you have stopped / Our revolution marches on" (101/64).

57. "The unemployed can not wait any longer, nor can I wait any longer. There is too much suffering" (99, translation modified/60).

58. Hence, *Die Maßnahme* dramatizes the conflict between ethics and politics that Derrida has explored in a series of essays inspired by Levinas. In various writings Derrida opposes two different "logics" or "orders" of justice, one in which justice is understood as a response to the call of a singular other and another conception of justice that in its attempt to codify this responsibility in a set of laws, or politicize it in the form of a program, effectively effaces precisely the unique call for justice that grounds both law and politics. See Jacques Derrida, "Force of Law: The 'Mystical Foundation of Authority," in *Acts of Religion*, ed. Gil Anidjar (New York: Routledge, 2002), 228–298; Jacques Derrida, *Adieu to Emmanuel Levinas*, trans. Pascale-Anne Brault and Michael Naas (Stanford, CA: Stanford University Press, 1999), 116 ff; Jacques Derrida, *The Gift of Death*, transl. David Will (Chicago: University of Chicago Press, 1996), 77 ff. For helpful discussions see Simon Critchley, *Ethics, Politics, Subjectivity: Essays on Derrida, Levinas and Contemporary French Thought* (London: Verso, 1999), 158 ff.; and Hent de Vries, "Hospitable Thought: Before and beyond Cosmopolitanism," in *Religion and Violence: Philosophical Perspectives from Kant to Derrida* (Baltimore: Johns Hopkins University Press, 2002), 293–398.

59. Arendt notes: "*Persona*, at any event, originally referred to the actor's mask that covered his individual 'personal' face and indicated to the spectator the role and part of the actor of the play. But in this mask, which was designed and determined by the play, there existed a broad opening at the place of the mouth through which the individual, undisguised voice of the actor could sound. It is from this sounding through that the word persona was derived: *per-sonare*, 'to sound through,' is the verb of which *persona*, the mask, is the noun. . . . It is through this role, sounding through it as it were, that something else manifests itself, something entirely idiosyncratic and indefinable" (Arendt, "Prologue," in *Responsibility and Judgment*, 12–13).

60. The ABC of communism, however, is not exactly a *law*. The Party tries to establish a new, more just law; it wants to overthrow the law in the name of justice. In *The ABC of Communism*, Bukharin and E. Preobrazhensky, define "Bourgeois Justice"—that is, the "law"—as one of the "various institutions of bourgeois society which serve to oppress and deceive the working masses" (quoted in Keith Dickson, *Towards Utopia: A Study of Brecht* [Oxford, UK:

Clarendon Press, 1978], 146). The ABC, then, points to a contradiction between "justice" and "legality" in capitalist society. However, as an "ABC," it stands for an attempt to *codify* the revolutionary call for justice into a set of *rules*.

61. It is tempting to read this scene allegorically and to understand the young comrade as a representation of something *in* the four comrades, from which they have to distance themselves in order to become true communists. Martin Esslin, for example, suggests that the four surviving comrades take turns playing the young comrade because "he represents a part of their own nature, the part they have to suppress and kill in themselves" (Esslin, *A Choice of Evils*, 142).

62. Lacan, *The Seminar of Jacques Lacan*, 254 ff.

63. Hannah Arendt defines a "hero" as someone whose acts disclose who he is. See Arendt, *The Human Condition*, 183–188.

64. Ernst Bloch, *The Principle of Hope, Volume 3*, trans. Neville Plaice (Cambridge, MA: MIT Press, 1995), 1173. See also Ernst Boch, *Das Prinzip Hoffnung* (Frankfurt am Main: Suhrkamp, 1959), 137.

65. "Only one kind of person can get by on the way to death almost without traditional consolation: the red hero . . . [He} goes clearly, coldly, consciously into the nothingness in which, as a freethinker, he has been taught to believe." Employing religious language to characterize what he calls its "magnificence," Bloch continues, "His sacrifice is therefore different from that of previous martyrs . . . The communist hero . . . sacrifices himself without hope of resurrection . . . His Good Friday is not mitigated or even cancelled out by an Easter Sunday on which he personally will be re-awakened to life" (Bloch, *Principle of Hope*, 1172).

66. Precisely this anticipation to a future moment of redemption or resolution reveals the plays relation to Stalinism and the Moscow trials. As Slavoj Žižek has argued, a crucial aspect of Stalinism was precisely that it tended to justify its worse atrocities by referring to a future moment of justice. It considers the present from the vantage point of a "Last Judgment"; historical events will receive their signification retroactively. Stalinism dictates that "we are obliged, implicitly at least, to view the historical process from the perspective of 'Last Judgment': of a final settling of accounts, of a point of accomplished symbolization/ historicization, of the 'end of history,' when every event will receive retroactively its definitive meaning, its final place in the total narration. Actual history occurs, so to speak, on credit; only subsequent development will decide retroactively if the current revolutionary violence will be forgiven, legitimated, or if it will continue to exert a pressure on the shoulders of the present generation as its guilt, as its unsettled debt" (Žižek, *The Sublime Object of Ideology* [London: Verso, 1989], 142). This anticipatory logic was evoked by Maurice Merleau-Ponty's infamous defense of the Moscow trials of 1947. Merleau-Ponty states that even though the victims may have been innocent, the justness of the trials can be judged only in the future, when its historical role will be fully comprehended: "The trials do not go beyond the subjective and never approach what one calls 'true'

justice, objective and timeless, because they bear upon facts which are still open toward the future, which consequently are not yet univocal and only acquire a definitively criminal character when they are viewed from the perspective on the future held by the men in power" (Maurice Merleau-Ponty, *Humanism and Terror: The Communist Problem*, trans. John O'Neill [New Brunswick, NJ: Transaction Publishers, 2000], 27). As John O'Neill has argued, this anticipatory logic was also adopted by some of the defendants during the trial, most notably Bukharin, who "confessed" that he was "objectively guilty,"—that is, in the eyes of history—even though he had not considers his acts criminal when he committed them. See John O'Neill, "Merleau-Ponty's Critique of Marxist Scientism," in *Phenomenology and Marxism*, ed. Bernhard Waldenfels, Jan Broekman, and Ante Pazanin (New York: Routledge, 1984), 276–304. Ernst Bloch employs a similar logic to justify the trials in his "Jubilee for Renegades" (1937), *New German Critique* 45 (1988), 4. See also Ernst Bloch, "Kritik einer Prozeßkritik" (1937), in *Vom Hazard zur Katastrophe. Politische Aufsaetze aus den Jahren 1934–1939* (Frankfurt am Main: Suhrkamp Verlag, 1972), 195–205.

67. In a broadcast of *Das Literarische Quartett devoted to the 50th anniversary of Brecht's death* (August 11, 2006).

68. Eric Bentley, "Introduction," in Brecht, *The Jewish Wife*, 8. In "A Brecht Commentary," Bentley compares the description of the young comrade with descriptions of Stephan, the first martyr in the New Testament (Eric Bentley, "A Brecht Commentary (continued)," in *Perspectives and Personalities: Studies in Modern German Literature Honoring Claude Hill*, ed. Ralph Ley [Heidelberg: Carl Winter Universitätsverlag, 1978], 26).

69. Demetz, "Introduction," in *Brecht: A Collection of Critical Essays*, 8.

70. "Participation in *die Maßnahme* is a secularized act of ritual; it is a demonstration of faith" (201) (Antony Tatlow, *The Mask of Evil: Brecht's Response to the Poetry, Theatre and Thought of China and Japan: A Comparative and Critical Evaluation* [Bern: Peter Lang, 1977], 201).

71. Sigrid Thielking, "*L'homme Statue*? Brechts Inschriften im Kontext von Denkmalsdiskurs und Erinnerungspolitik," *Brecht Jahrbuch* 24 (2000) 57.

72. Brecht, *Gesammelte Werke* VIII: Gedichte 1: 305 (my translation).

73. Cited in Thielking, 57 (my translation).

74. Bertolt Brecht, *Poems 1913–1956*, ed. John Willet (London: Routledge, 1987), 264–265. "Einst dachte ich: in fernen Zeiten / Wenn die Häuser zerfallen sind, in denen ich wohne / Und die Schiffe verfault, aud denen ich fuhr / Wird mein Name nog genannt werden / Mit andren. . . . Wird mein Name noch genannt / werden auf einem Stein . . . Aber heute / bin ich einverstanden daß er vergessen wird. . . . Warum / Soll man nach dem Bäcker fragen, wenn genügend Brot da ist? / Warum / Soll der Schnee gerühmt werden, der geschmolzen ist / Wenn neue Schneefälle bevorstehen? / Warum / Soll es eine Vergangenheit geben, wenn es eine / Zukunft gibt?" (Brecht, *Gesammelte Werke IX*, 561–562).

75. Brecht, *Gesammelte Werke IX: Gedichte 2*, 666–668.

76. Brecht, *Poems*, 175. "So nützen sie sich, indem sie Lenin ehrten und / ehrten ihn, indem sie sich nützen, und hatten ihn / also verstanden" (Brecht, *Gesammelte Werke IX: Gedichte 2*, 667).

77. Quoted in Susan Buck-Morss, *Dreamworld and Catastrophe: The Passing of Mass Utopia in East and West* (Cambridge, MA: MIT Press, 2000), 72. Buck-Morss points out that the decision to mummify Lenin's body came from Stalin, who proclaimed a day after Lenin's death: "We, the communists are people of a special make. We are special material. The communist body does not decay" (71), thereby effectively ordering the mummification of Lenin. Slavoj Žižek describes how Lenin was suspicious of state funerals—including his own: "The idea of his funeral as a great state event he found repulsive. This was not modesty: he was simply indifferent to the fate of his body, regarding it as an instrument to be ruthlessly exploited and discarded when no longer useful." Žižek opposes this attitude, in which the body of the leader is thoroughly instrumentalized on behalf of the revolution, to the Stalinist era in which the body becomes an "'objectively beautiful' celebrated public image, whose body needs to be preserved and worshipped after his death" (Žižek, "Attempts to Escape the Logic of Capitalism." *London Review of Books*, 21, no. 21. [1999]: 5).

78. Tretiakov's remarks are quoted by Hubertus Gaßner, "Sowjetische Denkmaler im Aufbau," in: *Mo(nu)mente. Formen und Funktionen ephemerer Denkmäler*, ed. Michael Diers and Andreas Beyer (Berlin: Akademie Verlag, 1993), 155.

79. See Boris Groys, *The Total Art of Stalinism. Avant-Garde, Aesthetic Dictatorship and Beyond*, trans. Charles Rougle (Princeton, NJ: Princeton University Press, 1992); and Boris Groys and Michael Hagemeister, eds., *Die Neue Menschheit. Biolopolitische Utopien in Russland zu Beginn des 20. Jahrhunderts.* (Frankfurt: Suhrkamp, 2005). See also Claude Lefort, "The Death of Immortality" in *Democracy and Political Theory*, 256. Lefort suggests that the notion of immortality changed profoundly in the years following the French Revolution, as it was no longer a person but his deeds that became immortal. Citing Lefort, Joan Copjec suggests, in "The Tomb of Perseverance: On Antigone," that in postrevolutionary France immortality is no longer understood as a breakout of time, but that "in modernity the deed was reconceived as affording one the possibility of transcending historical time *within* time. . . . The great social revolutions at the end of the eighteenth century may have severed all ties with the past, but they did so, paradoxically, in order to establish a permanence in time, a durability, of human deeds that was not possible previously" (Joan Copjec, "The Tomb of Perseverance: On *Antigone*," in *Giving Ground: The Politics of Propinquity*, ed. Joan Copjec and Michael Sorkin [London: Verso, 1999], 240). See also: Irene Masing-Delic, *Abolishing Death: A Salvation Myth of Russian Twentieth-Century Literature* (Stanford, CA: Stanford University Press, 1992), who analyzes the topos in

Soviet funeral oratory of the resurrection of the dead by extrapolation from the traces their labor left in the material world. Ernst Bloch's *The Principle of Hope* also notes the changed attitude toward the corpses of the deceased under communism: "In short, his belief in a mechanical universe meant that the red hero, when, as a corpse, he was utterly transformed into a dead mechanism, returned without pleasure but also without pantheism to dust; —yet this materialist dies as if all eternity were his" (1173).

80. Brecht, *Poems*, 132.

81. Benjamin, *Understanding Brecht*, 60.

82. Brecht, *Poems* 133.

83. Benjamin, *Understanding Brecht*, 134.

84. "The expulsion of the Jews from Germany was (until the pogroms of 1938) carried out in the spirit described in this poem" (Ibid., 62).

85. Tretiakov, "Bert Brecht," 17.

86. Tretiakov was arrested on July 26, 1937, in a ward of the Kremlin hospital where he was recovering from an illness. For a historical reconstruction of Tretiakov's arrest, see Vladimir Kolyazin, "'How Will He Go to His Death?' An Answer to Brecht's Question about the Death of His Teacher the 'Tall and Kindly' Tretiakov," *The Brecht Yearbook* 22 (1997): 169–179.

87. Walter Benjamin, "Conversations with Brecht," *Reflections*, 214. Ernst Ottwald was the coauthor of the film *Kulhe Wampe*. He had accompanied Brecht during his trip to Moscow in the spring of 1935. Kolyazin argues that he was arrested for "fascist agitation"; see Kolyazin, "'How Will He Go?'" 169. In a letter to Karl Korsch written in November 1993, Brecht writes: "Since Tretiakov was arrested (as a Japanese spy I believe) my contacts with the Soviet Union have been very meager" (Brecht, *Letters 1913–1956*, trans. Ralph Manheim, ed. John Willett [London: Methuen, 1990], 272).

88. Bertolt Brecht, *Journals*, trans. Hugh Rorrison, ed. John Willett (London: Methuen, 1993); written January 20, 1939.

89. Brecht, *Poems*, 331–333. "Mein Lehrer / Der große, freundliche / Ist erschossen worden, verurteilt durch ein Volksgericht. / Als ein Spion. Sein Name is Verdammt. / Seine Bücher sind vernichtet. Das Gespräch über ihn / Ist verdächtig und verstummt. . . . Gesetzt, er ist unschuldig? / Wie mag er zum Tod gehen?" (Brecht, *Gesammelte Werke IX: Gedichte 2*, 741–743).

90. See "Notes on Individual Poems" in Brecht, *Poems*, 576.

91. "From the Testimony of Berthold Brecht [sic]—Hearings of the House Committee on Un-American Activities" in Demetz, *Brecht: A Collection of Essays*, 37.

92. Ibid.

93. Ibid., 38.

94. See Julie Cassiday, "Marble Columns and Jupiter Lights: Theatrical and Cinematic Modeling of Soviet Show Trials in the 1920s," *The Slavic and East European Journal*, vol. 42, no. 4 (Winter, 1998), 640–660. See also Julie Cassiday, *The Enemy on Trial: Early Soviet Courts on Stage and Screen* (DeKalb: Northern

Illinois University Press, 2000). Cassiday points out how Lenin, as early as 1917, expressed interest in "the educational role" of certain *model* trials, whose proceedings were publicized and accompanied by the distribution of books, pamphlets, and lectures that spelled out the lessons the masses were supposed to learn from these legal spectacles, often repeated in "demonstration trials" outside the courtroom (Cassiday, "Marble Columns," 641; *Enemy on Trial*, 37).

95. Cassiday, "Marble Columns," 642.

96. *Arbeitsjournal*, October 30,1947, quoted by Steinweg, *Brecht's Modell*, 186–187 (my translation).

97. Lehmann and Lethen and Nägele point to an excess of violence that lingers beyond the closure of the plays. See Nägele, "Brecht's Theater of Cruelty," in *Reading after Freud*, 111–134; and Hans-Thies Lehmann and Helmut Lethen, "Ein Vorschlag zur Güte. Zu doppelten Polarität der Lehrstücke," in Reiner Steinweg, ed., *Auf Anregung Bertolt Brechts: Lehrstücke mit Schülern, Arbeitern, Theaterleuten* (Frankfurt: Suhrkamp, 1978), 302–318.

98. "Brechts Dramaturgie verheimlicht in keinem Moment die Gewalttätigkeit mit der eine Art Maschine, heiße sie Dialektik, Geschichte oder Partei, dem Einzelnen sein Todesurteil auf den Leib schreibt" (Lehmann and Lethen, "Ein Vorschlag," 302).

99. "Der stumme Protest der Körperlichkeit" (Ibid., 302).

100. Felman, *The Juridical Unconscious*.

101. FBI file 100-18112. I

102. Bertolt Brecht, *Die Antigone des Sophokles. Materialen zur "Antigone"* (Frankfurt am Main: Suhrkamp, 1965); "The Antigone of Sophocles," translated by David Constantine, in *The Collected Plays, Volume 8*, edited by Tom Kuhn and David Constantine (London: Methuen, 2003), 1–51.

103. Brecht, "Antigone," 4–5 (translation modified); *Die Antigone*, 11.

104. Brecht, "Antigone," 7; "Da sah ich meine Schwester an. / Sollt sie in eigner Todespein / Jetzt gehn, den Bruder zu befrein? / Er mochte nicht gestorben sein" (Brecht, *Die Antigone*, 14).

105. "Laß das Vergangne" (let go of the past), Ismene tells Antigone in the first act of the play, be happy that you have survived: "Vergangenes, gelassen/ Bleibt nicht vergangen" is Antigone's answer, "the past, left alone, does not remain the past" (17). She insists: "Ich aber / folge dem Brauch und begrabe den Bruder" (Brecht, *Die Antigone*, 17).

106. Brecht, *Poems*, 414 "Komm aus dem Dämmer und geh / Vor uns her eine Zeit / Freundliche, mit dem leichten Schritt / Der ganz Bestimmten, schrecklich / Den Schrecklichen" (Brecht, *Die Antigone*, n.p.).

107. Walter Benjamin, "Kommentare zu Gedichten von Brecht," in *Versuche über Brecht*, 64–96; Walter Benjamin, "Commentaries on Poems by Brecht," in *Understanding Brecht*, trans. Anna Bostock (London: Verso, 1989), 43–74.

108. Quoted in Benjamin, "Commentaries," in *Understanding Brecht*, 72.

109. Ibid., 74.

110. Ibid., 74.

111. In a gloss on Hegel's allusion to Antigone's fidelity to the dead as the "eternal irony of the community," Derrida evokes the etymology of the word *eironeia* as meaning "to dissimulate." The sense of justice evoked by Antigone, the *dike*, Derrida suggests, refers in the play not to a harmonizing sense of justice but to something that throws our community "out of joint" (Derrida, *Gift of Death*, 76 ff). See also Derrida's *Specters of Marx* for a deconstruction of Heidegger's reading of *dike* (as evoked in Anaximander) as justice as a gathering force (Derrida, *Specters of Marx: The State of Debt, the Work of Mourning and the New International*, trans. Peggy Kamuf [New York: Routledge, 1994], 23 ff).

112. See Esslin, *Brecht: A Choice of Evils*, 179–180.

113. Brecht, *Poems*, 319–320. "Ihr, die ihr auftauchen werdet aus der Flut / In der wir untergegangen sind / Gedenkt / Wenn ihr von unseren Schwächen sprecht / Auch der finsteren Zeit / Der ihr entronnen seid. / . . . / Ach, wir / Die wir den Boden bereiten wollten für Freundlichkeit / Konnten selber nicht freundlich sein. // Ihr aber, wenn es so weit sein wird / Daß der Mensch dem Menschen ein Helfer ist / Gedenkt unsrer / Mit Nachsicht" (Brecht, *Gesammelte Werke IX: Gedichte 2*, 724).

114. George Tabori, *Die Brecht-Akte*, trans. in German by Ursula Grützmacher-Tabori, *Theater der Zeit* vol 2., no. 55 (2000): 56–72. See also Holger Teschke, "Hollywood-Elegien. Holger Teschke spricht mit George Tabori," *Theater der Zeit* vol. 2, no. 55 (2000): 8–10. Tabori had earlier worked on a film project under the same title. See Martin Kagel, "Brecht Files: Conversations with George Tabori," *The Brecht Yearbook/Theater der Zeit* 23 (1997), 70–75.

115. Tabori, *Brecht-Akte*, 70 (my translation from the German).

116. Tabori's play seems to suggest the latter, as a final scene follows the above dialogue, in which Brecht is at the airport, the day after the hearing, waiting for the plane that would take him to Switzerland. When he is asked whether he would recant his testimony, Tabori lets him answer with a quote taken from Brecht's play on Galileo: "Whatever you do, or I do, the world will keep turning," thereby suggesting that Brecht has dodged important moral issues.

117. Arendt, "Bertolt Brecht: 1898–1956," in *Men in Dark Times*, 207–249.

118. Steinweg, *Das Lehrstück*, 60 (my translation).

119. Ibid., 61 (my translation).

CONCLUSION

1. J. L. Austin, *How to Do Things with Words*, ed. J. O. Urmson and Marina Sbisa (Cambridge, MA: Harvard University Press, 1962), 153.

2. It has become conventional to distinguish between the study of law *in* literature and law *as* literature. "Essentially, 'law *in* literature' examines the possible relevance of literary texts, particularly those which present themselves as telling a legal story, as texts appropriate for study by legal scholars . . . 'Law *as* literature,'

on the other hand, seeks to apply the techniques of literary criticism to legal texts" (Ian Ward, *Law and Literature: Possibilities and Perspectives* [Cambridge, MA: Cambridge University Press, 1995], 3). My remarks concern of course the study of law in literature.

3. Martha Nussbaum, *Poetic Justice: The Literary Imagination and Public Life* (Boston: Beacon Press, 1995).

4. Ibid., 96.

5. Guyora Binder and Robert Weisberg's historical overview of Law and Literature argues that "many scholars have contended that reading great literature addressing legal problems can expand and enhance moral sensibility with which we approach questions of justice" (Guyora Binder and Robert Weisberg, eds., *Literary Criticisms of Law* [Princeton, NJ: Princeton University Press, 2000], 3).

6. In Peter Brooks and Paul Gewirtz, eds., *Law's Stories: Narrative and Rhetoric in the Law* (New Haven, CT: Yale University Press, 1998).

7. James Boyd White, *When Words Lose Their Meaning: Constitutions and Reconstitutions of Language, Character and Community* (Chicago: University of Chicago Press, 1984), 190.

8. Markus Dirk Dubber, *The Sense of Justice: Empathy in Law and Punishment* (New York: NYU Press, 2006). Ian Ward points to the argument, ubiquitous in defenses of law and literature, that literature "humanizes." Richard Weisberg, for example, insists in an exchange with Richard Posner that "novels about the law . . . are the path to human understanding" (quoted in Ward, *Law and Literature*, 9).

9. Nussbaum writes, "But in order to be fully rational, judges must also be capable of fancy and sympathy. They must educate not only their technical capacities but also their capacity for humanity. In the absence of that capacity their impartiality will be obtuse and their justice blind" (Nussbaum, *Poetic Justice*, 121).

10. I rely on Vismann, who explicates Legendre in the following terms: "The main task of the trial is not to investigate the truth, since this can be done outside of the courtroom, at the backside of the stage, but to dramatize, and hence discursify, the violation within an instituted legal frame" (Cornelia Vismann, "'Rejouer les crimes': Theater vs. Video," *Cardozo Studies in Law and Literature* vol. 13, no. 119 (2001), 166). See also Pierre Legendre, *Law and the Unconscious: A Legendre Reader*, ed. Peter Goodrich, trans. Peter Goodrich with Alain Pottage, and Anton Schütz (Basingstoke, UK: Macmillan, 1997).

11. Arendt, *The Human Condition*, 240, n.78.

12. Ibid., 240, 241.

13. Ibid., 241. "The alternative to forgiveness, but by no means its opposite, is punishment, and both have in common that they attempt to put an end to something that without interference could go on endlessly. It is therefore quite significant, a structural element in the realm of human affairs, that men are unable to forgive what they cannot punish and that they are unable to punish what turned out to be unforgiveable" (241).

14. See Harris, *Tyranny on Trial*, 199 ff.

15. Jacques Derrida, *The Politics of Friendship*, trans. George Collins (London: Verso, 1997), x.

16. Paul Ricoeur, "Le pardon, peut-il guérir?" in *Esprit* 3–4 (1995), 77–82.

17. Arendt, "On Humanity in Dark Times: Thoughts about Lessing," in *Men in Dark Times*, 20.

18. Ibid., 20.

19. As Adorno writes, "It is now virtually in art alone that suffering can still find its own voice, consolation, without immediately being betrayed by it" (Adorno, "Commitment" [1962], in *The Essential Frankfurt School Reader*, ed. Andrew Arato and Eike Gebhardt [New York: Continuum, 1982], 318).

20. Quoted in Young-Bruehl, *Hannah Arendt*, 448.

Bibliography

Abel, Lionel. *The Intellectual Follies: A Memoir of the Literary Venture in New York and Paris*. New York: Norton, 1984.

Adorno, Theodor. "Was bedeutet: Aufarbeitung der Vergangenheit?" *Gesammelte Schriften*. Vol. 10, pt. 2, 555–572. Frankfurt am Main: Suhrkamp Verlag, 1977. (Originally published in 1959.)

———. "Commitment" (1962). In *The Essential Frankfurt School Reader*. Edited by Andrew Arato and Eike Gebhardt, 300–318. New York: Continuum, 1982.

———. "What Does Coming to Terms with the Past Mean?" Translated by Timothy Bahti. In *Bitburg in Moral and Political Perspective*. Edited by Geoffrey Hartman, 114–129. Bloomington: Indiana University Press, 1986.

———. *Notes to Literature, Volume 2*. Edited by Rolf Tiedemann and translated by Sherry Nicholson. New York: Columbia University Press, 1993.

———. "Education after Auschwitz (1967)." Translated by Henry Pickford. In *Can One Live after Auschwitz? A Philosophical Reader*. Edited by Rolf Tiedemann, 19–33. Stanford, CA: Stanford University Press, 2003.

Agamben, Giorgio. *Homo Sacer: Sovereign Power and Bare Life*. Translated by Daniel Heller-Roazen. Stanford, CA: Stanford University Press, 1998.

———. *Remnants of Auschwitz: The Witness and the Archive*. Translated by Daniel Heller-Roazen. New York: Zone Books, 1999.

———. *Means without End: Notes on Politics*. Translated by Vincenzo Binetti and Cesare Casarino. Minneapolis: University of Minnesota Press, 2000.

Alphen, Ernst van. *Caught by History: Holocaust Effects in Contemporary Art, Literature, and Theory*. Stanford, CA: Stanford University Press, 1997.

———. "Caught by Images." In *Art in Mind: How Contemporary Images Shape Thought*, 163–179. Chicago: University of Chicago Press, 2005.

———. "Giving Voice: Charlotte Salomon and Charlotte Delbo." In *Reading Charlotte Salomon*. Edited by Michael Steinberg and Monica Bohm-Duchen, 114–125. Ithaca, NY: Cornell University Press, 2006.

Amstutz, Mark. *The Healing of Nations: The Promise and Limits of Political Forgiveness*. Lanham, MD: Rowman & Littlefield, 2005.

Arendt, Hannah. *The Origins of Totalitarianism*. New York: Harcourt Brace, 1994. (Originally published in 1951).

————. *The Human Condition.* Chicago: University of Chicago Press, 1958.

————. *Between Past and Future: Six Exercises in Political Thought.* New York: Penguin, 2006. (Originally published in 1961.)

————. "A Reporter at Large: Eichmann in Jerusalem." *New Yorker* 39 (1963): 40–113.

————. "A Reporter at Large: Eichmann in Jerusalem (continued)." *New Yorker* 40 (1963): 40–111.

————. *Eichmann in Jerusalem: A Report on the Banality of Evil.* New York: Penguin, 1963.

————. *On Revolution.* New York: Penguin Books, 1977. (Originally published in 1963.)

————. *Men in Dark Times.* New York: Harcourt Brace, 1968.

————. "Thinking and Moral Considerations: A Lecture." *Social Research* 38, no. 3 (1971): 430–455.

————. *The Jew as Pariah: Jewish Identity and Politics in the Modern Age.* Edited by Ron H. Feldman. New York: Grove Press, 1978.

————. *The Life of the Mind. One-volume edition.* New York: Harcourt Brace Jovanovich, 1978. (Originally published in 1971.)

————. *Lectures on Kant's Political Philosophy.* Edited by Ronald Beiner. Chicago: University of Chicago Press, 1982.

————. "Social Science Techniques and the Study of Concentration Camps." In *Echoes from the Holocaust: Philosophical Reflections on a Dark Time.* Edited by Alan Rosenberg and Gerald E. Myers, 365–378. Philadelphia: Temple University Press, 1988. (Originally written in 1950.)

————. *Essays in Understanding: 1930–1954.* Edited by Jerome Kohn. New York: Harcourt Brace, 1994.

————. *Love And Saint Augustine.* Edited by Joanna Vecchiarelli Scott and Judith Chelius Stark. Chicago: University of Chicago Press, 1996.

————. *The Portable Hannah Arendt.* Edited by Peter Baehr. New York, Penguin: 2000.

————. *Responsibility and Judgment.* Edited by Jerome Kohn. New York: Schocken, 2003.

Arendt, Hannah, and Karl Jaspers. *Correspondence 1926–1969.* Edited by Lotte Kohler and Hans Saner and translated by Robert Kimber and Rita Kimber. New York: Harcourt Brace, 1992.

Arendt, Hannah, and Mary McCarthy. *Between Friends: The Correspondence of Hannah Arendt and Mary McCarthy, 1949–1975.* Edited by Carol Brightman. New York: Harcourt Brace, 1995.

Austin, J. L. *How to Do Things with Words.* Edited by J. O. Urmson and Marina Sbisa. Cambridge, MA: Harvard University Press, 1962.

————. *Sense and Sensibilia.* Edited by G. J. Warnock. Oxford, UK: Oxford University Press, 1962.

_____. *Philosophical Papers*. Edited by J. O. Urmson and G. J. Warnock. Oxford, UK: Oxford University Press, 1970.

Baer, Ulrich. *Remnants of Song: Trauma and the Experience of Modernity in Charles Baudelaire and Paul Celan*. Stanford, CA: Stanford University Press, 2000.

Bal, Mieke. *Double Exposures: The Subject of Cultural Analysis*. New York: Routledge, 1996.

_____. *Travelling Concepts in the Humanities: A Rough Guide*. Toronto: University of Toronto Press, 2002.

Beiner, Ronald. "Interpretive Essay." In *Lectures on Kant's Political Philosophy* by Hannah Arendt, 89–155. Chicago: University of Chicago Press, 1992.

Benhabib, Seyla. "Identity, Perspective and Narrative in Hannah Arendt's *Eichmann in Jerusalem*." *History and Memory* 8, no. 2 (1996): 48–53.

Benjamin, Walter. *Reflections: Essays, Aphorisms, Autobiographical Writings*. Edited by Peter Demetz and translated by Edmund Jephcott. New York: Schocken Books, 1978.

_____. *Versuche über Brecht*. Edited by Rolf Tiedemann. Frankfurt am Main: Suhrkamp Verlag, 1978.

_____. *Understanding Brecht*. Translated by Anna Bostock. London: Verso, 1998.

Bennett, Jill. *Empathic Vision: Affect, Trauma and Contemporary Art*. Stanford, CA: Stanford University Press, 2005.

Bentley, Eric, ed. *The Storm over the Deputy*. New York: Grove Press, 1964.

_____, ed. *Thirty Years of Treason: Excerpts from the Hearings before the House Committee on Un-American Activities, 1938–1968*. New York: Viking Press, 1971.

_____. "A Brecht Commentary (continued)." In *Perspectives and Personalities. Studies in Modern German Literature Honoring Claude Hill*. Edited by Ralph Ley, 15–27. Heidelberg: Carl Winter Universitätsverlag, 1978.

Benveniste, Emile. "Subjectivity in Language." In *Critical Theory since 1965*. Edited by Hazard Adams and Leroy Searle, 728–732. Tallahassee: Florida State University Press, 1986.

_____. "The Nature of Pronouns." In *Problems in General Linguistics*. Translated by Mary Elizabeth Meek, 210–220. Coral Gables, FL: University of Miami Press, 1971.

Bernstein, Richard. "Judging: The Actor and the Spectator." In *Philosophical Profiles: Essays in a Pragmatic Mode*, 221–238. Cambridge, UK: Polity Press, 1986.

Binder, Guyora. "Representing Nazism: Advocacy and Identity at the Trial of Klaus Barbie." *Yale Law Review* 98 (1989): 1309–1321.

Binder, Guyora, and Robert Weisberg, eds. *Literary Criticisms of Law*. Princeton, NJ: Princeton University Press, 2000.

Bloch, Ernst. *Das Prinzip Hoffnung*. Frankfurt am Main: Suhrkamp, 1959.

————. "Jubilee for Renegades" (1937). *New German Critique* 45, no. 4 (1988): 17–25.

————. "Kritik einer Prozeßkritik" (1937). In *Vom Hazard zur Katastrophe. Politische Aufsätze aus den Jahren 1934–1939*, 195–205. Frankfurt am Main: Suhrkamp Verlag, 1972.

————. *The Principle of Hope. Volume 3*. Translated by Neville Plaice. Cambridge, MA: MIT Press, 1995.

Bodek, Richard. *Proletarian Performance: Agitprop, Chorus, and Brecht*. Columbia, SC: Camden House, 1997.

Boraine, Alex, and Janet Levy, eds. *The Healing of a Nation?* Cape Town, South Africa: Justice in Transition, 1995.

Bourdieu, Pierre. "The Force of Law: Toward a Sociology of the Juridical Field." *Hastings Law Journal* 38 (1987): 805–853.

Brecht, Bertolt. "Das Badener Lehrstück vom Einverständnis." In *Gesammelte Werke 2: Stücke 2*, 586–612. Frankfurt am Main: Suhrkamp Verlag, 1967). (Originally published in 1929.)

————. *Der Jasager und der Neinsager: Vorlagen, Fassungen, Materialen*. Edited by Peter Szondi. Frankfurt am Main: Suhrkamp, 1978. (Originally published in 1929/1930.)

————. *Die Maßnahme: Zwei Fassungen*. Frankfurt am Main: Suhrkamp Verlag, 1998. (Originally published in 1930.)

————. *Epiceskie dramy*. Moscow–Leningrad: Staatsverlag für künstlerische Literatur, 1934.

————. *Die Antigone des Sophokles. Materialen zur "Antigone."* Frankfurt am Main: Suhrkamp, 1965. (Originally published in 1948).

————. "The Measures Taken." In *The Jewish Wife and Other Short Plays*. Edited and translated by Eric Bentley. New York: Grove Press, 1965.

————. *Gesammelte Werke IX: Gedichte 2*. Frankfurt am Main: Suhrkamp, 1967.

————. *Poems 1913–1956*. Edited and translated by John Willet. London and New York: Routledge, 1987.

————. *Letters 1913–1956*. Translated by Ralph Manheim and edited by John Willett. London: Methuen, 1990.

————. *Journals*. Translated by Hugh Rorrison and edited by John Willett. London: Methuen, 1993.

————. "The Antigone of Sophocles." Translated by David Constantine. In *The Collected Plays, Volume 8*. Edited by Tom Kuhn and David Constantine, 1–51. London: Methuen, 2003.

Brenner, Charles. "Working Through: 1914–1984." *Psychoanalytic Quarterly* LVI (1987): 88–108.

Brooks, Peter, and Paul Gewirtz, eds. *Law's Stories: Narrative and Rhetoric in the Law*. New Haven, CT: Yale University Press, 1998.

Buck-Morss, Susan. *Dreamworld and Catastrophe: The Passing of Mass Utopia in East and West.* Cambridge, MA: MIT Press, 2000.

Bukharin, Nicolai, and E. Preobrazhensky. *The ABC of Communism.* Translated by Eden and Cedar Paul. Harmondsworth, UK: Penguin, 1969.

Butler, Judith. *Antigones Claim. Kinship between Life and Death.* New York: Columbia University Press, 2000.

———. *Precarious Life: The Powers of Mourning and Violence.* London: Verso, 2004.

———. *Frames of War: When Is Life Grievable?* London: Verso, 2009.

Carlson, Marvin. *Theories of the Theatre. A Historical and Critical Survey, from the Greeks to the Present.* Ithaca, NY: Cornell University Press, 1993.

Caruth, Cathy, ed. *Trauma: Explorations in Memory.* Baltimore: Johns Hopkins University Press, 1995.

———. *Unclaimed Experience: Trauma, Narrative, and History.* Baltimore: Johns Hopkins University Press, 1996.

———. "The Claims of the Dead: History, Haunted Property and the Law." *Critical Inquiry* 28 (winter 2002): 419–441.

Cassiday, Julie. "Marble Columns and Jupiter Lights: Theatrical and Cinematic Modeling of Soviet Show Trials in the 1920s." *The Slavic and East European Journal* 42, no. 4 (1998): 640–660.

———. *The Enemy on Trial: Early Soviet Courts on Stage and Screen.* DeKalb: Northern Illinois University Press, 2000.

Ceplair, Larry and Steven Englund. *The Inquisition in Hollywood: Politics in the Film Community, 1930–1960.* Berkeley: University of California Press, 1983.

Chapman, Audrey, and Patrick Ball. "The Truth of the Truth Commissions: Comparative Lessons from Haiti, South Africa and Guatamala." *Human Rights Quarterly* 23, no. 1 (2001): 1–43.

Clark, Katerina. *The Author As Producer: Cultural Revolution in Berlin and Moscow.* New Haven, CT: Typoscript, 2003.

Cohen, Barbara, and Dragan Kojundzic, eds. *Provocations to Reading: J. Hillis Miller and the Democracy to Come.* New York: Fordham University Press, 2005.

Cohen, Roger. "The German Army Hero, Updated." *Sunday New York Times,* May 12, 2000, section 2.

Cohen, Stanley. "Memory Wars and Peace Commissions." *Index on Censorship* 1 (2001): 38–47.

———. *States of Denial: Knowing about Atrocities and Suffering.* Cambridge, UK: Polity Press, 2001.

Cook, Bruce. *Brecht in Exile.* New York: Holt, Rinehart and Winston, 1982.

Copjec, Joan. "The Tomb of Perseverance: On *Antigone.*" In *Giving Ground: The Politics of Propinquity.* Edited by Joan Copjec and Michael Sorkin, 233–266. London: Verso, 1999.

Crimp, Douglas. "Mourning and Militancy." *October* 51 (Winter 1989): 3–18.

Critchley, Simon. *Ethics, Politics, Subjectivity: Essays on Derrida, Levinas and Contemporary French Thought.* London: Verso, 1999.

Delaney, Sheila. "The Politics of the Signified in Bertolt Brecht's *The Measures Taken.*" *CLIO. A Journal of Literature, History and the Philosophy of History* 16, no. 1 (1986): 67–80.

Delbo, Charlotte. *Le convoi du 24 janvier.* Paris: Minuit, 1965.

———. *Auschwitz et après: Aucun de nous ne reviendra.* Paris: Minuit, 1970.

———. *Une connaissance inutile.* Paris: Minuit, 1970.

———. *Mesure de nos jours.* Paris: Minuit, 1971.

———. "Phantoms, My Companions." Translated by Rosette Lamont. *Massachusetts Review* vol. 12, no. 1 (1971): 20–21.

———. *Spectres, mes compagnons.* Lausanne: Maurice Bridel, 1977.

———. *La Mémoire et les jours.* Paris: Berg International, 1985.

———. *Auschwitz and After.* Translated by Rosette C. Lamont. New Haven, CT: Yale University Press, 1995.

———. *Convoy to Auschwitz: Women of the French Resistance.* Translated by Carol Cosman. Boston: Northeastern University Press, 1997.

———. *Days and Memory.* Translated by Rosette Lamont. Evanston, IL: The Marlboro Press/Northwestern University Press, 2001.

Demetz, Peter, ed. *Brecht: A Collection of Critical Essays.* Englewood Cliffs, NJ: Prentice Hall, 1962.

Derrida, Jacques. *Memoires for Paul de Man. Revised Edition.* Translated by Cecile Lindsay c.s. New York: Columbia University Press, 1989.

———. "Force of Law," in *Deconstruction and the Possibility of Justice.* Edited by David Carlson, Drucilla Cornell, and Michel Rosenfeld, 3–67. New York: Routledge, 1992.

———. "Shibboleth." Translated by Joshua Wilner. *Acts of Literature.* Edited by Derek Attridge, 370–413. London and New York: Routlege, 1992.

———. *Specters of Marx: The State of Debt, the Work of Mourning and the New International.* Translated by Peggy Kamuf. London and New York: Routledge, 1994.

———. *The Gift of Death.* Translated by David Will. Chicago: University of Chicago Press, 1996.

———. *The Politics of Friendship.* Translated by George Collins. London: Verso, 1997.

———. *Adieu to Emmanuel Levinas.* Translated by Pascale-Anne Brault and Michael Naas. Stanford, CA: Stanford University Press, 1999.

———. *On Cosmopolitanism and Forgiveness.* Translated by Richard Kearney. New York: Routledge, 2001.

———. *The Work of Mourning.* Edited by Pascale-Anne Brault and Michael Naas. Chicago: University of Chicago Press, 2001.

————. "Declarations of Independence." In *Negotiations: Interventions and Interviews 1971–2001*. Edited and translated by Elizabeth Rottenberg, 46–54. Stanford, CA: Stanford University Press, 2002.

Des Pres, Terence. "Holocaust Laughter?" In *Writing and the Holocaust*. Edited by Berel Lang, 216–233. New York: Holmes and Meier, 1988.

Dickey, W. J. "Forgiveness and Crime: The Possibilities of Restorative Justice." In *Exploring Forgiveness*. Edited by R. D. Enright and J. North, 104–121. Madison: The University of Wisconsin Press, 1998.

Dickson, Keith. *Towards Utopia: A Study of Brecht*. Oxford, UK: Clarendon Press, 1978.

Douglas, Lawrence. *The Memory of Judgment: Making Law and History in the Trials of the Holocaust*. New Haven, CT: Yale University Press, 2001.

Dubber, Markus Dirk. *The Sense of Justice: Empathy in Law and Punishment*. New York: New York University Press, 2006.

Dümling, Albrecht. *Laßt euch nicht verführen: Brecht und die Musik*. Munich: Kindler, 1985.

Durham Peters, John. *Courting the Abyss: Free Speech and the Liberal Tradition*. Chicago: University of Chicago Press, 2005.

Eaton, Katerine. "Die Pionierin und Feld-Herren vorm Kreidekreis. Bemerkungen zu Brecht und Tretjakow." In *Brecht Jahrbuch 1979*, 19–29. Frankfurt am Main: Atheneum Verlag, 1979.

Elkins, James R. "On the Emergence of Narrative Jurisprudence: The Humanistic Perspective Finds a New Path," *Legal Studies Forum* 9 (1985): 123–156.

Elsaesser, Thomas. "Antigone Agonistes: Urban Guerilla or Guerilla Urbanism? The Red Army Faction, *Germany in Autumn* and *Death Game*." In *Giving Ground: The Politics of Propinquity*. Edited by Joan Copjec and Michael Sorkin, 267–302. London: Verso, 1999.

Esslin, Martin *Brecht. A Choice of Evils. A Critical Study of the Man, His Work and His Opinions*. London: Eyre Methuen, 1980.

Felman, Shoshana. *The Literary Speech Act: Don Juan with J.L. Austin, or Seduction in Two Languages*. Translated by Catherine Porter. Ithaca, NY: Cornell University Press, 1983.

————. *Jacques Lacan and the Adventure of Insight: Psychoanalysis in Contemporary Culture*. Cambridge, MA: Harvard University Press, 1987.

————. *The Juridical Unconscious: Trials and Traumas in the Twentieth Century*. Cambridge, MA: Harvard University Press, 2002.

————. *The Claims of Literature: A Shoshana Felman Reader*. Edited by Ulrich Baer, Eyal Peretz, and Emily Sun. New York: Fordham University Press, 2007.

Felman, Shoshana, and Dori Laub. *Testimony: Crises of Witnessing in Literature, Psychoanalysis, and History*. New York: Routledge, 1992.

Finkielkraut, Alain. *La mémoire vaine: du crime contre l'humanité*. Paris: Gallimard, 1989.

Fischer, Ruth. *Stalin and German Communism: A Study in the Origins of the State Party.* Cambridge, MA: Harvard University Press, 1948.

Fisher, Jo. *Mothers of the Disappeared.* Boston: South End Press, 1989.

Friedländer, Saul. *Memory, History, and the Extermination of the Jews in Europe.* Bloomington: Indiana University Press, 1993.

Friedrich. Rainer. "Brecht and Postmodernism." *Philosophy and Literature* 23, no. 1 (1999): 44–64.

Freud, Sigmund. "Remembering, Repeating and Working-through (Further Recommendations on the Teaching of Psycho-Analysis)." In *The Standard Edition of the Complete Psychological Works of Sigmund Freud XII.* 145–156. Translated by James Strachey. London: Hogarth and the Institute of Psychoanalysis, 1957. (Originally Published in 1914.)

————. "Mourning and Melancholia." *The Standard Edition of the Complete Psychological Works of Sigmund Freud XIV*, 239–258. Translated by James Strachey. London: Hogarth and the Institute of Psychoanalysis, 1957. (Originally published in 1917.)

"From the Testimony of Berthold Brecht [sic]—Hearings of the House Committee on Un-American Activities." In *Brecht: A Collection of Essays.* Edited by Peter Demetz, 30–42. Englewood Cliffs, NJ: Prentice-Hall, 1962.

Fuegi, John. *Brecht & Company: Sex, Politics and the Making of the Modern Drama.* New York: Grove Press, 1994.

Gaßner, Hubertus. "Sowjetische Denkmaler im Aufbau." In *Mo(nu)mente. Formen und Funktionen ephemerer Denkmäler.* Edited by Michael Diers and Andreas Beyer, 152–176. Berlin: Akademie Verlag, 1993.

Getty, J. Arch, and Oleg V. Naumov, eds. *The Road to Terror. Stalin and the Self-Destruction of the Bolsheviks, 1932–1939.* New Haven, CT: Yale University Press, 1999.

Giraudoux, Jean. *Ondine.* Paris: Éditions Bernard Grasset, 1939.

————. "Ondine," In *Drama in the Modern World. Plays and Essays.* Translated and edited by Samuel Abba Weiss, 37–365. Boston: Heath, 1968.

Glade, Henry. "Brecht and the Soviet Theater: A 1971 Overview." *Brecht Heute/ Brecht Today. Jahrbuch der Internationalen Brecht Gesellschaft*, 2 (1972): 164–173.

Goodrich, Peter, and David Carlson, eds. *Law and the Postmodern Mind: Essays on Psychoanalysis and Jurisprudence.* Ann Arbor: University of Michigan Press, 1998.

Groys, Boris. *The Total Art of Stalinism. Avant-Garde, Aesthetic Dictatorship and Beyond.* Translated by Charles Rougle. Princeton, NJ: Princeton University Press, 1992.

Groys, Boris, and Michael Hagemeister, eds. *Die Neue Menschheit. Biolopolitische Utopien in Russland zu Beginn des 20. Jahrhunderts.* Frankfurt: Suhrkamp, 2005.

Habermas, Jürgen. "On the Public Use of History." In *The New Conservatism: Cultural Criticism and the Historian's Debate.* Edited and translated by Shierry Weber Nicholson, 229–240. Cambridge, MA: MIT Press, 1989.

Harms, Kathy, Lutz Reuter, and Volker Dürr, eds. *Coping with the Past: Germany and Austria after 1945.* Madison: University of Wisconsin Press, 1990.

Harris, Whitney. *Tyranny on Trial: The Trial of the Major German War Criminals at the End of World War II in Germany, 1954–1946.* Dallas, TX: Southern Methodist University Press, 1999.

Hartman, Geoffrey. "On Traumatic Knowledge and Literary Studies." *New Literary History* vol. 26, no. 3 (1995): 537–563.

———. *The Longest Shadow: In the Aftermath of the Holocaust.* Bloomington: Indiana University Press, 1996.

———. *The Geoffrey Hartman Reader.* Edited by Geoffrey Hartman and Daniel O'Hara. New York: Fordham University Press, 2004.

Hayes, Graham. "We Suffer Our Memories: Thinking about the Past, Healing and Reconciliation." *American Imago* 55, no. 1 (1998): 29–50.

Hayner, Priscilla B. "Fifteen Truth Commissions—1974–1994: A Comparative Study," *Human Rights Quarterly*, 16, no. 4 (1994), 597–655.

———. *Unspeakable Truth: Confronting State Terror and Atrocity.* New York: Routledge, 2001.

Hecht, Werner. *Brechts Weg zum epischen Theater: Beitrag zur Entwicklung des epischen Theaters 1918 bis 1933.* Berlin: Henschelverlag, 1962.

———, ed. *Brecht Chronik: 1898–1956.* Frankfurt am Main: Suhrkamp, 1997.

Hegel, George. *The Phenomenology of Spirit.* Translated by H. P. Kainz. University Park: Pennsylvania State University Press, 1994.

Hochhuth, Rolf. *Der Stellvertreter: ein Schauspiel.* Reinbek bei Hamburg: Rowohlt, 1963.

———. "Soll das Theater die heutige Welt darstellen? Antworten auf Fragen der Zeitschrift *Theater Heute*." In *Die Hebamme: Komödie, Erzählungen, Gedichte, Essays.* Reinbek bei Hamburg: Rowohlt, 1971.

———. *The Representative: A Christian Tragedy.* Translated by Robert MacDonald. London: Oberon, 1998.

Honig, Bonnie. "Declarations of Independence: Arendt and Derrida on the Problem of Founding a Republic." *American Political Science Review* 85, no. 1 (March 1991): 97–113.

———. "Arendt's Accounts of Action and Authority." In *Political Theory and the Displacement of Politics*, 76–103. Ithaca, NY: Cornell University Press, 1993.

Hoover, Marjorie. "Brecht's Soviet Connection: Tretiakov." *Brecht Heute/Brecht Today. Jahrbuch der Internationalen Brecht Gesellschaft* 3 (1973): 39–56.

Huyssen, Andreas. *After the Great Divide: Modernism, Mass Culture, Postmodernism.* London: MacMillan Press, 1986.

Ignatieff, Michael. "Articles of Faith." *Index on Censorship* 5 (1996): 110–122.

———. "Digging Up the Dead." *New Yorker*, November 10, 1997: 84–93.

Jameson, Frederic. *Brecht and Method*. London and New York: Verso, 1998.

Jaspers, Karl. *The Question of German Guilt*. Translated by E. B. Ashton. New York: Capricorn Books, 1961.

———. "On *The Deputy*." In *The Storm over the Deputy*. Edited by Eric Bentley and translated by Salvator Attanasio, 99–102. New York: Grove Press, 1964.

Jolles, André. *Einfache Formen: Legende, Sage, Mythe, Rätsel, Spruch, Kasus, Memorabile, Märchen, Witz*. Leipzig: Halle, 1930.

Kagel, Martin. "Brecht Files: Conversations with George Tabori," *The Brecht Yearbook/Theater der Zeit* 23 (1997), 70–75.

Kahn, Gordon. *Hollywood on Trial*. New York: Boni and Gaer, 1948.

Kaldiris, Dimitris. *The Drama of Kalavryta*. N.P.: Society of Natives of Kalavryta, 1998.

Kant, Immanuel. *Critique of Judgment*. Translated by Werner Pluhar. Indianapolis: Hackett, 1987.

Kaplan, Alice Yaeger. Introduction to *Remembering in Vain*, by Alain Finkielkraut, ix–xxxvi. New York: Columbia University Press, 1992.

Keenan, Thomas. *Fables of Responsibility: Aberrations and Predicaments in Ethics and Politics*. Stanford, CA: Stanford University Press, 1997.

———. "Introduction to 'Humanism without Borders: A Dossier on Humanitarianism and Human Rights.'" *Alphabet City* 7 (2000): 35–43.

Kojève, Alexandre. *Introduction to a Reading of Hegel*. Translated by J. H. Nichols. New York: Basic Books, 1965.

Kolyazin, Vladimir. "'How Will He Go to His Death?' An Answer to Brecht's Question about the Death of his Teacher the 'Tall and Kindly' Tretiakov." *The Brecht Yearbook* 22 (1997): 169–179.

Kopelew, Leo. "Brecht und die Russische Theaterrevolution." *Brecht Heute/ Brecht Today* 3 (1973): 19–38.

Kristeva, Julia. *Hannah Arendt*. Translated by Ross Guberman. New York: Columbia University Press, 2001.

Krog, Antjie. *Country of My Skull*. London: Jonathan Cape, 1998.

Lacan, Jacques. *The Seminar of Jacques Lacan, Book VII: The Ethics of Psychoanalysis (1959–60)*. Edited by Jacques-Alain Miller and translated by Dennis Porter. New York: Norton & Co., 1992.

LaCapra, Dominick. "Representing the Holocaust: Reflections on the Historian's Debate." In *Probing the Limits of Representation: Nazism and the "Final Solution."* Edited by Saul Friedländer, 108–127. Cambridge, MA: Harvard University Press, 1992.

———. *Representing the Holocaust: History, Theory, Trauma*. Ithaca, NY: Cornell University Press, 1994.

———. *History and Memory after Auschwitz*. Ithaca, NY: Cornell University Press, 1998.

————. *Writing History, Writing Trauma*. Baltimore: Johns Hopkins University Press, 2001.

Langer, Lawrence. *Holocaust Testimonies: The Ruins of Memory*. New Haven, CT: Yale University Press, 1991.

————. Introduction to *Auschwitz and After*, by Charlotte Delbo, ix–xviii. New Haven, CT: Yale University Press, 1995.

————. *Admitting the Holocaust. Collected Essays*. Oxford, UK: Oxford University Press, 1996.

————. *America, Europe, and the Soviet Union: Selected Essays*. Piscataway, NJ: Transaction Publishers, 1983.

Laub, Dori. "The Empty Circle: Children of Survivors and the Limits of Reconstruction." *Journal of the American Psychoanalytic Association* 46, no. 2 (1998): 507–529.

Laub, Dori, and Nanette Auerhahn. "Knowing and Not Knowing Massive Psychic Trauma: Forms of Traumatic Memory." *International Journal of Psychoanalysis* 74 (1993): 287–302.

Leach, Robert. "Brecht's Teacher." *Modern Drama* 32, no. 4 (December 1989): 502–511.

Lefort, Claude. *Democracy and Political Theory*. Translated by David Macey. Cambridge, UK: Polity Press, 1988.

Legendre, Pierre. *Law and the Unconscious: A Legendre Reader*. Edited by Peter Goodrich, Translated by Peter Goodrich with Alain Pottage, and Anton Schütz. Basingstoke, UK: Macmillan, 1987.

————. "Id Efficit, Quod Figurat (It Is the Symbol Which Produces Effects): The Social Constitution of Speech and the Development of the Normative Role of Images." *Legal Studies Forum* 20 (1996): 247–263.

————. "The Other Dimension of Law." *Law and the Postmodern Mind: Essays on Psychoanalysis and Jurisprudence*. Edited by Peter Goodrich and David Carlson, 175–192. Ann Arbor: University of Michigan Press, 1998.

Lehmann, Hans-Thies. *Postdramatic Theatre*. Translated by Karen Jürs-Munby. New York: Routledge, 2006.

Lehmann, Hans Thies, and Helmut Lethen. "Ein Vorschlag zur Güte. Zu doppelten Polarität der Lehrstücke." In *Auf Anregung Bertolt Brechts: Lehrstücke mit Schülern, Arbeitern, Theaterleuten*. Edited by Reiner Steinweg, 302–318. Frankfurt: Suhrkamp, 1978.

Levine, Michael. *The Belated Witness: Literature, Testimony and the Question of the Holocaust*. Stanford, CA: Stanford University Press, 2006.

Lewis, Jon. "We Do Not Ask You to Condone This: How the Blacklist Saved Hollywood." *Cinema Journal* 39, no. 2 (2000): 3–30.

Lyon, James. "Das FBI als Literaturhistoriker. Die Akte Bertolt Brechts." *Akzente* 4 (August 1980): 362–383.

————, ed. *Brecht in den USA*. Frankfurt am Main: Suhrkamp, 1994.

Maier, Charles. *The Unmasterable Past: History, Holocaust and German National Identity.* Cambridge, MA: Harvard University Press, 1988.

Man, Paul de. *Allegories of Reading: Figural Language in Rousseau, Nietzsche, Rilke and Proust.* New Haven, CT: Yale University Press, 1979.

———. "Autobiography as De-Facement." In *The Rhetoric of Romanticism*, 67–83. New York: Columbia University Press, 1984.

———. "The Resistance to Theory." In *The Resistance to Theory*, 3–20. Minneapolis: University of Minnesota Press, 1986.

———. "The Concept of Irony." In *Aesthetic Ideology.* Edited by Andrzej Warminski, 163–184. Minneapolis: University of Minnesota Press, 1996.

Marrus, Michael, ed. *Nuremberg War Crimes Trial, 1945–46: A Documentary History.* Boston: Bedford Books, 1997.

Marshall, David. *The Figure of Theater: Shaftesbury, Defoe, Adam Smith and George Eliot.* New York: Columbia University Press, 1986.

———. *The Surprising Effects of Sympathy: Marivaux, Diderot, Rousseau and Mary Shelley.* Chicago: University of Chicago Press, 1988.

Masing-Delic, Irene. *Abolishing Death: A Salvation Myth of Russian Twentieth-Century Literature.* Stanford, CA: Stanford University Press, 1992.

Merleau-Ponty, Maurice. *Humanism and Terror. The Communist Problem.* Translated by John O'Neill. New Brunswick, NJ: Transaction Publishers, 2000.

Mierau, Fritz. "Tretiakov: Gesicht und Name." In *Gesichter der Avantgarde: Porträts—Essays—Briefe*, 447–459. Berlin and Weimer: Aufbau Verlag, 1985.

Miller, J. Hillis. "Three Literary Theorists in Search of o." In *Provocations to Reading: J. Hillis Miller and the Democracy to Come.* Edited by Barbara Cohen and Dragan Kujundzic, 210–227. New York: Fordham University Press, 2005.

Minow, Martha. *Between Vengeance and Forgiveness. Facing History after Genocide and Mass Violence.* Boston: Beacon Press, 1998.

———. *Breaking the Cycles of Hatred: Memory, Law, and Repair.* Edited by Nancy Rosenblum. Princeton, NJ: Princeton University Press, 2002.

Mitscherlich, Alexander, and Margarete Mitscherlich. *Die Unfähigkeit zu trauern: Grundlagen kollektiven Verhaltens.* Munich: Piper, 1977 [1967].

Mittenzwei, Werner. "Die Spur der Brechtschen Lehrstück—Theorie Gedanken zur neueren Lehrstück-Interpretation." In *Brechts Modell der Lehrstücke: Zeugnisse, Diskussion, Erfahrungen.* Edited by Reiner Steinweg, 225–254. Frankfurt am Main: Suhrkamp, 1976.

Müller, Roswitha. "Learning for a New Society: 'The Lehrstück.'" In *The Cambridge Companion to Brecht.* Edited by Peter Thomson and Glendyr Sacks, 79–95. Cambridge, UK: Cambridge University Press, 1994.

Nägele, Rainer. "Brecht's Theater der Grausamkeit: Lehrstücke und Stückwerke." In *Brechts Dramen.* Edited by Walter Hinderer, 300–315. Stuttgart: Reclam, 1984.

————. *Reading after Freud. Essays on Goethe, Hölderlin, Habermas, Nietzsche, Brecht, Celan and Freud.* New York: Columbia University Press, 1987.

Nancy, Jean-Luc. "Laughter, Presence." In *The Birth to Presence.* Translated by Brian Holmes, 368–392. Stanford, CA: Stanford University Press, 1993.

Neier, Aryeh. "The Quest for Justice." *New York Review of Books,* March 8, 2001.

Nelson, Deborah. "Suffering and Thinking: The Scandal of Tone in *Eichmann in Jerusalem.*" In *Compassion: the Culture and Politics of an Emotion.* Edited by Lauren Berlant, 219–244. New York: Routledge, 2004.

Nussbaum, Laureen. "The German Documentary Theater of the Sixties: A Stereopsis of Contemporary History." *German Studies Review* 4, no. 2 (1981), 237–255.

Nussbaum, Martha. *Poetic Justice: The Literary Imagination and Public Life.* Boston: Beacon Press, 1995.

O'Neill, John. "Merleau-Ponty's Critique of Marxist Scientism." In *Phenomenology and Marxism.* Edited by Bernhard Waldenfels, Jan Broekman, and Ante Pazanin, 276–304. New York: Routledge: 1984.

Osiel, Marc. *Mass Atrocity, Collective Memory and the Law.* New Brunswick, NJ: Transaction Publishers, 1997.

Passerin D'Entrèves, Maurizio. "Arendt's Theory of Judgment." In *The Cambridge Companion to Hannah Arendt.* Edited by Dana Richard Villa, 245–260. Cambridge, UK: Cambridge University Press, 2000.

Pearlman, Moshe. *The Capture and Trial of Adolf Eichmann.* New York: Simon and Schuster, 1963.

Piscator, Erwin, "Vorwort." In *Der Stellvertreter: ein Schauspiel* by Rolf Hochhuth, 7–11. Reinbek bei Hamburg: Rowohlt, 1963.

Rabinbach, Anson. *In the Shadow of Catastrophe: German Intellectuals between Apocalypse and Enlightenment.* Berkeley: University of California Press, 1997.

————. "The German as Pariah: Karl Jaspers and the Question of German Guilt." *Radical Philosophy* 75 (January 1996): 15–25.

Raddatz, Fritz, ed. *Summa Iniuria: oder Durfte der Pabst schweigen? Hochhuth's "Stellvertreter" in der öffentlichen Kritik.* Reinbek bei Hamburg: Rowohlt, 1963.

Ricoeur, Paul. "Le pardon, peut-il guérir?" *Esprit,* no. 3–4 (1995): 77–82.

————. "Aesthetic Judgment and Political Judgment according to Hannah Arendt." In *The Just.* Translated by David Pellauer, 94–108. Chicago: University of Chicago Press, 2000.

Rosen, Alan. *Sounds of Defiance: The Holocaust, Multilingualism and the Problem of English.* Lincoln: University of Nebraska Press, 2005.

Rousso, Henry. *The Vichy Syndrome: History and Memory in France since 1944.* Translated by Arthur Goldhammer. Cambridge, MA: Harvard University Press, 1991.

Sanders, Mark. "Ambiguities of Mourning: Law, Custom, and Testimony of Women Before South Africa's Truth and Reconciliation Commission." In *Loss: the Politics of Mourning*. Edited by David Eng and David Kazanjian, 77–98. Berkeley: University of California Press, 2003.

————. *Ambiguities of Witnessing: Law and literature in the Time of a Truth Commission*. Stanford, CA: Stanford University Press, 2007.

Santner, Eric. *Stranded Objects: Mourning, Memory and Film in Postwar Germany*. Ithaca, NY: Cornell University Press, 1993.

————. "History beyond the Pleasure Principle: Some Thoughts on the Representation of Trauma." In *Probing the Limits of Representation: Nazism and the "Final Solution."* Edited by Saul Friedländer, 143–154. Cambridge, MA: Harvard University Press, 1992.

Sarat, Austin, and Thomas Kearns, eds. *History, Memory and the Law*. Ann Arbor: University of Michigan Press, 2002.

Schlögel, Karl. *Berlin Ostbahnhoff Europas. Russen und Deutsche in ihrem Jahrhundert*. Berlin: Siedler Verlag, 1998.

Scholem, Gershom. *Gershom Scholem: A Life in Letters, 1914–1982*. Edited and translated by David Skinner. Cambridge, MA, and London: Harvard University Press, 2002.

Searle, John. *Expression and Meaning: Studies in the Theory of Speech Acts*. Cambridge, UK: Cambridge University Press, 1979.

Segev, Tom. *The Seventh Million: The Israelis and the Holocaust*. New York: Hill and Wang, 1993.

Shklar, Judith. *Legalism: Law, Morals, and Political Trials*. Cambridge, MA; Harvard University Press, 1986.

Simpson, Gerry. *Law, War and Crime: War Crimes Trials and the Reinvention of International Law*. Cambridge, UK: Polity, 2007.

Sontag, Susan. "Reflections on *The Deputy*." In *The Storm over the Deputy*. Edited by Eric Bentley, 117–123. New York: Grove Press, 1964.

Sophocles. "Antigone," In *The Oedipus Cycle*. Translated by Dudley Fitts and Robert Fitzgerald. New York: Harcourt Brace, 1949.

Steiner, George. *Antigones*. New York: Clarendon Press, 1984.

Steinweg, Reiner. *Das Lehrstück. Brecht's Theorie einer politisch-ästhetischen Erziehung*. Stuttgart: Metzlersche, 1972.

————, ed. *Brechts Modell der Lehrstücke: Zeugnisse, Diskussion, Erfahrungen*. Frankfurt am Main: Suhrkamp, 1976.

————, ed. *Auf Anregung Bertolt Brechts: Lehrstücke mit Schülern, Arbeitern, Theaterleuten*. Frankfurt am Main: Suhrkamp, 1978.

Stephan, Alexander. *Im Visier des FBI. Deutsche Exilschriftsteller in den Akten amerikanischer Geheimdienste*. Stuttgart: Metzler, 1995.

————. "Enemy Alien. Die Überwachung des exilierten Komponisten Hanns Eisler durch FBI, HUAC und INS." *The Brecht Yearbook* 22 (1997): 181–193.

_____. " ' . . . Advocates Communist World Revolution by Violent Means.' Brecht, Eisler und The Measures Taken in den Dossiers von FBI und HUAC." In *Massnehmen: Bertolt Brecht/ Hanns Eislers Lehrstück* Die Massnahme. *Theater der Zeit Recherchen* 1 (1998), 116.

Storey, Walter R. "Bert Brecht, GPU Songbird Liked Hollywood Fine," *New Leader*, September 19, 1949, 12.

Tabori, Georg. *Die Brecht-Akte*. Translated to German by Ursula Grützmacher-Tabori. *Theater der Zeit* vol. 2, no. 55 (2000): 56–72.

Tatlow, Antony. "Theory and Practice of the Didactic Play." *Brecht Heute/Brecht Today. Jahrbuch der Internationalen Brecht Gesellschaft* 3 (1972): 255–260.

_____. *The Mask of Evil: Brecht's Response to the Poetry, Theatre and Thought of China and Japan: A Comparative and Critical Evaluation*. Bern: Peter Lang, 1977.

Taylor, Diana. "Making a Spectacle. The Mothers of the Plaza de Mayo." In *Radical Street Performance. An International Anthology*. Edited by J. Cohen-Cruz, 74–85. London and New York: Routledge, 1998.

_____. "Trapped in Bad Scripts: The Mothers of Plaza de Mayo." In *Disappearing Acts: Spectacles of Gender and Nationalism in Argentina's "Dirty War,"* 183–222. Durham, NC: Duke University Press, 1997.

Taylor, Telford. "Large Questions in the Eichmann Case." *New York Times Magazine*, January 22, 1961: 21–25.

Teschke, Holger. "Hollywood-Elegien. Holger Teschke spricht mit George Tabori." *Theater der Zeit* 2, no. 55 (2000): 8–10.

Thielking, Sigrid. *"L'homme Statue*? Brechts Inschriften im Kontext von Denkmalsdiskurs und Erinnerungspolitik." *Brecht Jahrbuch* 24 (2000): 53–67.

Trejakow, Sergej. *Gesichter der Avantgarde: Porträts—Essays—Briefe*. Berlin and Weimar: Aufbau Verlag, 1985.

Tretiakov, Sergey. "Bert Brecht." In *Brecht: A Collection of Critical Essays*. Edited by Peter Demetz, 16–29. Englewood Cliffs, NJ: Prentice-Hall, 1962.

_____. *Lyrik, Dramatik Prosa*. Leipzig: Verlag Philipp Reclam, 1972.

_____. *Gesichter der Avantgarde: Porträts—Essays—Briefe*. Berlin and Weimar: Aufbau Verlag, 1985.

Truth and Reconciliation Commission of South Africa Report, Vol. 1–5. Cape Town: Juta, 1998.

Tutu, Desmond. *No Future without Forgiveness*. New York: Doubleday, 1999.

Villa-Vicencio, Charles. "A Different Kind of Justice: The South African Truth and Reconciliation Commission." *Contemporary Justice Review* 1 (1999): 407–428.

Vismann, Cornelia. " '*Rejouer les crimes*': Theater vs. Video." *Cardozo Studies in Law and Literature* 13 (2001): 119–135.

Vries, Hent de. "Hospitable Thought: Before and Beyond Cosmopolitanism." In *Religion and Violence: Philosophical Perspectives from Kant to Derrida*, 293–398. Baltimore: Johns Hopkins University Press.

Ward, Ian. *Law and Literature: Possibilities and Perspectives*. Cambridge, UK: Cambridge University Press, 1995.

White, James Boyd. *When Words Lose Their Meaning: Constitutions and Reconstitutions of Language, Character and Community*. Chicago: University of Chicago Press, 1984.

Wieviorka, Annette. *Le Procès Eichmann, 1961*. Brussels: Editions Complexe, 1989.

———. *The Era of the Witness*. Translated by Jared Stark. Ithaca, NY: Cornell University Press, 2006.

Wirth, Andrzej. "The Lehrstück as Performance." *The Drama Review* 43, no. 3 (1999): 113–121.

Wolin, Richard. "The Ambivalences of German-Jewish Identity: Hannah Arendt in Jerusalem." *History & Memory* 8, no. 2 (1996): 9–35.

Wood, Nancy. *Vectors of Memory: Legacies of Trauma in Postwar Europe*. Oxford, UK, and New York: Berg, 1999.

———. "Memory on Trial in Contemporary France. The Case of Maurice Papon," *History and Memory* vol. 11, no. 1 (1999), 41–76

Yar, Majid. "From Actor to Spectator: Hannah Arendt's Two Theories of Judgement." *Philosophy and Social Criticism* 26, no. 2 (2000): 1–27.

Young-Bruehl, Elizabeth. *Hannah Arendt: For Love of the World, Second Edition*. New Haven, CT: Yale University Press, 2004. (Originally published in 1982.)

Zertal, Idith. *Israel's Holocaust and the Politics of Nationhood*. Trans. Chaya Galai. Cambridge, UK: Cambridge University Press, 2005.

Žižek, Slavoj. *The Sublime Object of Ideology*. London: Verso, 1989.

———. *Enjoy Your Symptom! Jacques Lacan in Hollywood and Out*. New York: Routledge, 1993.

———. "When the Party Commits Suicide." *New Left Review* 238 (November/December 1999): 26–47.

———. "Attempts to Escape the Logic of Capitalism." *London Review of Books* 21, no. 21 (October 1999): 3–6.

———. *Did Somebody Say Totalitarianism?* New York, London: Verso, 2001.

———. *Welcome to the Desert of the Real*. New York: Wooster Press, 2001.

Index

Abel, Lionel: on Eichmann trial, 23–24, 25, 26, 153n23; on founding of Israel, 23–24, 26

Adorno, Theodor: on art and suffering, 183n19; "Education after Auschwitz," 143n4; on Freud, 144n4; on Hochhuth's *Der Stellvertreter*, 155n38; on public enlightenment, 2–3, 4, 143n4; on spell of the past, 7; "Was bedeutet: Aufarbeitung der Vergangenheit?," 1–3, 4, 7, 133, 134, 139, 143nn1,3, 144n6

Agamben, Giorgio: *Homo Sacer*, 162n21; *Means without End*, 162n21; *Remnants of Auschwitz*, 162n21

amnesty, 6, 8–9

Amstutz, Mark: on retributive vs. restorative justice, 147n21

anacoluthon, 39, 41, 158nn56,65

Arendt, Hannah: on banality of evil, 17–19, 33–35, 36–37, 42–43, 44, 45, 136–37, 138, 157n51; vs. Brecht, 9, 12–13, 14, 99, 133–34, 135–38, 139; on Brecht and Stalinism, 131–32; on Brecht's *Die Maßnahme*, 99; on citizenship, 163n26; on collective guilt, 47; on comedy in Eichmann trial, 10, 16, 19, 33–39, 43–45, 137, 151n6, 157nn51,53; on common-sense judgments, 41–42; on compassion and empathy, 24–25, 135, 136, 154nn28,29; on crimes against humanity, 50–51, 57–60, 63, 138, 163nn25,27,28; on crimes against Jewish people, 50–55, 63, 163n27;

on criminal guilt, 47, 49–50; on Declaration of Independence, 56, 162n24; vs. Delbo, 9, 12–13, 14, 62, 133–34, 138–39; on *Eichmann in Jerusalem*, 15–16, 17–18; on Eichmann's language, 37–39, 41, 157n53; on Eichmann's thoughtlessness, 17, 18, 29, 30, 36, 39–41, 157n51; on Eichmann trial's didactic impact, 9–10, 19, 20–22, 31, 34–37, 42–43, 44, 135–37; on Eichmann trial's location, 51, 52–53; on empty speech, 38, 157n54; on exemplary judgments, 31–32, 43, 136, 156nn46,47; on Faulkner's *A Fable*, 140; on forgiveness, 138, 183n13; on the hero, 177n63; on Hochhuth's *Der Stellvertreter*, 28; on human rights vs. citizens' rights, 53–55, 57, 162n22; on ideological thinking, 40–42, 158n64; on individual responsibility, 30, 155n42; on Jewish suffering, 21–23, 24, 28–29, 50; on judgment and general rules, 30–32, 136, 156n44; on justice and trials, 10, 21, 24, 61–62; on Kant and judgment, 39, 136, 156nn44,47; on Kant and laughter, 35; on lamentations, 140; on laughter, 35, 44; on law and public life, 25, 154n31, 161n16, 167n34; on legal judgment, 9–10, 22–23, 24–25, 26, 28–29, 47, 49–50, 64–65, 131, 136, 163n25; on logic, 40, 158n63; on mastering the past, 140; on Nazi anti-Semitism as new, 57–58;

Cultural Memory | *in the Present*

214 *Cultural Memory in the Present*

Diane Perpich, *The Ethics of Emmanuel Levinas*

Marcel Detienne, *Comparing the Incomparable*

François Delaporte, *Anatomy of the Passions*

René Girard, *Mimesis and Theory: Essays on Literature and Criticism, 1959–2005*

Richard Baxstrom, *Houses in Motion: The Experience of Place and the Problem of Belief in Urban Malaysia*

Jennifer L. Culbert, *Dead Certainty: The Death Penalty and the Problem of Judgment*

Samantha Frost, *Lessons from a Materialist Thinker: Hobbesian Reflections on Ethics and Politics*

Regina Mara Schwartz, *Sacramental Poetics at the Dawn of Secularism: When God Left the World*

Gil Anidjar, *Semites: Race, Religion, Literature*

Ranjana Khanna, *Algeria Cuts: Women and Representation, 1830 to the Present*

Esther Peeren, *Intersubjectivities and Popular Culture: Bakhtin and Beyond*

Eyal Peretz, *Becoming Visionary: Brian De Palma's Cinematic Education of the Senses*

Diana Sorensen, *A Turbulent Decade Remembered: Scenes from the Latin American Sixties*

Hubert Damisch, *A Childhood Memory by Piero della Francesca*

José van Dijck, *Mediated Memories in the Digital Age*

Dana Hollander, *Exemplarity and Chosenness: Rosenzweig and Derrida on the Nation of Philosophy*

Asja Szafraniec, *Beckett, Derrida, and the Event of Literature*

Sara Guyer, *Romanticism After Auschwitz*

Alison Ross, *The Aesthetic Paths of Philosophy: Presentation in Kant, Heidegger, Lacoue-Labarthe, and Nancy*

Gerhard Richter, *Thought-Images: Frankfurt School Writers' Reflections from Damaged Life*

Bella Brodzki, *Can These Bones Live? Translation, Survival, and Cultural Memory*

Rodolphe Gasché, *The Honor of Thinking: Critique, Theory, Philosophy*

Brigitte Peucker, *The Material Image: Art and the Real in Film*

Natalie Melas, *All the Difference in the World: Postcoloniality and the Ends of Comparison*

Jonathan Culler, *The Literary in Theory*

Michael G. Levine, *The Belated Witness: Literature, Testimony, and the Question of Holocaust Survival*

Jennifer A. Jordan, *Structures of Memory: Understanding German Change in Berlin and Beyond*

Christoph Menke, *Reflections of Equality*

Marlène Zarader, *The Unthought Debt: Heidegger and the Hebraic Heritage*

Jan Assmann, *Religion and Cultural Memory: Ten Studies*

Jean-Luc Nancy, *The Speculative Remark: (One of Hegel's bon mots)*
Jean-François Lyotard, *Soundproof Room: Malraux's Anti-Aesthetics*
Jan Patočka, *Plato and Europe*
Hubert Damisch, *Skyline: The Narcissistic City*
Isabel Hoving, *In Praise of New Travelers: Reading Caribbean Migrant Women Writers*
Richard Rand, ed., *Futures: Of Jacques Derrida*
William Rasch, *Niklas Luhmann's Modernity: The Paradoxes of Differentiation*
Jacques Derrida and Anne Dufourmantelle, *Of Hospitality*
Jean-François Lyotard, *The Confession of Augustine*
Kaja Silverman, *World Spectators*
Samuel Weber, *Institution and Interpretation: Expanded Edition*
Jeffrey S. Librett, *The Rhetoric of Cultural Dialogue: Jews and Germans in the Epoch of Emancipation*
Ulrich Baer, *Remnants of Song: Trauma and the Experience of Modernity in Charles Baudelaire and Paul Celan*
Samuel C. Wheeler III, *Deconstruction as Analytic Philosophy*
David S. Ferris, *Silent Urns: Romanticism, Hellenism, Modernity*
Rodolphe Gasché, *Of Minimal Things: Studies on the Notion of Relation*
Sarah Winter, *Freud and the Institution of Psychoanalytic Knowledge*
Samuel Weber, *The Legend of Freud: Expanded Edition*
Aris Fioretos, ed., *The Solid Letter: Readings of Friedrich Hölderlin*
J. Hillis Miller / Manuel Asensi, *Black Holes / J. Hillis Miller; or, Boustrophedonic Reading*
Miryam Sas, *Fault Lines: Cultural Memory and Japanese Surrealism*
Peter Schwenger, *Fantasm and Fiction: On Textual Envisioning*
Didier Maleuvre, *Museum Memories: History, Technology, Art*
Jacques Derrida, *Monolingualism of the Other; or, The Prosthesis of Origin*
Andrew Baruch Wachtel, *Making a Nation, Breaking a Nation: Literature and Cultural Politics in Yugoslavia*
Niklas Luhmann, *Love as Passion: The Codification of Intimacy*
Mieke Bal, ed., *The Practice of Cultural Analysis: Exposing Interdisciplinary Interpretation*
Jacques Derrida and Gianni Vattimo, eds., *Religion*